The Dirty Pair™

FATAL BUT NOT SERIOUS

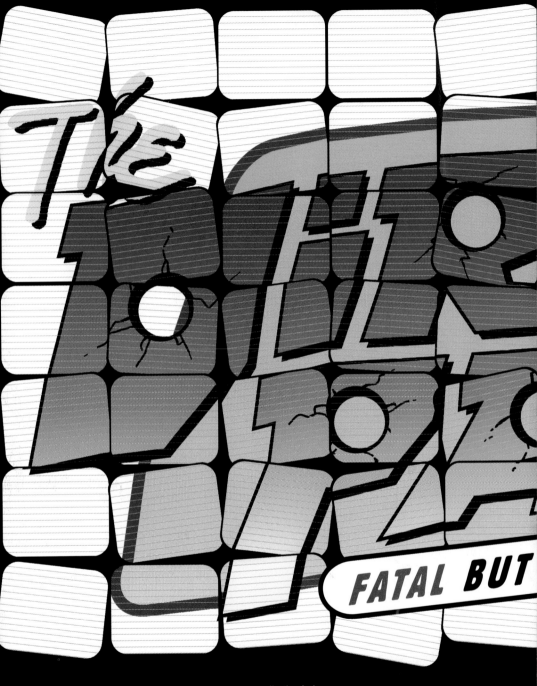

FATAL BUT

series editor
PEET JANES

collection designer
HARALD GRAHAM

collection editor
LYNN ADAIR

collection design manager
BRIAN GOGOLIN

NOT SERIOUS

story and pencils
ADAM WARREN

inks
ADAM WARREN
KARL STORY
TOM SIMMONS
ROBERT DEJESUS
JASON MARTIN
JIM ROYAL

colors
JOE ROSAS
DAVE NESTELLE
GINA GOING

lettering
STEVE DUTRO
TOMOKO SAITO

Based on characters and
situations created by
Haruka Takachiho

DARK HORSE COMICS®

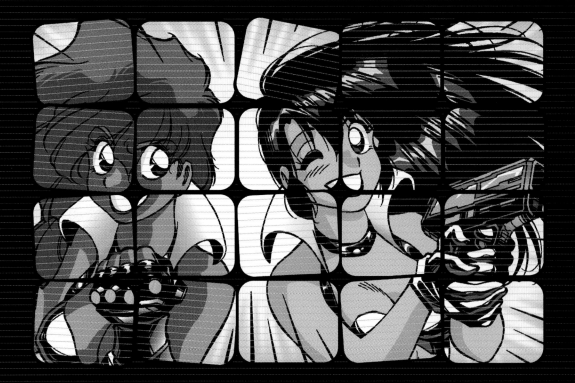

publisher
Mike Richardson

executive vice president
Neil Hankerson

vice president of publishing
David Scroggy

vice president of sales & marketing
Lou Bank

vice president of finance
Andy Karabatsos

general counsel
Mark Anderson

director of editorial adm.
Meloney C. Chadwick

creative director
Randy Stradley

director of production & design
Cindy Marks

art director
Mark Cox

computer graphics director
Sean Tierney

director of sales
Michael Martens

director of licensing
Tod Borleske

director of operations
Mark Ellington

director of m.i.s.
Dale LaFountain

THE DIRTY PAIR™:
FATAL BUT NOT SERIOUS

This book collects issues one through five of the Dark
Horse comic-book series *The Dirty Pair*™:
Fatal but not Serious.

Published by
Dark Horse Comics. Inc.
10956 SE Main Street
Milwaukie. OR 97222

First edition: August 1996
ISBN: 1-56971-172-0

10 9 8 7 6 5 4 3 2 1

Printed in Canada

YOU'RE UPLINKED TO **HYPERNET**™, THE UNITED GALACTICA'S **#1** HYPERWAVE-BROADCAST, INSTANTANEOUS INFORMATION NETWORK!

SWEET SMART SMOOTH TALK TALK TALK TALK

HEART TO HEA[RT] TALK TALK TA[LK]

Cory!

EMERSON

HYPERNET™ NODE: **CORY!** @MIDDLEBROW.TALK.SHOWS//UNIV.MEDIA.NTWB

THE **WORLDS WELFARE WORK ASSOCIATION.** GOOFY NAME, BUT A GOOD IDEA, IN **THEORY.**

THE **"3WA"** IS A PANGALACTIC, SUPRAGOVERNMENTAL ORGANIZATION SET UP TO COUNTER ANY **"THREATS TO HUMANITY"** THAT INDIVIDUAL WORLDS CAN'T HANDLE ON THEIR OWN.

WHEN PLANETARY AUTHORITIES PETITION FOR HELP, THE 3WA DISPATCHES TEAMS OF ELITE OPERATIVES CALLED **"TROUBLE CONSULTANTS."**

MY GUESTS ON TODAY'S **"CORY!"** ARE SUPPOSEDLY THE 3WA'S **TOP** TROUBLE CONSULTANTS. WHENEVER THEY'RE CALLED IN TO DEAL WITH A PROBLEM, IT GETS SOLVED. **ALWAYS.**

BUT...

Cory!

...ALONG THE WAY, SOMETHING ALWAYS GOES WRONG, AND **DISASTER** STRIKES.

THOUSANDS, EVEN **MILLIONS**, ARE WOUNDED OR KILLED. ENTIRE ECONO- MIES AND BIOSPHERES ARE DISRUPTED OR DESTROYED. CITIES, NATIONS, AND PLANETS ARE LEFT IN **RUINS.**

I'VE SEEN THIS HAPPEN, PEOPLE, AND BELIEVE ME, IT'S **NOT** PRETTY.

NOW, MY TWO GUESTS ARE OFFICIALLY CODENAMED "THE **LOVELY ANGELS**," BUT ARE BETTER KNOWN BY A LESS **COMPLIMENTARY** SOBRIQUET REFERRING TO THEIR PENCHANT FOR **DESTRUCTION.**

THEY'RE **VIOLENT!** THEY'RE **CONTROVERSIAL!** THEY'RE **SCANTILY CLAD!**

"DIRTY PAIR" BLAMED
KILL[ED]
chaos
dea[d]
CALY[...]
CERTAIN DOOM?

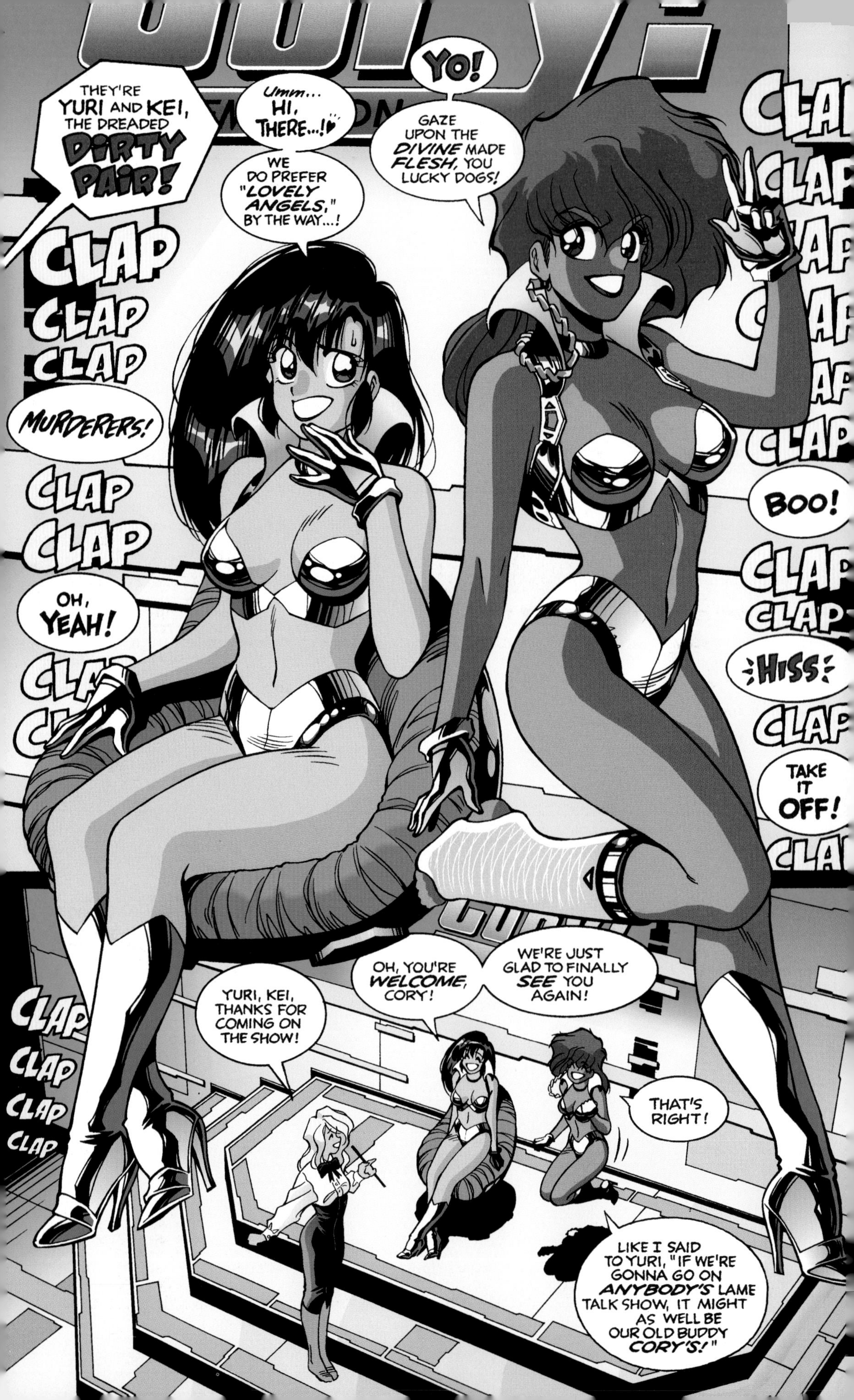
THEY'RE YURI AND KEI, THE DREADED DIRTY PAIR!
Umm... HI, THERE...!♥
WE DO PREFER "LOVELY ANGELS," BY THE WAY...!
YO!
GAZE UPON THE DIVINE MADE FLESH, YOU LUCKY DOGS!
CLAP
CLAP
CLAP
MURDERERS!
CLAP
CLAP
OH, YEAH!
CLAP
BOO!
CLAP
CLAP
HISS
CLAP
TAKE IT OFF!
CLAP
CLAP
CLAP
CLAP
YURI, KEI, THANKS FOR COMING ON THE SHOW!
OH, YOU'RE WELCOME, CORY!
WE'RE JUST GLAD TO FINALLY SEE YOU AGAIN!
THAT'S RIGHT!
LIKE I SAID TO YURI, "IF WE'RE GONNA GO ON ANYBODY'S LAME TALK SHOW, IT MIGHT AS WELL BE OUR OLD BUDDY CORY'S!"

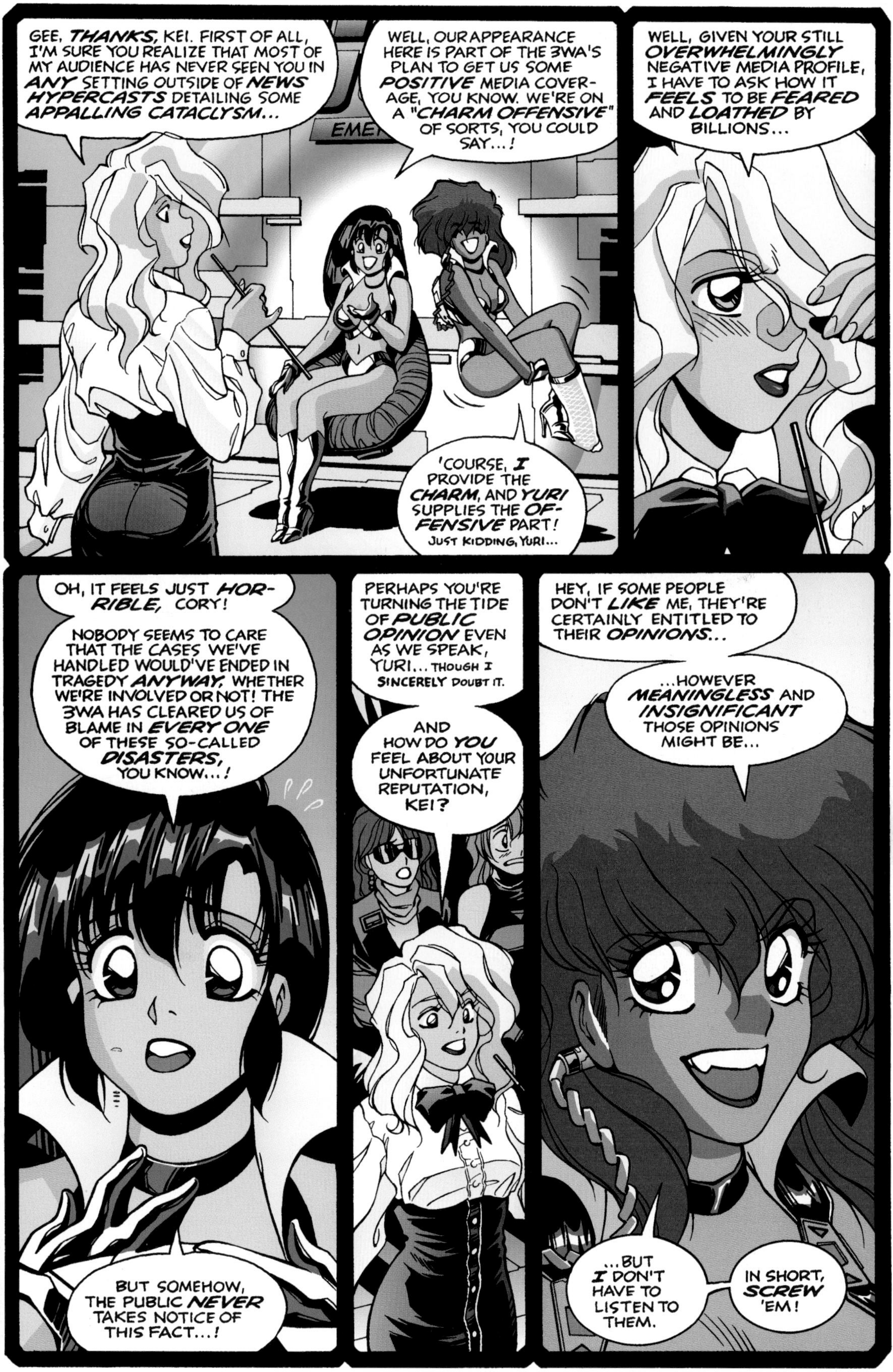
GEE, THANKS, KEI. FIRST OF ALL, I'M SURE YOU REALIZE THAT MOST OF MY AUDIENCE HAS NEVER SEEN YOU IN ANY SETTING OUTSIDE OF NEWS HYPERCASTS DETAILING SOME APPALLING CATACLYSM...
WELL, OUR APPEARANCE HERE IS PART OF THE 3WA'S PLAN TO GET US SOME POSITIVE MEDIA COVERAGE, YOU KNOW. WE'RE ON A "CHARM OFFENSIVE" OF SORTS, YOU COULD SAY...!
'COURSE, I PROVIDE THE CHARM, AND YURI SUPPLIES THE OFFENSIVE PART! JUST KIDDING, YURI...
EME
WELL, GIVEN YOUR STILL OVERWHELMINGLY NEGATIVE MEDIA PROFILE, I HAVE TO ASK HOW IT FEELS TO BE FEARED AND LOATHED BY BILLIONS...
OH, IT FEELS JUST HORRIBLE, CORY!
NOBODY SEEMS TO CARE THAT THE CASES WE'VE HANDLED WOULD'VE ENDED IN TRAGEDY ANYWAY, WHETHER WE'RE INVOLVED OR NOT! THE 3WA HAS CLEARED US OF BLAME IN EVERY ONE OF THESE SO-CALLED DISASTERS, YOU KNOW...!
BUT SOMEHOW, THE PUBLIC NEVER TAKES NOTICE OF THIS FACT...!
PERHAPS YOU'RE TURNING THE TIDE OF PUBLIC OPINION EVEN AS WE SPEAK, YURI... THOUGH I SINCERELY DOUBT IT.
AND HOW DO YOU FEEL ABOUT YOUR UNFORTUNATE REPUTATION, KEI?
HEY, IF SOME PEOPLE DON'T LIKE ME, THEY'RE CERTAINLY ENTITLED TO THEIR OPINIONS...
...HOWEVER MEANINGLESS AND INSIGNIFICANT THOSE OPINIONS MIGHT BE...
...BUT I DON'T HAVE TO LISTEN TO THEM.
IN SHORT, SCREW 'EM!

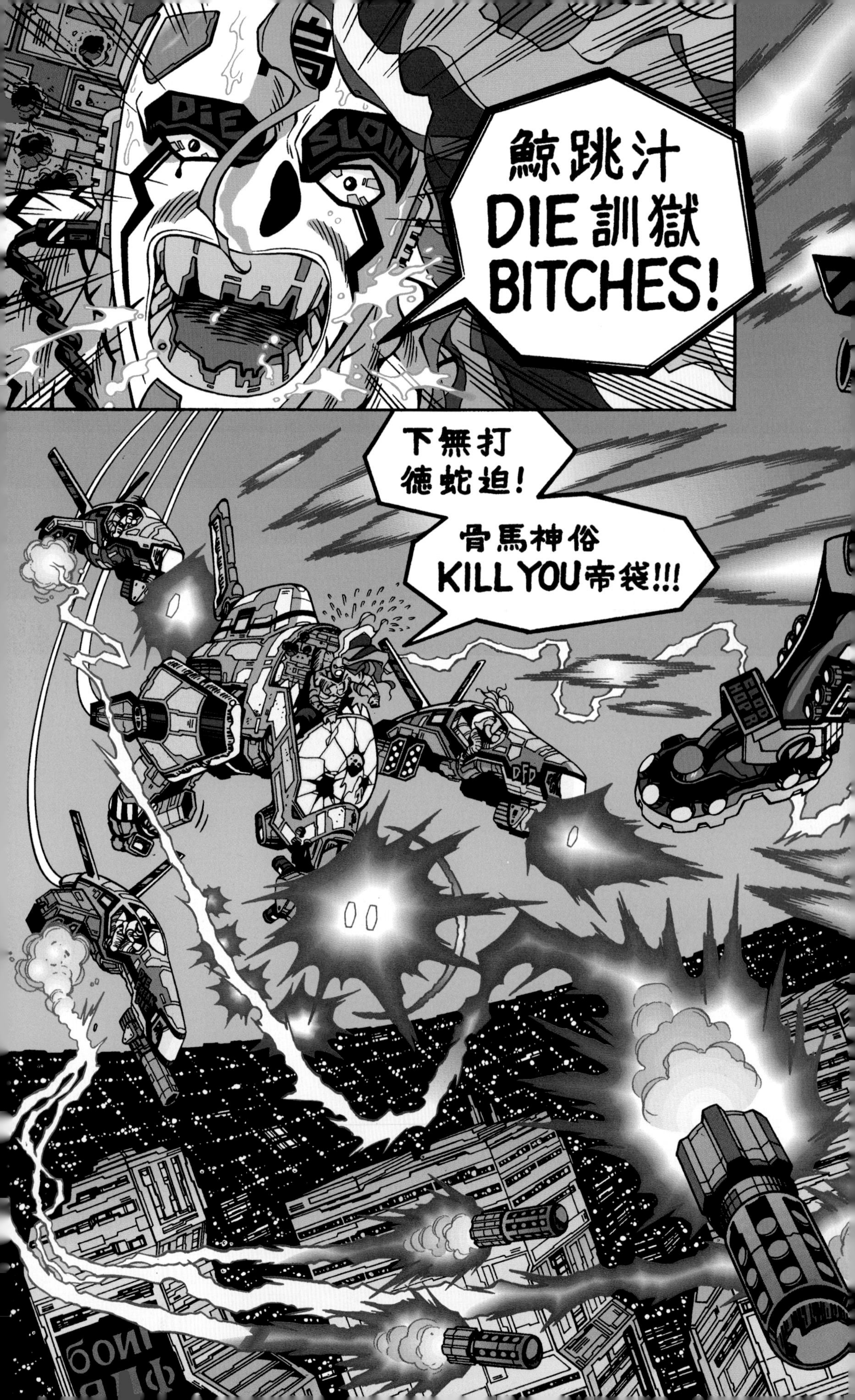
DIE SLOW
鯨跳汁 DIE 訓獄 BITCHES!
下無打 德蛇迫!
骨馬神俗 KILL YOU 帝袋!!!

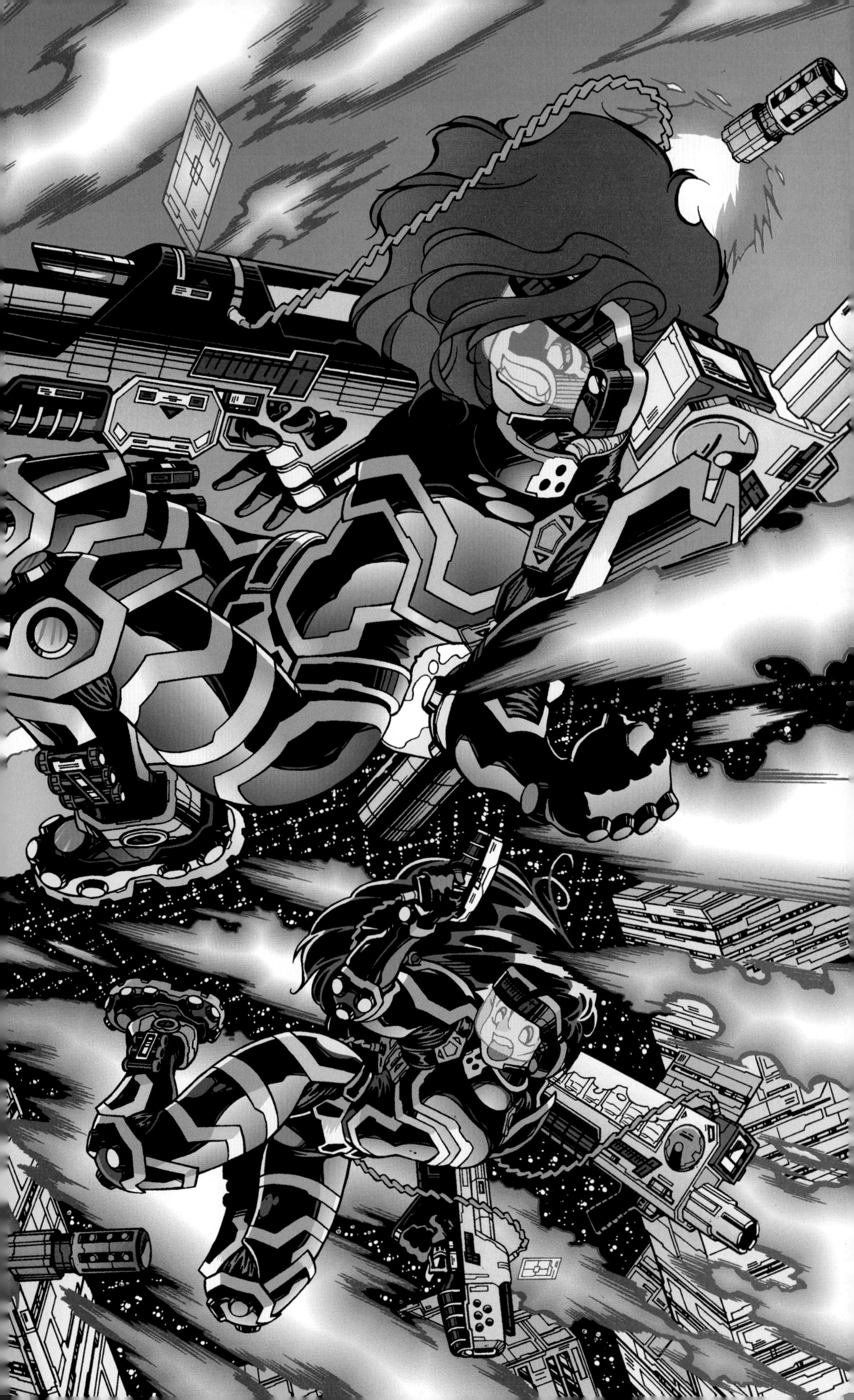

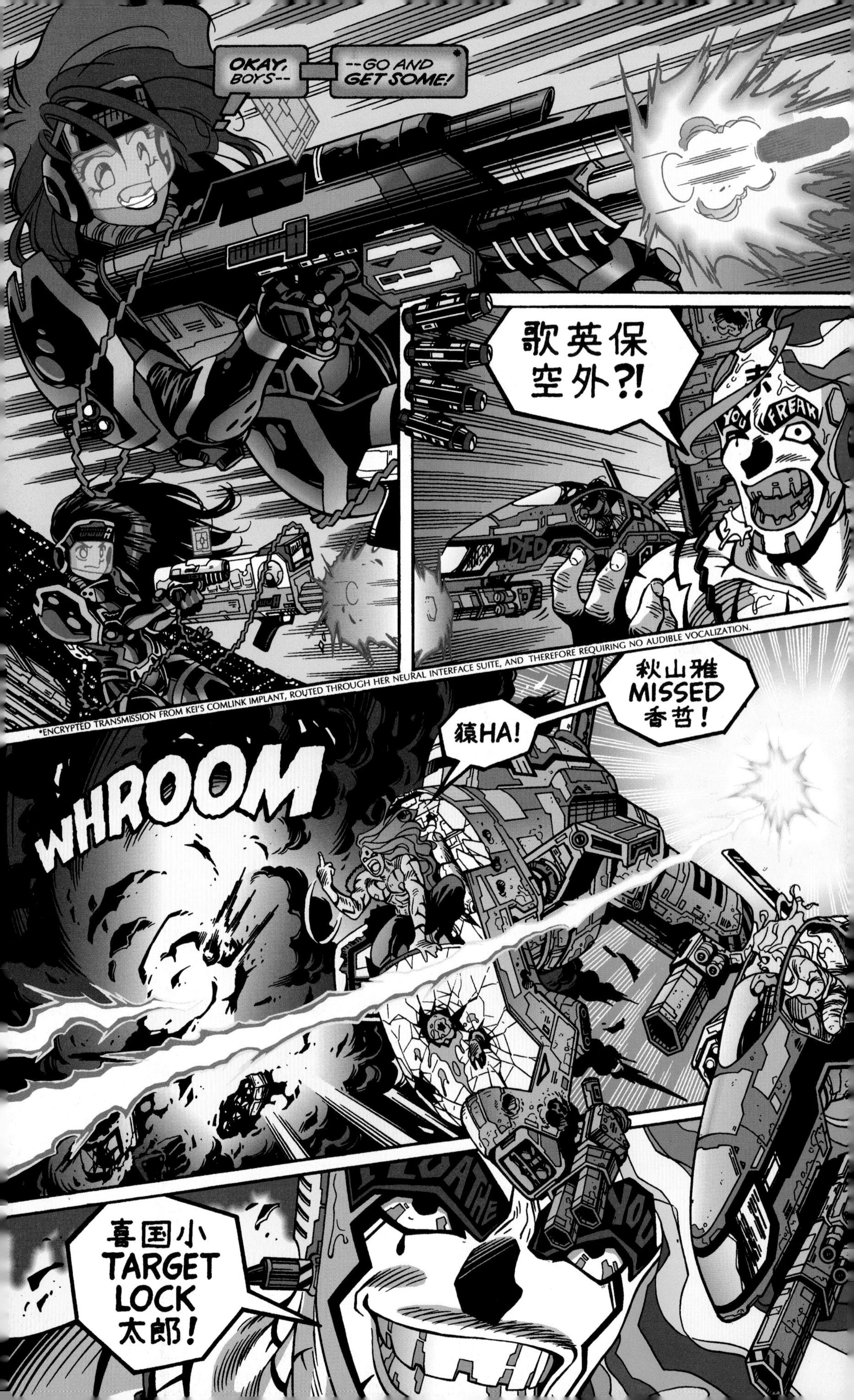
OKAY, BOYS--
--GO AND GET SOME!*
歌英保空外?!
YOU FREAK
*ENCRYPTED TRANSMISSION FROM KEI'S COMLINK IMPLANT, ROUTED THROUGH HER NEURAL INTERFACE SUITE, AND THEREFORE REQUIRING NO AUDIBLE VOCALIZATION.
WHROOM
猿HA!
秋山雅 MISSED 香哲!
喜国小 TARGET LOCK 太郎!

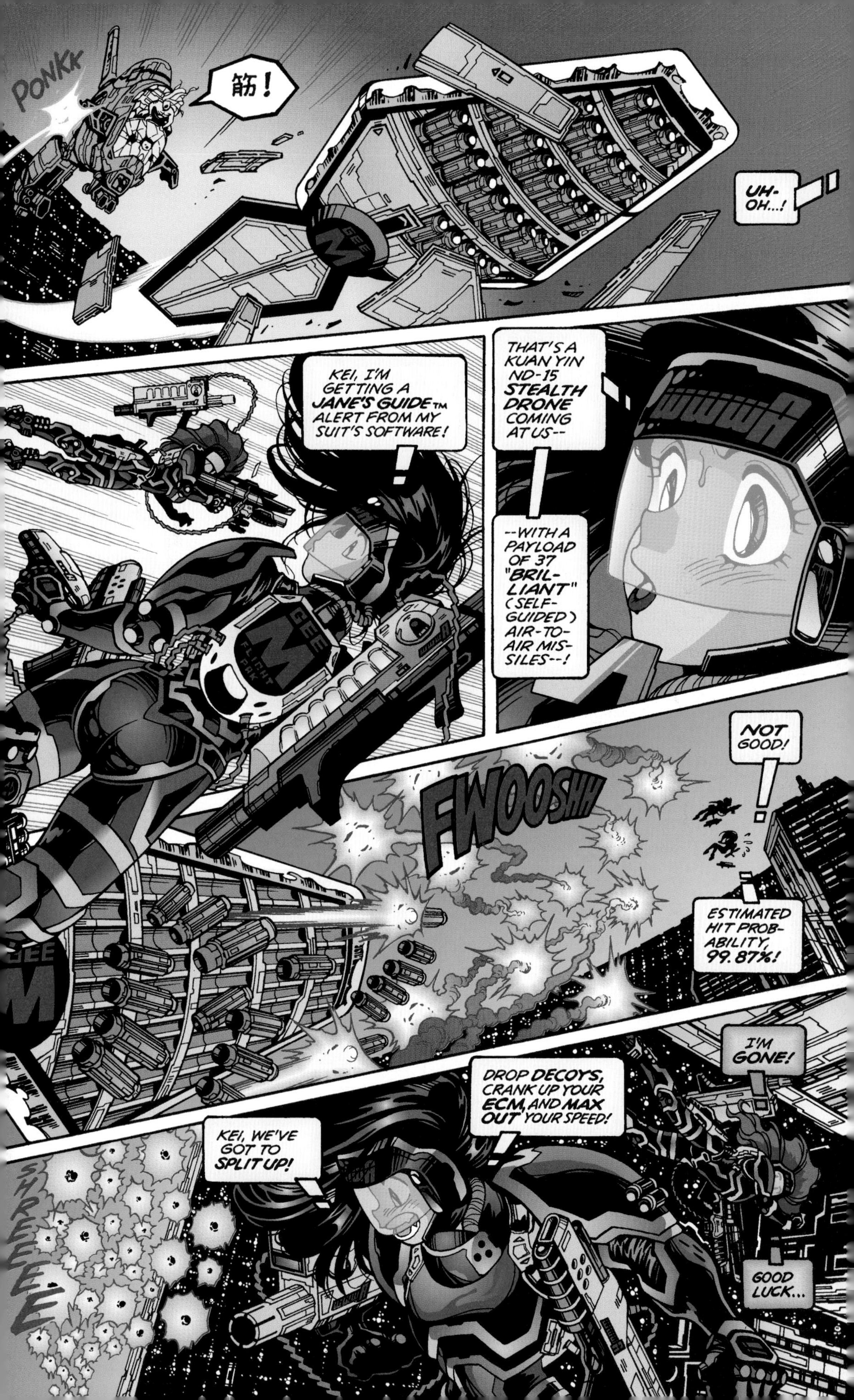
PONKK
筋！
UH-OH...!
KEI, I'M GETTING A JANE'S GUIDE™ ALERT FROM MY SUIT'S SOFTWARE!
THAT'S A KUAN YIN ND-15 STEALTH DRONE COMING AT US--
--WITH A PAYLOAD OF 37 "BRILLIANT" (SELF-GUIDED) AIR-TO-AIR MISSILES--!
FWOOSHH
NOT GOOD!
ESTIMATED HIT PROBABILITY, 99.87%!
SHREEEEE
KEI, WE'VE GOT TO SPLIT UP!
DROP DECOYS, CRANK UP YOUR ECM, AND MAX OUT YOUR SPEED!
I'M GONE!
GOOD LUCK...

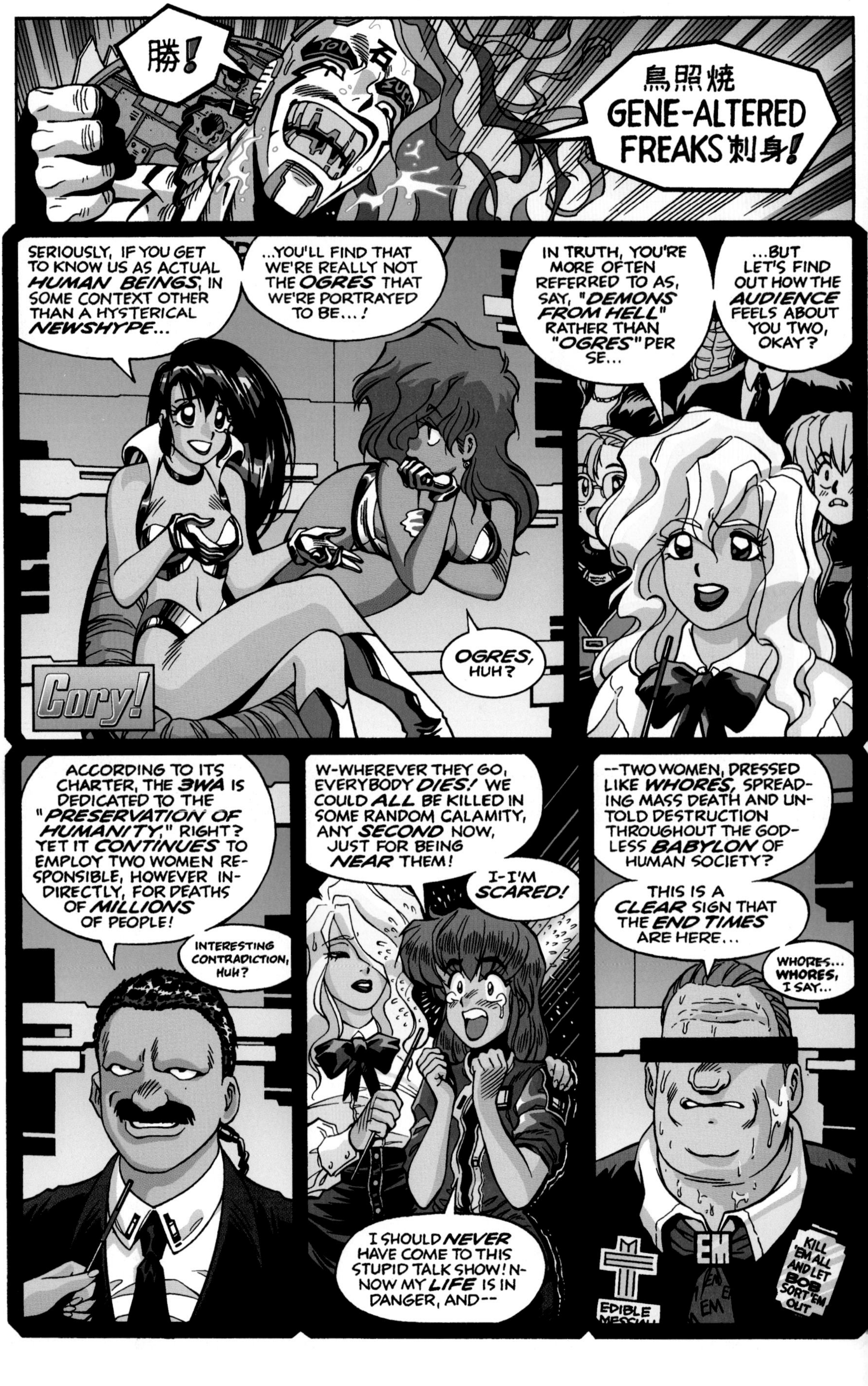
勝!
鳥照焼 GENE-ALTERED FREAKS 刺身!
SERIOUSLY, IF YOU GET TO KNOW US AS ACTUAL *HUMAN BEINGS*, IN SOME CONTEXT OTHER THAN A HYSTERICAL *NEWSHYPE*...
...YOU'LL FIND THAT WE'RE REALLY NOT THE *OGRES* THAT WE'RE PORTRAYED TO BE...!
OGRES, HUH?
Cory!
IN TRUTH, YOU'RE MORE OFTEN REFERRED TO AS, SAY, "*DEMONS FROM HELL*" RATHER THAN "*OGRES*" PER SE...
...BUT LET'S FIND OUT HOW THE *AUDIENCE* FEELS ABOUT YOU TWO, OKAY?
ACCORDING TO ITS CHARTER, THE *3WA* IS DEDICATED TO THE "*PRESERVATION OF HUMANITY*," RIGHT? YET IT *CONTINUES* TO EMPLOY TWO WOMEN RESPONSIBLE, HOWEVER INDIRECTLY, FOR DEATHS OF *MILLIONS* OF PEOPLE!
INTERESTING CONTRADICTION, HUH?
W-WHEREVER THEY GO, EVERYBODY *DIES!* WE COULD *ALL* BE KILLED IN SOME RANDOM CALAMITY, ANY *SECOND* NOW, JUST FOR BEING *NEAR* THEM!
I-I'M *SCARED!*
I SHOULD *NEVER* HAVE COME TO THIS STUPID TALK SHOW! N-NOW MY *LIFE* IS IN DANGER, AND--
--TWO WOMEN, DRESSED LIKE *WHORES*, SPREADING MASS DEATH AND UNTOLD DESTRUCTION THROUGHOUT THE GODLESS *BABYLON* OF HUMAN SOCIETY?
THIS IS A *CLEAR* SIGN THAT THE *END TIMES* ARE HERE...
WHORES... WHORES, I SAY...
EDIBLE
EM
KILL 'EM ALL AND LET BOB SORT 'EM OUT

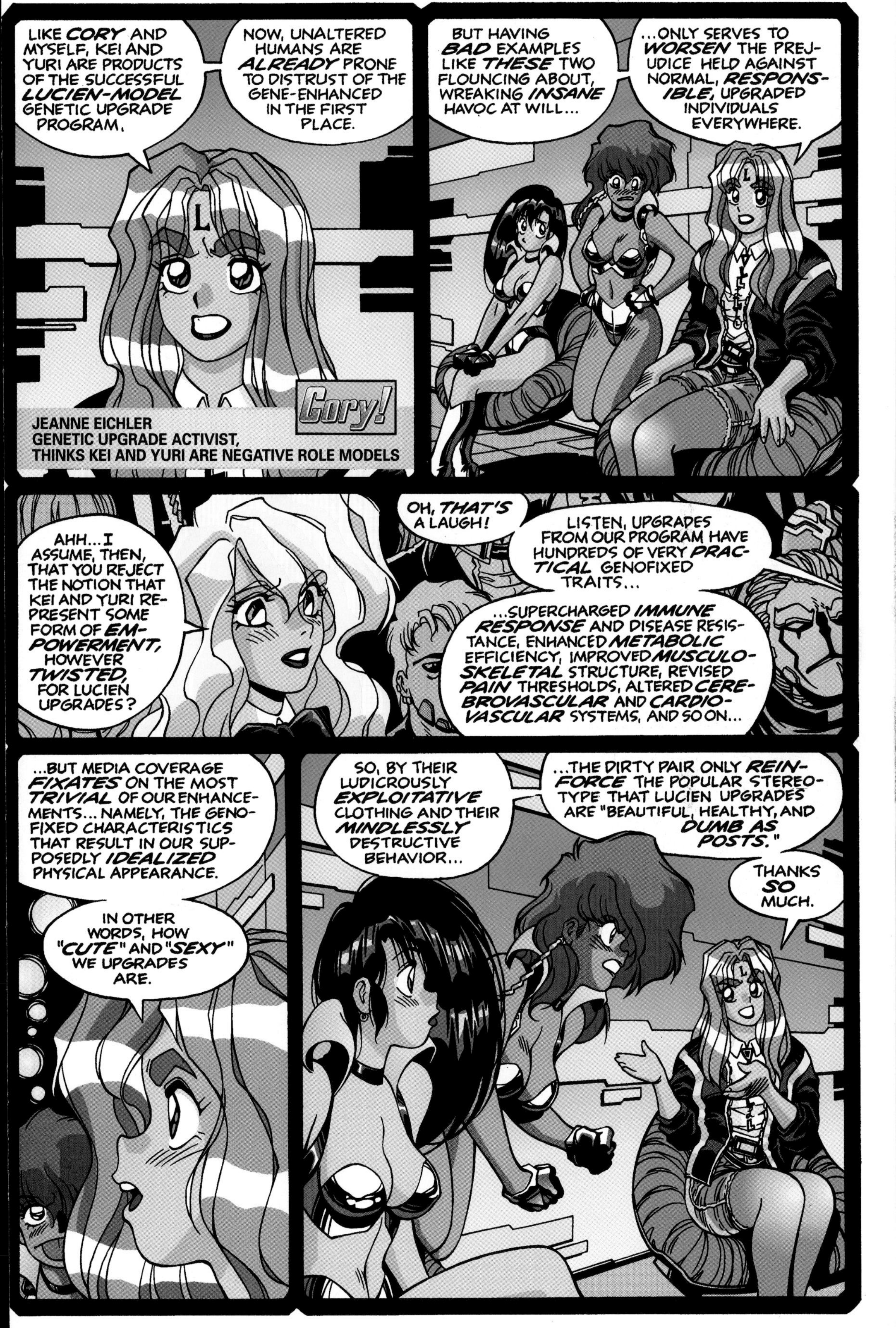
LIKE CORY AND MYSELF, KEI AND YURI ARE PRODUCTS OF THE SUCCESSFUL LUCIEN-MODEL GENETIC UPGRADE PROGRAM.
NOW, UNALTERED HUMANS ARE ALREADY PRONE TO DISTRUST OF THE GENE-ENHANCED IN THE FIRST PLACE.
Cory!
JEANNE EICHLER
GENETIC UPGRADE ACTIVIST,
THINKS KEI AND YURI ARE NEGATIVE ROLE MODELS
BUT HAVING BAD EXAMPLES LIKE THESE TWO FLOUNCING ABOUT, WREAKING INSANE HAVOC AT WILL...
...ONLY SERVES TO WORSEN THE PREJUDICE HELD AGAINST NORMAL, RESPONSIBLE, UPGRADED INDIVIDUALS EVERYWHERE.
AHH... I ASSUME, THEN, THAT YOU REJECT THE NOTION THAT KEI AND YURI REPRESENT SOME FORM OF EMPOWERMENT, HOWEVER TWISTED, FOR LUCIEN UPGRADES?
OH, THAT'S A LAUGH!
LISTEN, UPGRADES FROM OUR PROGRAM HAVE HUNDREDS OF VERY PRACTICAL GENOFIXED TRAITS...
...SUPERCHARGED IMMUNE RESPONSE AND DISEASE RESISTANCE, ENHANCED METABOLIC EFFICIENCY, IMPROVED MUSCULOSKELETAL STRUCTURE, REVISED PAIN THRESHOLDS, ALTERED CEREBROVASCULAR AND CARDIOVASCULAR SYSTEMS, AND SO ON...
...BUT MEDIA COVERAGE FIXATES ON THE MOST TRIVIAL OF OUR ENHANCEMENTS... NAMELY, THE GENOFIXED CHARACTERISTICS THAT RESULT IN OUR SUPPOSEDLY IDEALIZED PHYSICAL APPEARANCE.
IN OTHER WORDS, HOW "CUTE" AND "SEXY" WE UPGRADES ARE.
SO, BY THEIR LUDICROUSLY EXPLOITATIVE CLOTHING AND THEIR MINDLESSLY DESTRUCTIVE BEHAVIOR...
...THE DIRTY PAIR ONLY REINFORCE THE POPULAR STEREOTYPE THAT LUCIEN UPGRADES ARE "BEAUTIFUL, HEALTHY, AND DUMB AS POSTS."
THANKS SO MUCH.

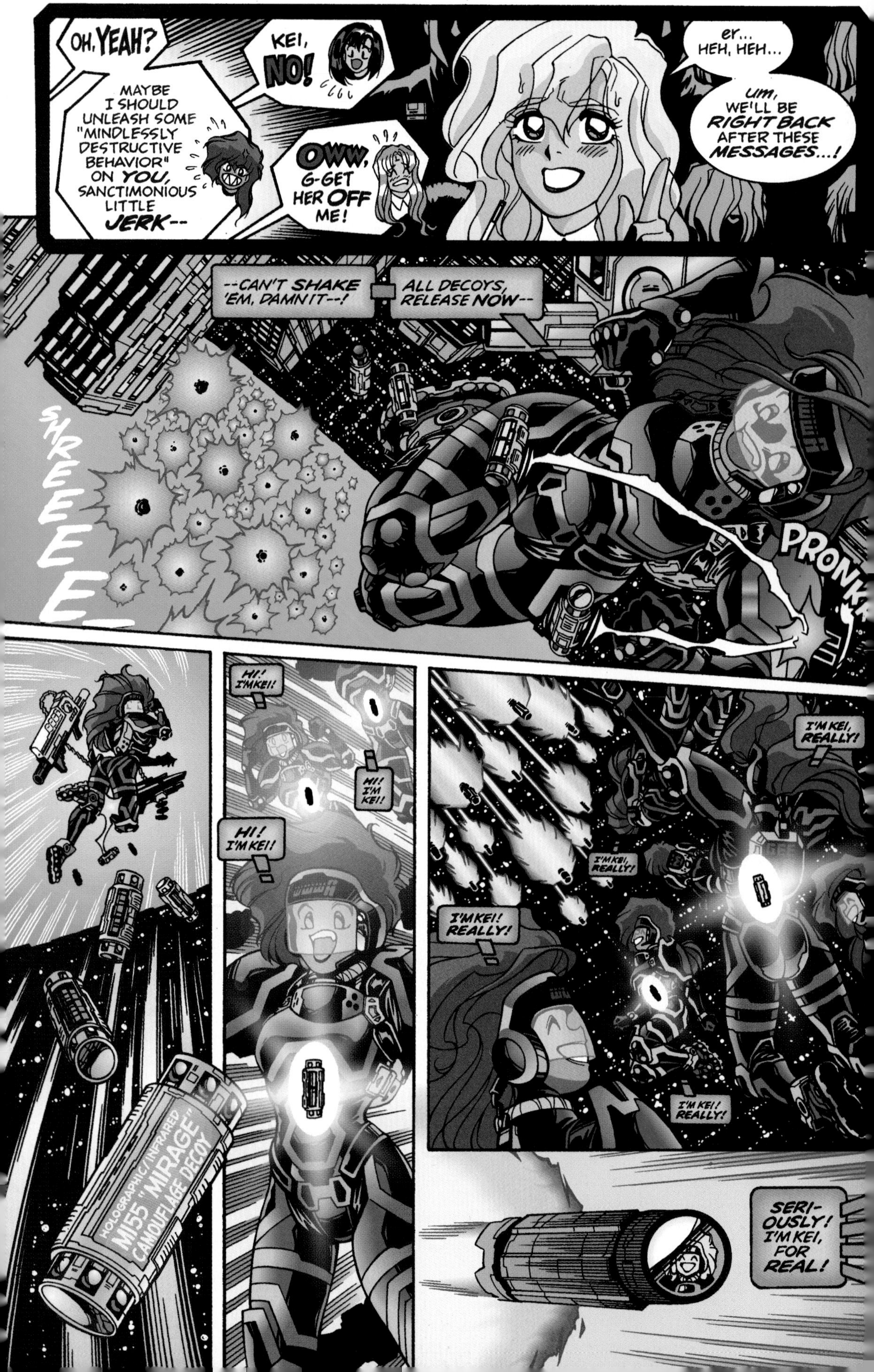
OH, YEAH?
MAYBE I SHOULD UNLEASH SOME "MINDLESSLY DESTRUCTIVE BEHAVIOR" ON YOU, SANCTIMONIOUS LITTLE JERK--
KEI, NO!
OWW, G-GET HER OFF ME!
er... HEH, HEH...
um, WE'LL BE RIGHT BACK AFTER THESE MESSAGES...!
--CAN'T SHAKE 'EM, DAMNIT--!
ALL DECOYS, RELEASE NOW--
SHREEEEE
PRONK
HOLOGRAPHIC/INFRARED M155 "MIRAGE" CAMOUFLAGE DECOY
HI! I'M KEI!
HI! I'M KEI!
HI! I'M KEI!
I'M KEI, REALLY!
I'M KEI, REALLY!
I'M KEI! REALLY!
I'M KEI! REALLY!
SERI-OUSLY! I'M KEI, FOR REAL!

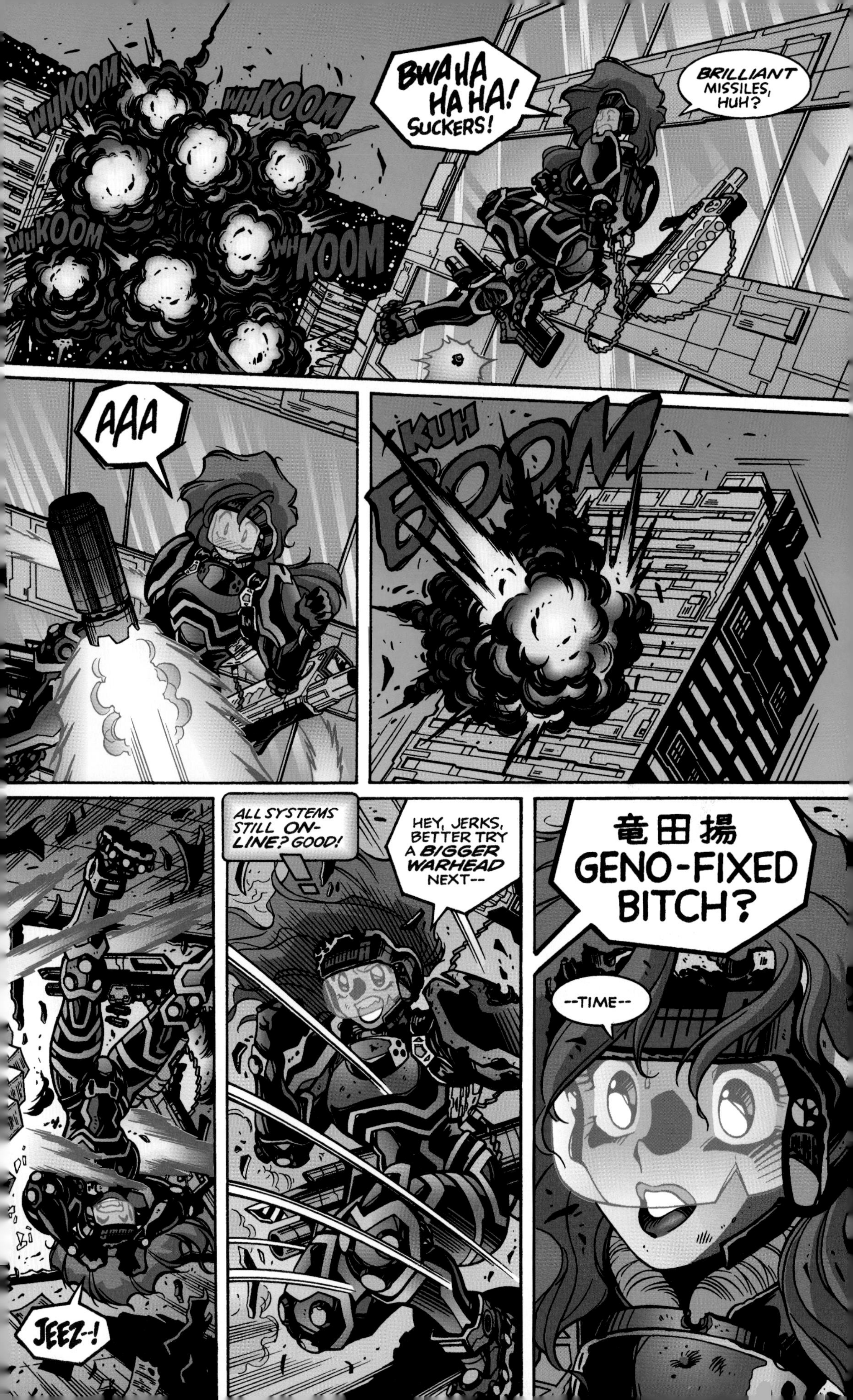
WHKOOM
WHKOOM
WHKOOM
WHKOOM
BWA HA HA HA! SUCKERS!
BRILLIANT MISSILES, HUH?
AAA
KUH BOOM
JEEZ--!
ALL SYSTEMS STILL ON-LINE? GOOD!
HEY, JERKS, BETTER TRY A BIGGER WARHEAD NEXT--
--TIME--
竜田揚 GENO-FIXED BITCH?

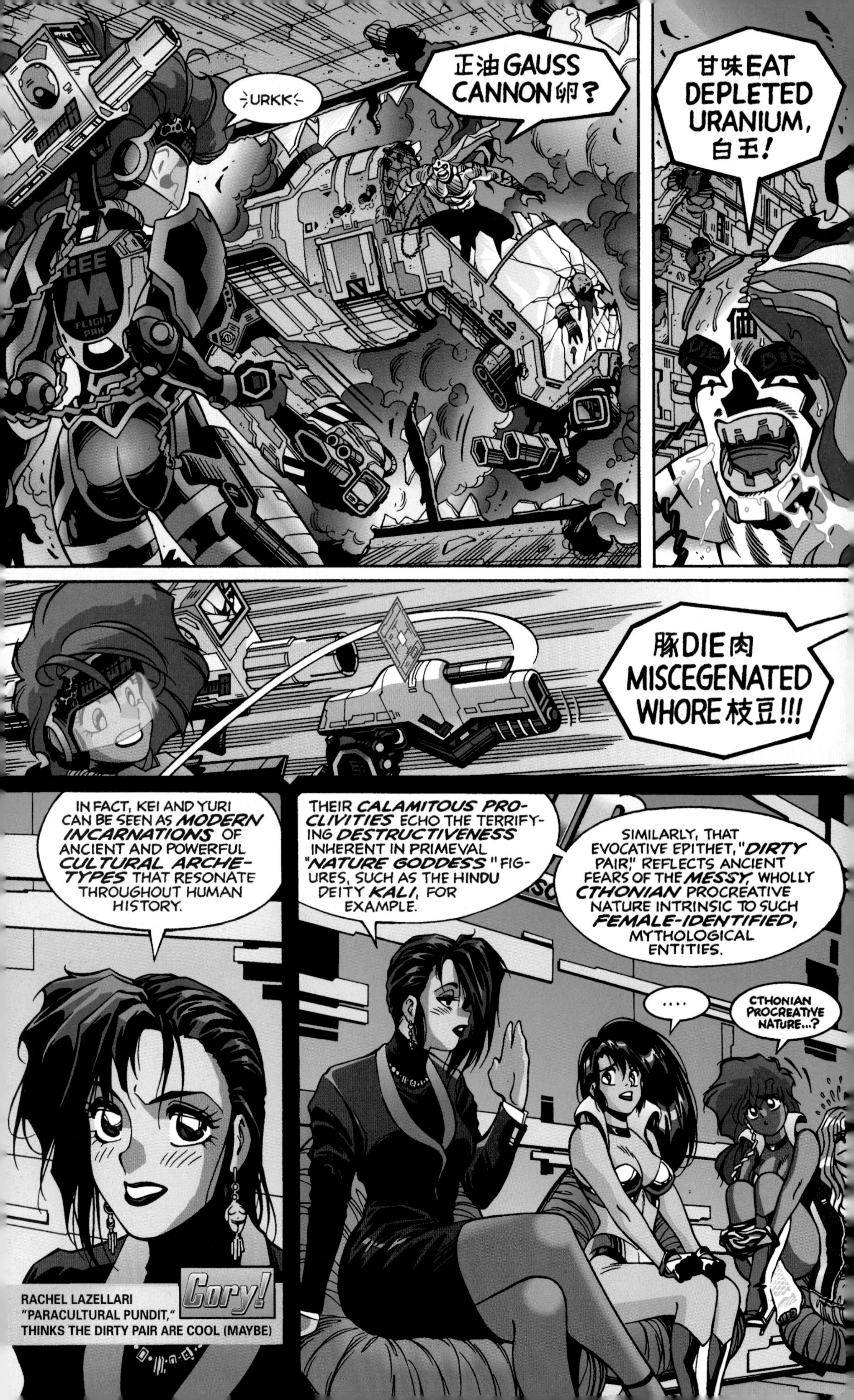
-URKK-
正油GAUSS CANNON卵?
甘味EAT DEPLETED URANIUM, 白玉!
豚DIE肉 MISCEGENATED WHORE枝豆!!!
IN FACT, KEI AND YURI CAN BE SEEN AS MODERN INCARNATIONS OF ANCIENT AND POWERFUL CULTURAL ARCHETYPES THAT RESONATE THROUGHOUT HUMAN HISTORY.
RACHEL LAZELLARI "PARACULTURAL PUNDIT," THINKS THE DIRTY PAIR ARE COOL (MAYBE)
Cory!
THEIR CALAMITOUS PROCLIVITIES ECHO THE TERRIFYING DESTRUCTIVENESS INHERENT IN PRIMEVAL "NATURE GODDESS" FIGURES, SUCH AS THE HINDU DEITY KALI, FOR EXAMPLE.
SIMILARLY, THAT EVOCATIVE EPITHET, "DIRTY PAIR," REFLECTS ANCIENT FEARS OF THE MESSY, WHOLLY CTHONIAN PROCREATIVE NATURE INTRINSIC TO SUCH FEMALE-IDENTIFIED, MYTHOLOGICAL ENTITIES.
....
CTHONIAN PROCREATIVE NATURE...?

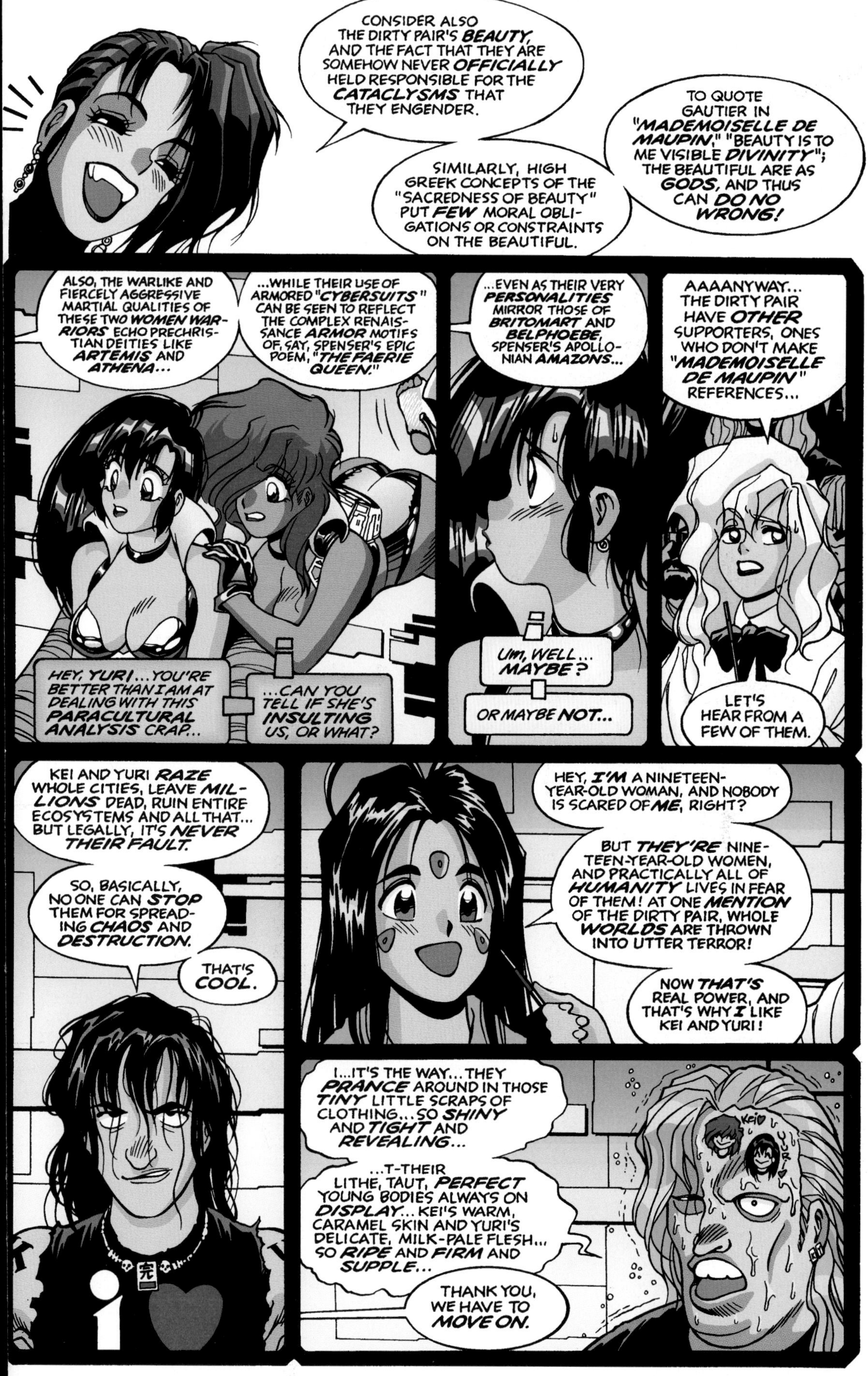
CONSIDER ALSO THE DIRTY PAIR'S BEAUTY, AND THE FACT THAT THEY ARE SOMEHOW NEVER OFFICIALLY HELD RESPONSIBLE FOR THE CATACLYSMS THAT THEY ENGENDER.
SIMILARLY, HIGH GREEK CONCEPTS OF THE "SACREDNESS OF BEAUTY" PUT FEW MORAL OBLIGATIONS OR CONSTRAINTS ON THE BEAUTIFUL.
TO QUOTE GAUTIER IN "MADEMOISELLE DE MAUPIN," "BEAUTY IS TO ME VISIBLE DIVINITY"; THE BEAUTIFUL ARE AS GODS, AND THUS CAN DO NO WRONG!
ALSO, THE WARLIKE AND FIERCELY AGGRESSIVE MARTIAL QUALITIES OF THESE TWO WOMEN WARRIORS ECHO PRECHRISTIAN DEITIES LIKE ARTEMIS AND ATHENA...
...WHILE THEIR USE OF ARMORED "CYBERSUITS" CAN BE SEEN TO REFLECT THE COMPLEX RENAISSANCE ARMOR MOTIFS OF, SAY, SPENSER'S EPIC POEM, "THE FAERIE QUEEN."
HEY, YURI... YOU'RE BETTER THAN I AM AT DEALING WITH THIS PARACULTURAL ANALYSIS CRAP...
...CAN YOU TELL IF SHE'S INSULTING US, OR WHAT?
...EVEN AS THEIR VERY PERSONALITIES MIRROR THOSE OF BRITOMART AND BELPHOEBE, SPENSER'S APOLLONIAN AMAZONS...
Um, WELL... MAYBE?
OR MAYBE NOT...
AAAANYWAY... THE DIRTY PAIR HAVE OTHER SUPPORTERS, ONES WHO DON'T MAKE "MADEMOISELLE DE MAUPIN" REFERENCES...
LET'S HEAR FROM A FEW OF THEM.
KEI AND YURI RAZE WHOLE CITIES, LEAVE MILLIONS DEAD, RUIN ENTIRE ECOSYSTEMS AND ALL THAT... BUT LEGALLY, IT'S NEVER THEIR FAULT.
SO, BASICALLY, NO ONE CAN STOP THEM FOR SPREADING CHAOS AND DESTRUCTION.
THAT'S COOL.
HEY, I'M A NINETEEN-YEAR-OLD WOMAN, AND NOBODY IS SCARED OF ME, RIGHT?
BUT THEY'RE NINETEEN-YEAR-OLD WOMEN, AND PRACTICALLY ALL OF HUMANITY LIVES IN FEAR OF THEM! AT ONE MENTION OF THE DIRTY PAIR, WHOLE WORLDS ARE THROWN INTO UTTER TERROR!
NOW THAT'S REAL POWER, AND THAT'S WHY I LIKE KEI AND YURI!
I...IT'S THE WAY... THEY PRANCE AROUND IN THOSE TINY LITTLE SCRAPS OF CLOTHING... SO SHINY AND TIGHT AND REVEALING...
...T-THEIR LITHE, TAUT, PERFECT YOUNG BODIES ALWAYS ON DISPLAY... KEI'S WARM, CARAMEL SKIN AND YURI'S DELICATE, MILK-PALE FLESH... SO RIPE AND FIRM AND SUPPLE...
THANK YOU, WE HAVE TO MOVE ON.

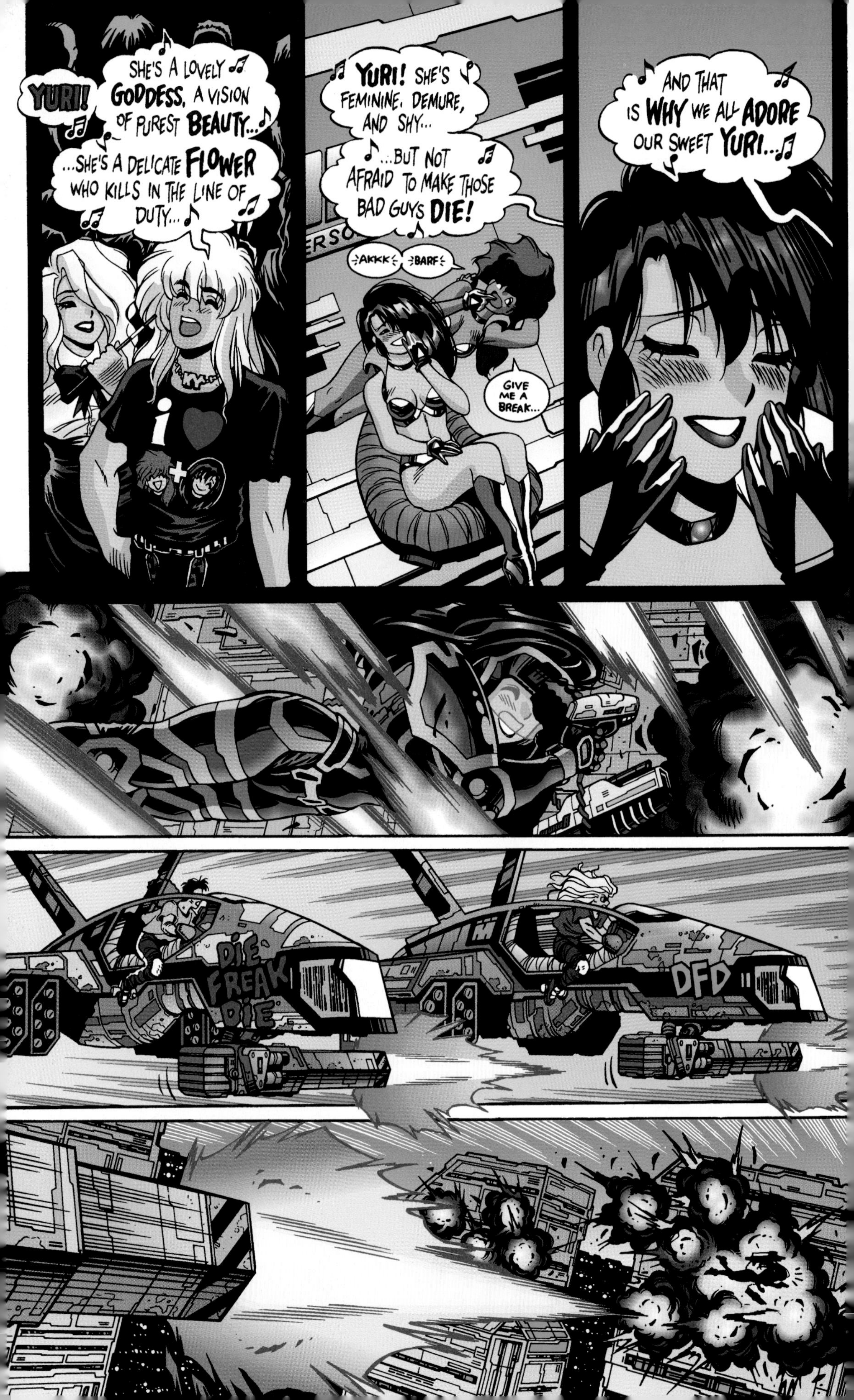
YURI!
SHE'S A LOVELY GODDESS, A VISION OF PUREST BEAUTY...
...SHE'S A DELICATE FLOWER WHO KILLS IN THE LINE OF DUTY...
YURI! SHE'S FEMININE, DEMURE, AND SHY...
...BUT NOT AFRAID TO MAKE THOSE BAD GUYS DIE!
AKKK
BARF
GIVE ME A BREAK...
AND THAT IS WHY WE ALL ADORE OUR SWEET YURI...
DIE FREAK DIE
DFD

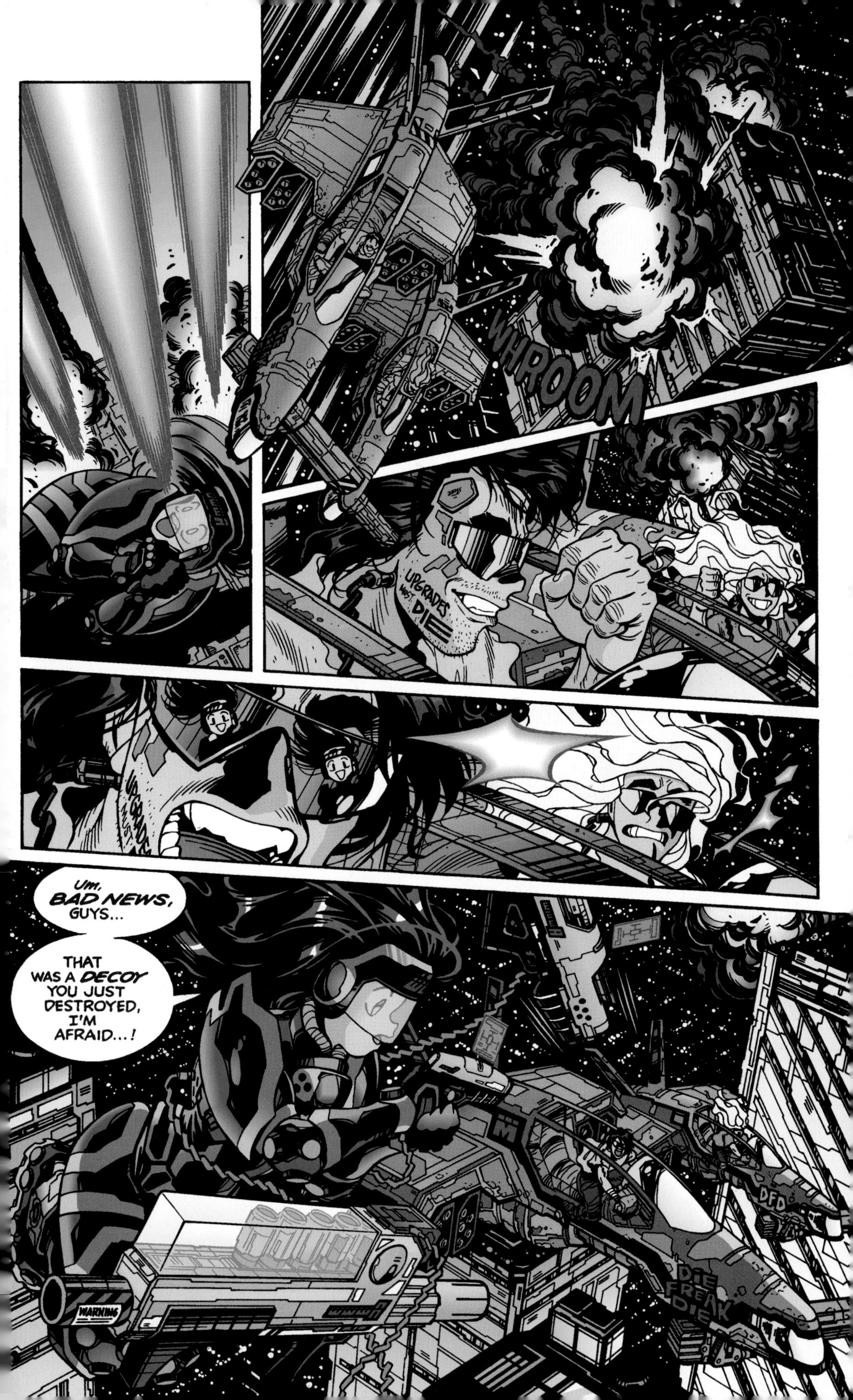
WHROOM
UPGRADES MUST DIE
Um, BAD NEWS, GUYS...
THAT WAS A DECOY YOU JUST DESTROYED, I'M AFRAID...!
WARNING
DFD

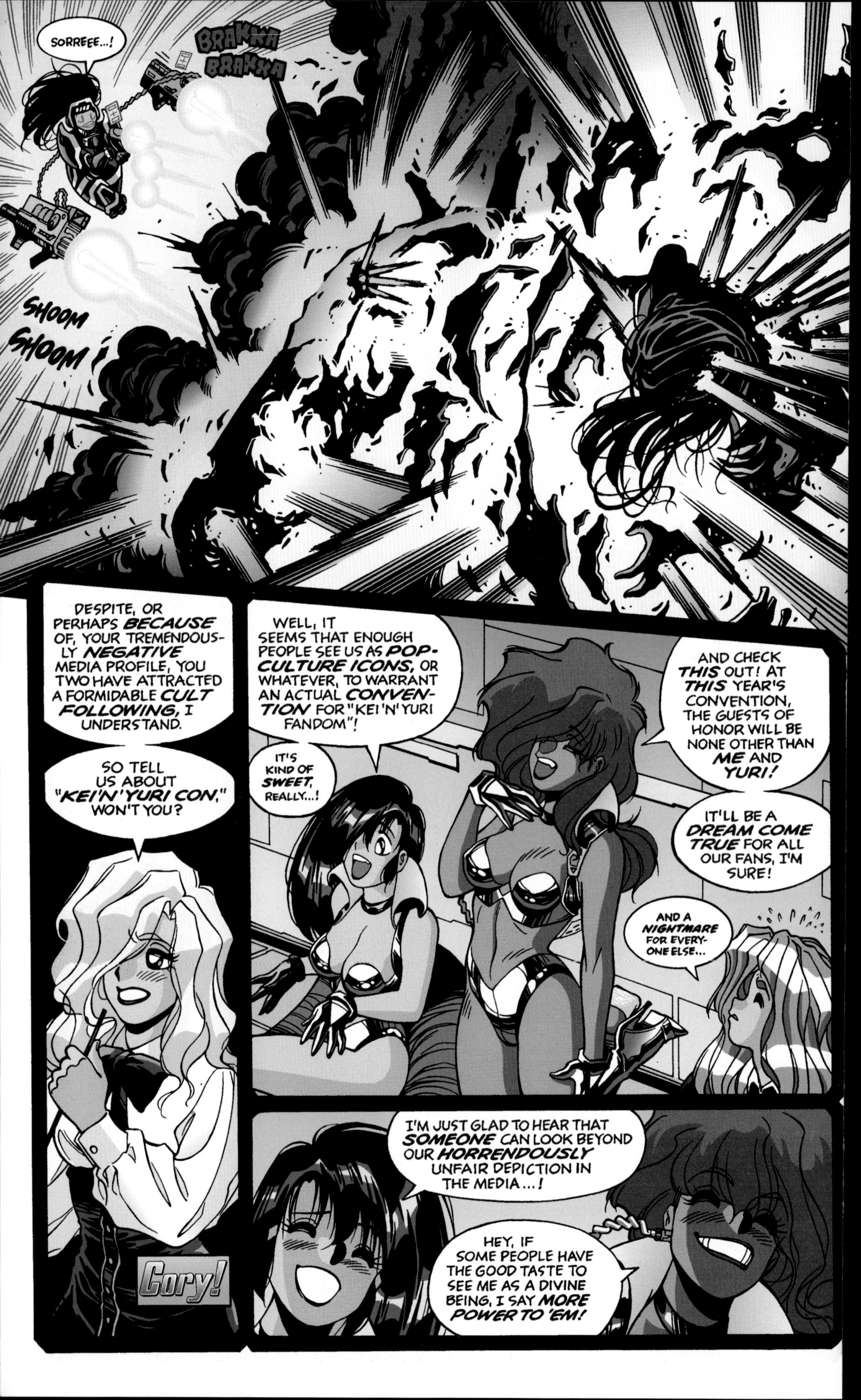
SORREEE...!
BRAKKA BRAKKA
SHOOM SHOOM
DESPITE, OR PERHAPS ***BECAUSE*** OF, YOUR TREMENDOUSLY ***NEGATIVE*** MEDIA PROFILE, YOU TWO HAVE ATTRACTED A FORMIDABLE ***CULT FOLLOWING,*** I UNDERSTAND.
SO TELL US ABOUT ***"KEI'N'YURI CON,"*** WON'T YOU?
Cory!
WELL, IT SEEMS THAT ENOUGH PEOPLE SEE US AS ***POP-CULTURE ICONS,*** OR WHATEVER, TO WARRANT AN ACTUAL ***CONVENTION*** FOR "KEI'N'YURI FANDOM"!
IT'S KIND OF ***SWEET,*** REALLY...!
AND CHECK ***THIS*** OUT! AT ***THIS*** YEAR'S CONVENTION, THE GUESTS OF HONOR WILL BE NONE OTHER THAN ***ME*** AND ***YURI!***
IT'LL BE A ***DREAM COME TRUE*** FOR ALL OUR FANS, I'M SURE!
AND A ***NIGHTMARE*** FOR EVERYONE ELSE...
I'M JUST GLAD TO HEAR THAT ***SOMEONE*** CAN LOOK BEYOND OUR ***HORRENDOUSLY*** UNFAIR DEPICTION IN THE MEDIA...!
HEY, IF SOME PEOPLE HAVE THE GOOD TASTE TO SEE ME AS A DIVINE BEING, I SAY ***MORE POWER TO 'EM!***

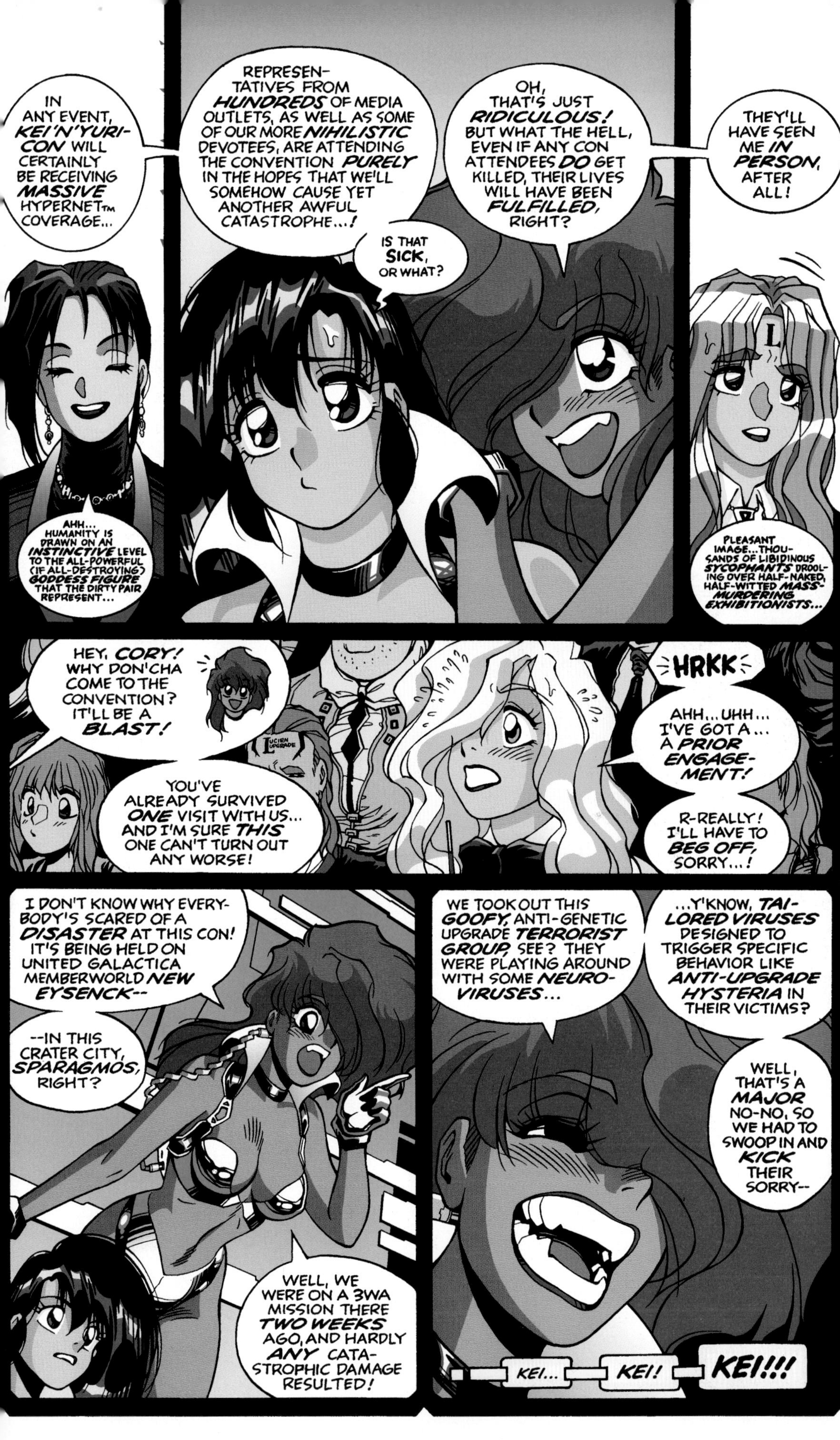
IN ANY EVENT, KEI'N'YURI-CON WILL CERTAINLY BE RECEIVING MASSIVE HYPERNET™ COVERAGE...
AHH... HUMANITY IS DRAWN ON AN INSTINCTIVE LEVEL TO THE ALL-POWERFUL (IF ALL-DESTROYING) GODDESS FIGURE THAT THE DIRTY PAIR REPRESENT...
REPRESEN-TATIVES FROM HUNDREDS OF MEDIA OUTLETS, AS WELL AS SOME OF OUR MORE NIHILISTIC DEVOTEES, ARE ATTENDING THE CONVENTION PURELY IN THE HOPES THAT WE'LL SOMEHOW CAUSE YET ANOTHER AWFUL CATASTROPHE...!
IS THAT SICK, OR WHAT?
OH, THAT'S JUST RIDICULOUS! BUT WHAT THE HELL, EVEN IF ANY CON ATTENDEES DO GET KILLED, THEIR LIVES WILL HAVE BEEN FULFILLED, RIGHT?
THEY'LL HAVE SEEN ME IN PERSON, AFTER ALL!
L
PLEASANT IMAGE...THOU-SANDS OF LIBIDINOUS SYCOPHANTS DROOL-ING OVER HALF-NAKED, HALF-WITTED MASS-MURDERING EXHIBITIONISTS...
HEY, CORY! WHY DON'CHA COME TO THE CONVENTION? IT'LL BE A BLAST!
LUCIEN UPGRADE
YOU'VE ALREADY SURVIVED ONE VISIT WITH US... AND I'M SURE THIS ONE CAN'T TURN OUT ANY WORSE!
HRKK
AHH...UHH... I'VE GOT A... A PRIOR ENGAGE-MENT!
R-REALLY! I'LL HAVE TO BEG OFF, SORRY...!
I DON'T KNOW WHY EVERY-BODY'S SCARED OF A DISASTER AT THIS CON! IT'S BEING HELD ON UNITED GALACTICA MEMBERWORLD NEW EYSENCK--
--IN THIS CRATER CITY, SPARAGMOS, RIGHT?
WELL, WE WERE ON A 3WA MISSION THERE TWO WEEKS AGO, AND HARDLY ANY CATA-STROPHIC DAMAGE RESULTED!
WE TOOK OUT THIS GOOFY, ANTI-GENETIC UPGRADE TERRORIST GROUP, SEE? THEY WERE PLAYING AROUND WITH SOME NEURO-VIRUSES...
...Y'KNOW, TAI-LORED VIRUSES DESIGNED TO TRIGGER SPECIFIC BEHAVIOR LIKE ANTI-UPGRADE HYSTERIA IN THEIR VICTIMS?
WELL, THAT'S A MAJOR NO-NO, SO WE HAD TO SWOOP IN AND KICK THEIR SORRY--
KEI...
KEI!
KEI!!!

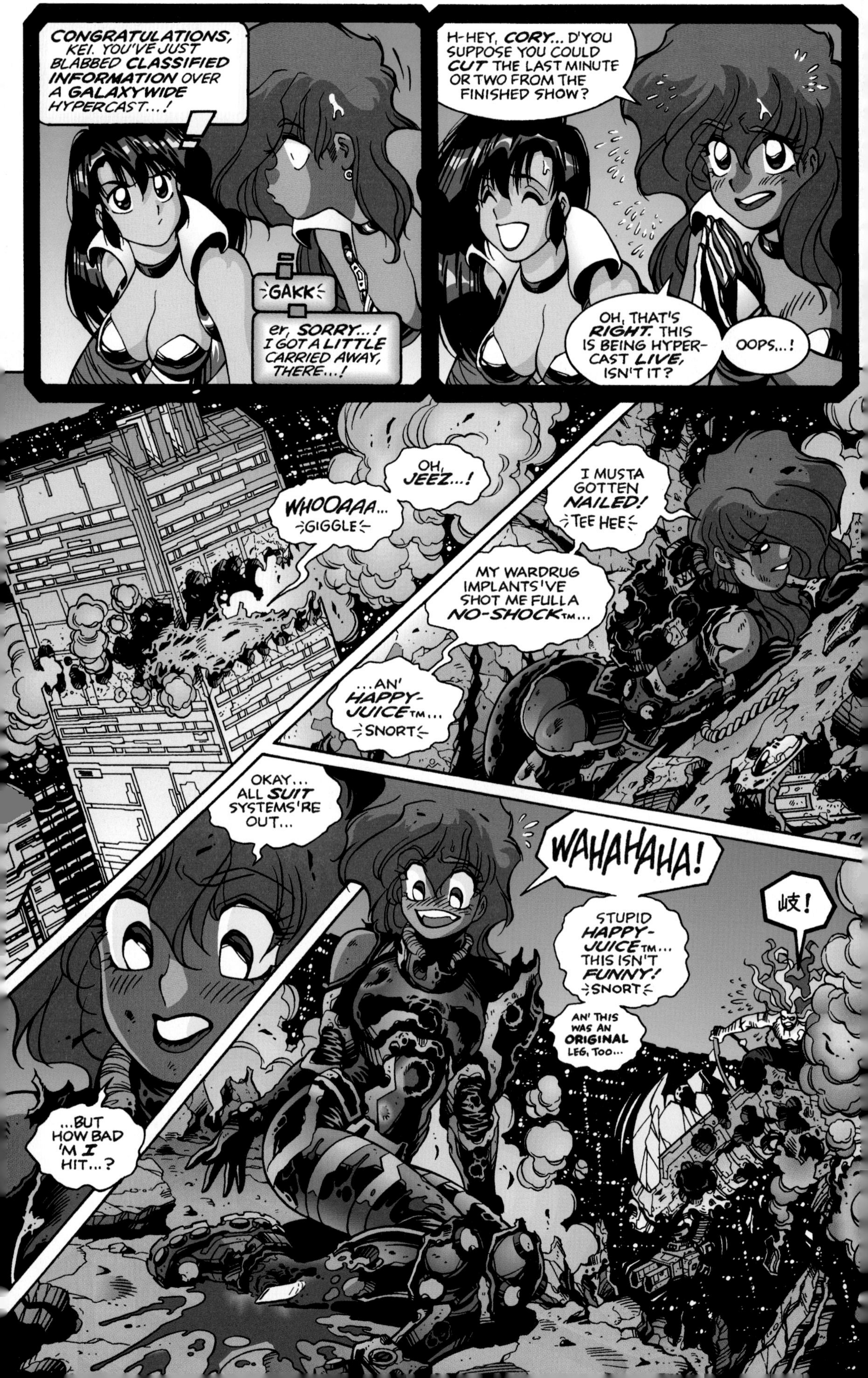
CONGRATULATIONS, KEI. YOU'VE JUST BLABBED CLASSIFIED INFORMATION OVER A GALAXYWIDE HYPERCAST...!
!
GAKK
er, SORRY...! I GOT A LITTLE CARRIED AWAY, THERE...!
H-HEY, CORY... D'YOU SUPPOSE YOU COULD CUT THE LAST MINUTE OR TWO FROM THE FINISHED SHOW?
OH, THAT'S RIGHT. THIS IS BEING HYPER-CAST LIVE, ISN'T IT?
OOPS...!
OH, JEEZ...!
WHOOAAA... GIGGLE
I MUSTA GOTTEN NAILED! TEE HEE
MY WARDRUG IMPLANTS'VE SHOT ME FULLA NO-SHOCK™...
...AN' HAPPY-JUICE™... SNORT
OKAY... ALL SUIT SYSTEMS'RE OUT...
...BUT HOW BAD 'M I HIT...?
WAHAHAHA!
STUPID HAPPY-JUICE™... THIS ISN'T FUNNY! SNORT
AN' THIS WAS AN ORIGINAL LEG, TOO...
岐!

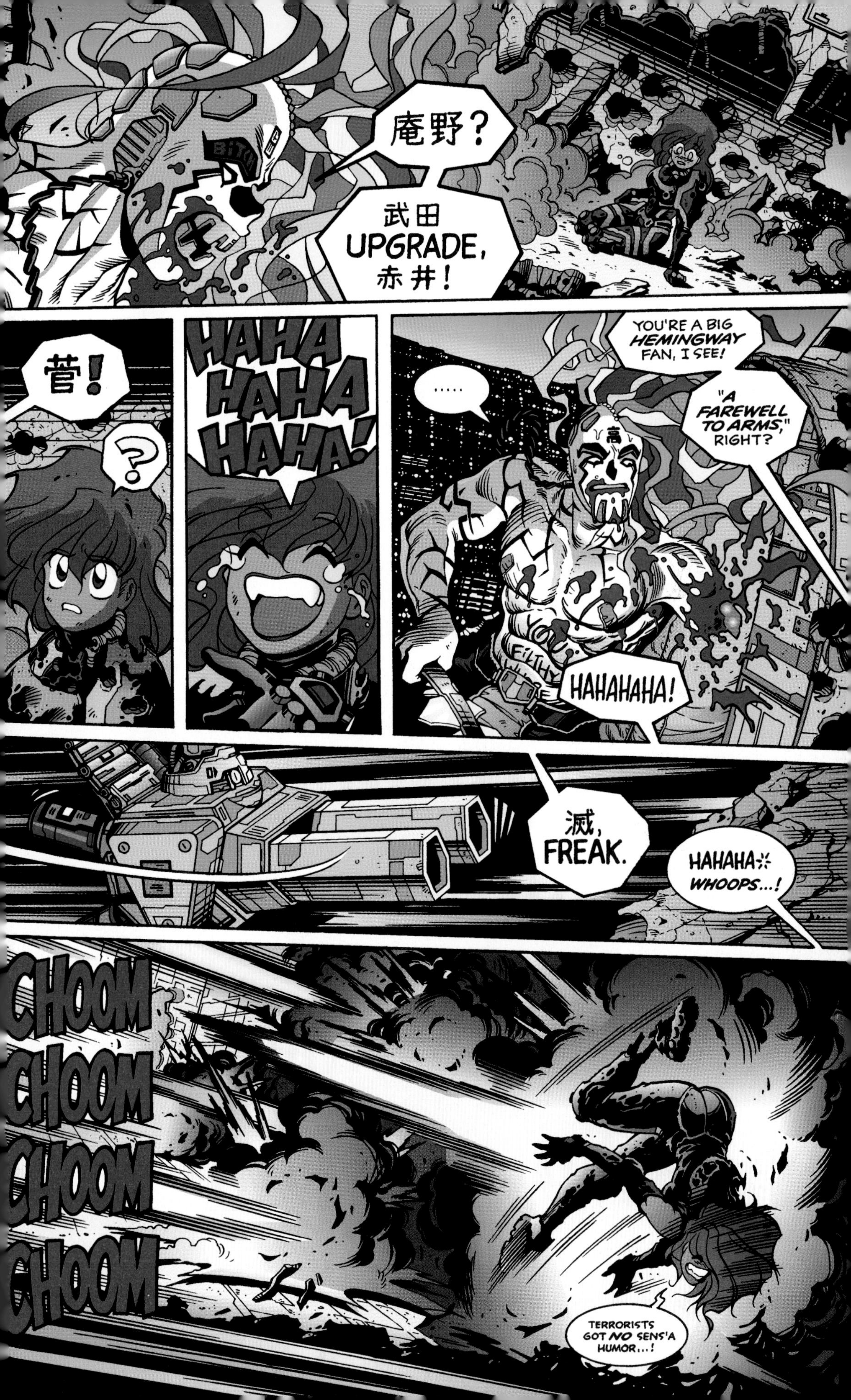
庵野？
武田 UPGRADE, 赤井！
菅！
?
HAHA HAHA HAHA!
.....
YOU'RE A BIG HEMINGWAY FAN, I SEE!
"A FAREWELL TO ARMS," RIGHT?
HAHAHAHA!
滅, FREAK.
HAHAHA-!! WHOOPS...!
CHOOM CHOOM CHOOM CHOOM
TERRORISTS GOT NO SENS'A HUMOR...!

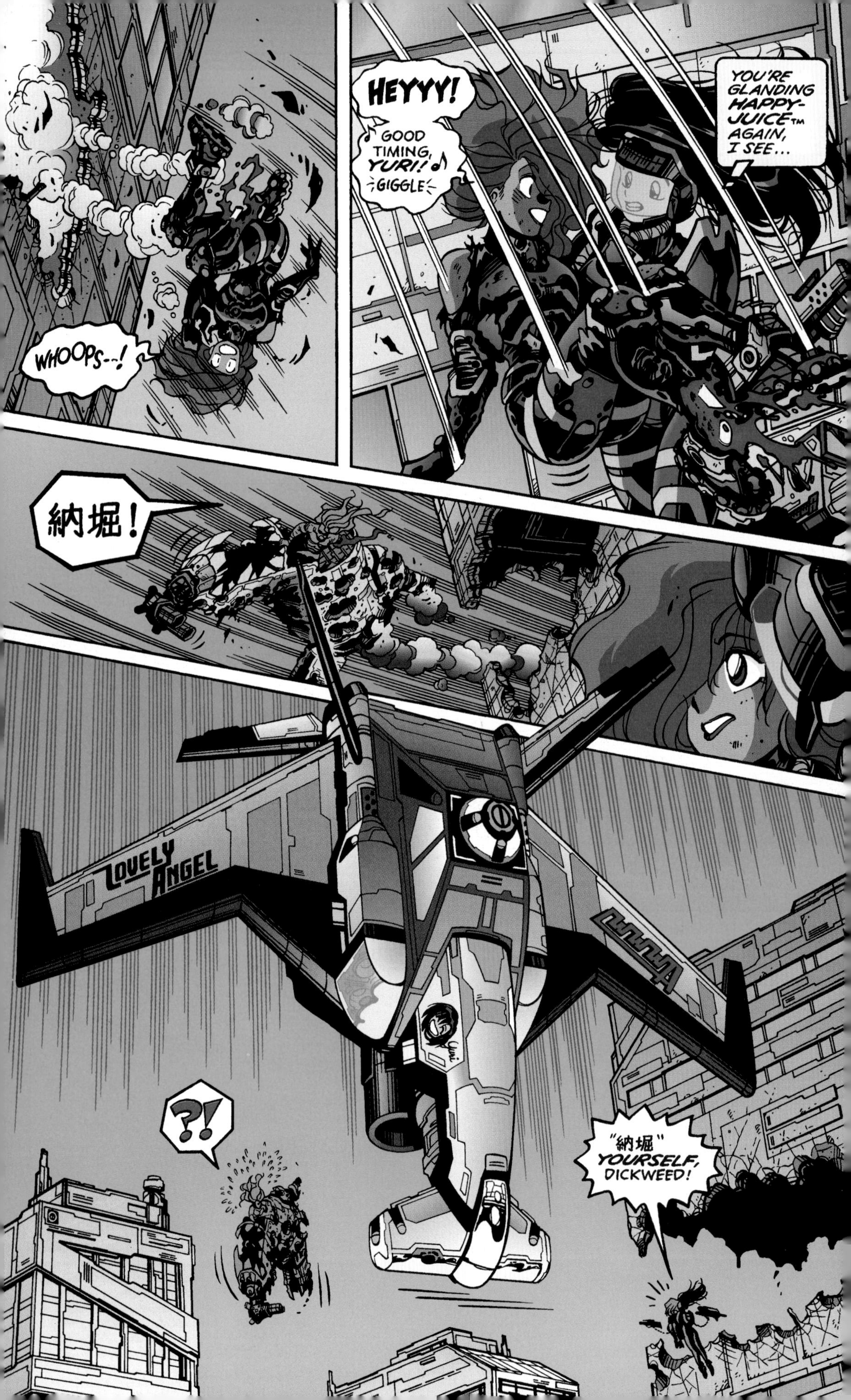
WHOOPS--!
HEYYY!
♪GOOD TIMING, YURI!♪ -GIGGLE-
YOU'RE GLANDING HAPPY-JUICE™ AGAIN, I SEE...
納堀！
LOVELY ANGEL
?!
"納堀" YOURSELF, DICKWEED!

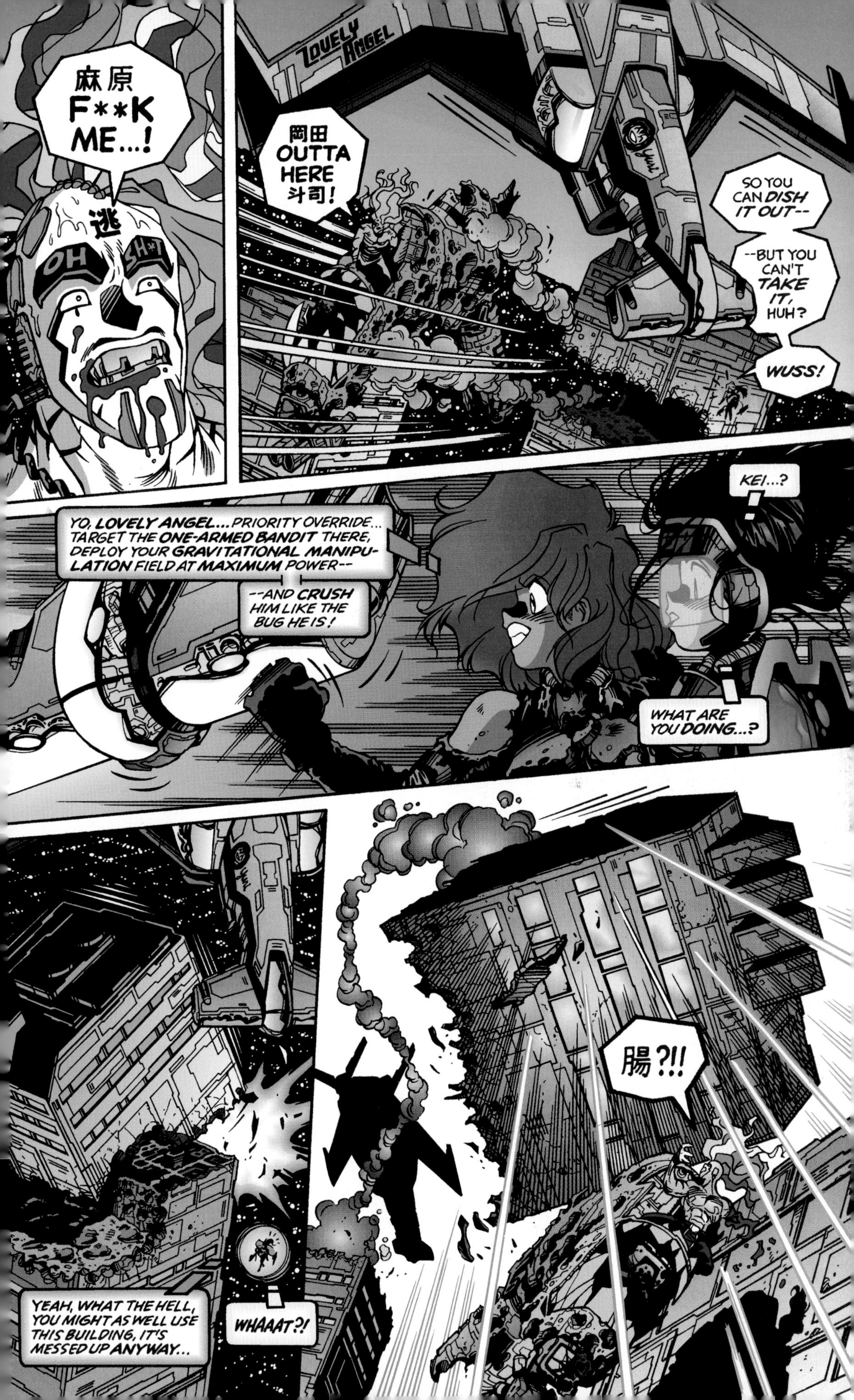

麻原 F**K ME...!
逃
OH
LOVELY ANGEL
岡田 OUTTA HERE 斗司!
SO YOU CAN DISH IT OUT--
--BUT YOU CAN'T TAKE IT, HUH?
WUSS!
YO, LOVELY ANGEL... PRIORITY OVERRIDE... TARGET THE ONE-ARMED BANDIT THERE, DEPLOY YOUR GRAVITATIONAL MANIPULATION FIELD AT MAXIMUM POWER--
--AND CRUSH HIM LIKE THE BUG HE IS!
KEI...?
WHAT ARE YOU DOING...?
YEAH, WHAT THE HELL, YOU MIGHT AS WELL USE THIS BUILDING, IT'S MESSED UP ANYWAY...
WHAAAT?!
腸?!!

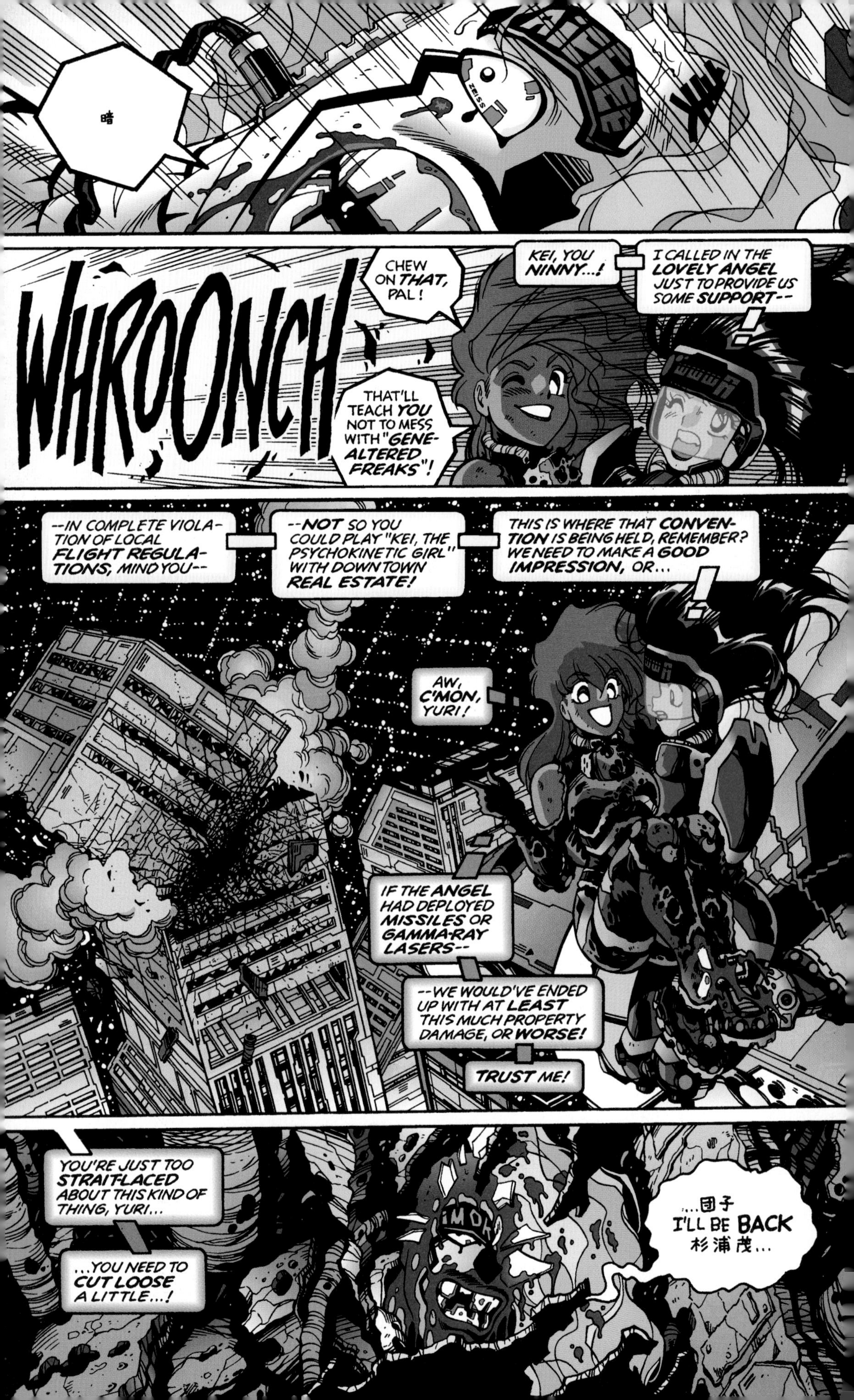
暗
WHROONCH
CHEW ON THAT, PAL!
THAT'LL TEACH YOU NOT TO MESS WITH "GENE-ALTERED FREAKS"!
KEI, YOU NINNY...!
I CALLED IN THE LOVELY ANGEL JUST TO PROVIDE US SOME SUPPORT--
!
--IN COMPLETE VIOLATION OF LOCAL FLIGHT REGULATIONS, MIND YOU--
--NOT SO YOU COULD PLAY "KEI, THE PSYCHOKINETIC GIRL" WITH DOWNTOWN REAL ESTATE!
THIS IS WHERE THAT CONVENTION IS BEING HELD, REMEMBER? WE NEED TO MAKE A GOOD IMPRESSION, OR...
!
AW, C'MON, YURI!
IF THE ANGEL HAD DEPLOYED MISSILES OR GAMMA-RAY LASERS--
--WE WOULD'VE ENDED UP WITH AT LEAST THIS MUCH PROPERTY DAMAGE, OR WORSE!
TRUST ME!
YOU'RE JUST TOO STRAIT-LACED ABOUT THIS KIND OF THING, YURI...
...YOU NEED TO CUT LOOSE A LITTLE...!
....团子 I'LL BE BACK 杉浦茂...

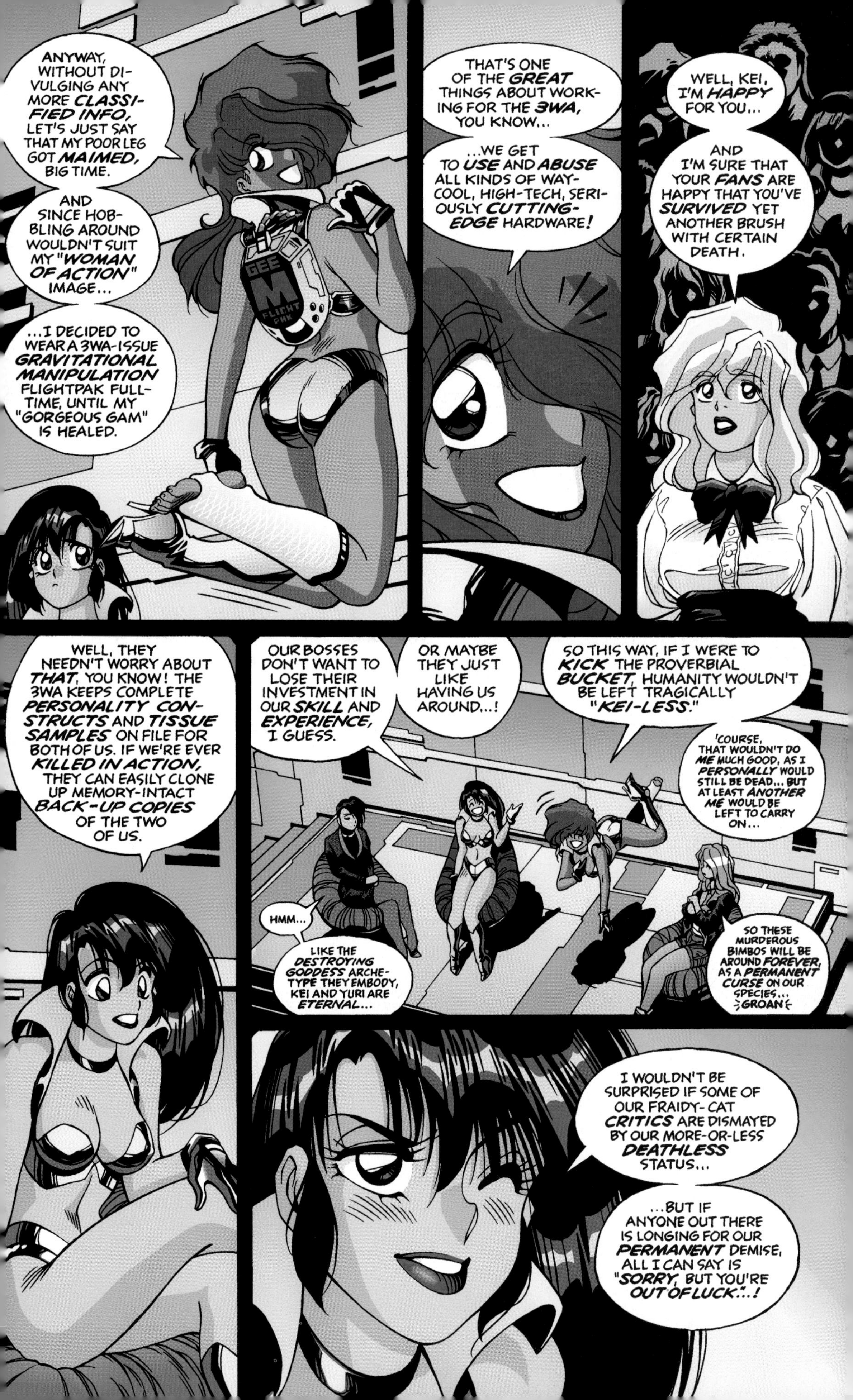
ANYWAY, WITHOUT DI-VULGING ANY MORE CLASSI-FIED INFO, LET'S JUST SAY THAT MY POOR LEG GOT MAIMED, BIG TIME.
AND SINCE HOB-BLING AROUND WOULDN'T SUIT MY "WOMAN OF ACTION" IMAGE...
...I DECIDED TO WEAR A 3WA-ISSUE GRAVITATIONAL MANIPULATION FLIGHTPAK FULL-TIME, UNTIL MY "GORGEOUS GAM" IS HEALED.
GEE M FLIGHT PAK
THAT'S ONE OF THE GREAT THINGS ABOUT WORK-ING FOR THE 3WA, YOU KNOW...
...WE GET TO USE AND ABUSE ALL KINDS OF WAY-COOL, HIGH-TECH, SERI-OUSLY CUTTING-EDGE HARDWARE!
WELL, KEI, I'M HAPPY FOR YOU...
AND I'M SURE THAT YOUR FANS ARE HAPPY THAT YOU'VE SURVIVED YET ANOTHER BRUSH WITH CERTAIN DEATH.
WELL, THEY NEEDN'T WORRY ABOUT THAT, YOU KNOW! THE 3WA KEEPS COMPLETE PERSONALITY CON-STRUCTS AND TISSUE SAMPLES ON FILE FOR BOTH OF US. IF WE'RE EVER KILLED IN ACTION, THEY CAN EASILY CLONE UP MEMORY-INTACT BACK-UP COPIES OF THE TWO OF US.
OUR BOSSES DON'T WANT TO LOSE THEIR INVESTMENT IN OUR SKILL AND EXPERIENCE, I GUESS.
OR MAYBE THEY JUST LIKE HAVING US AROUND...!
SO THIS WAY, IF I WERE TO KICK THE PROVERBIAL BUCKET, HUMANITY WOULDN'T BE LEFT TRAGICALLY "KEI-LESS."
'COURSE, THAT WOULDN'T DO ME MUCH GOOD, AS I PERSONALLY WOULD STILL BE DEAD... BUT AT LEAST ANOTHER ME WOULD BE LEFT TO CARRY ON...
HMM...
LIKE THE DESTROYING GODDESS ARCHE-TYPE THEY EMBODY, KEI AND YURI ARE ETERNAL...
SO THESE MURDEROUS BIMBOS WILL BE AROUND FOREVER, AS A PERMANENT CURSE ON OUR SPECIES... ≷GROAN≶
I WOULDN'T BE SURPRISED IF SOME OF OUR FRAIDY-CAT CRITICS ARE DISMAYED BY OUR MORE-OR-LESS DEATHLESS STATUS...
...BUT IF ANYONE OUT THERE IS LONGING FOR OUR PERMANENT DEMISE, ALL I CAN SAY IS "SORRY, BUT YOU'RE OUT OF LUCK"...!

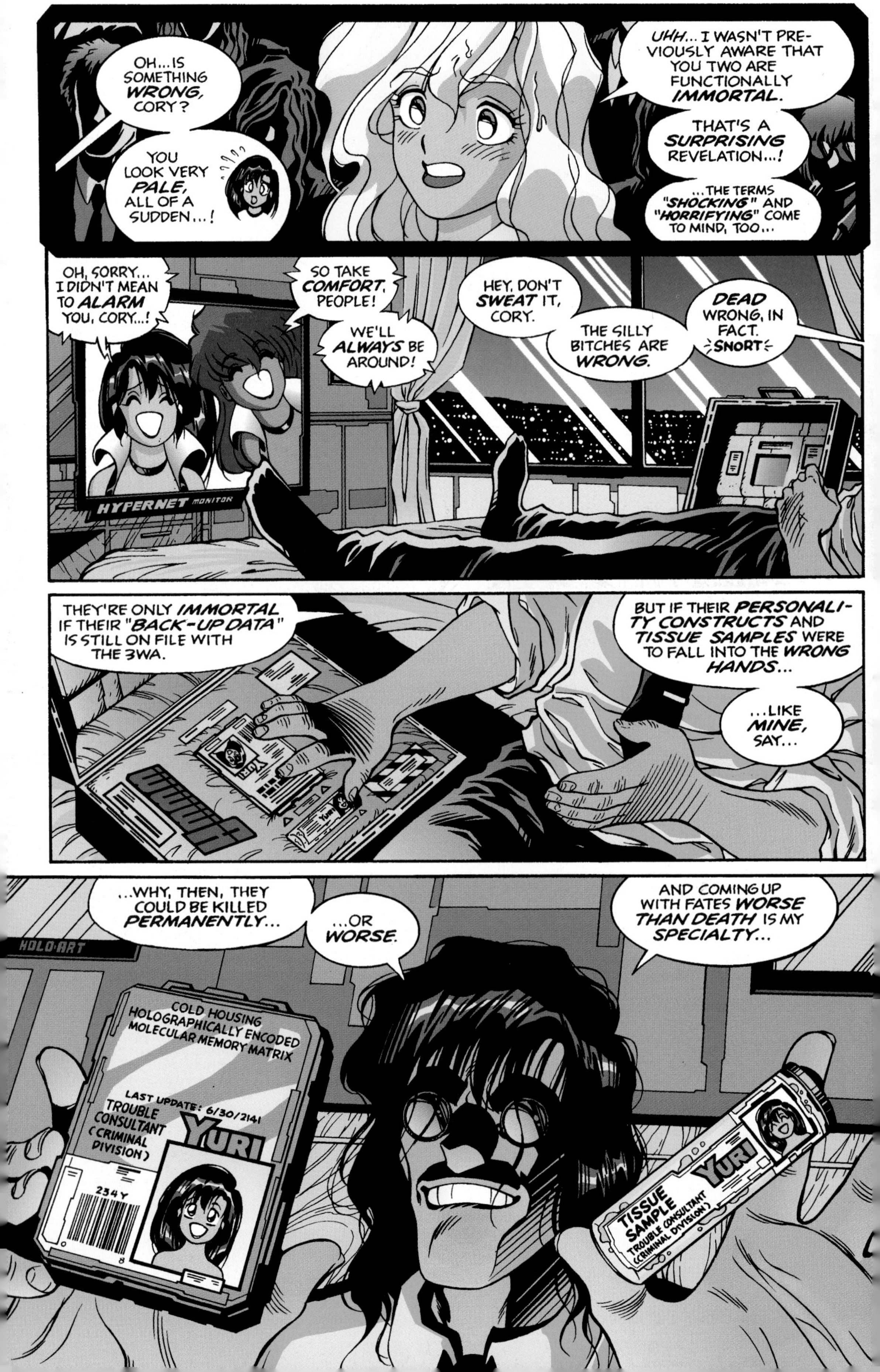

OH... IS SOMETHING WRONG, CORY?
YOU LOOK VERY PALE, ALL OF A SUDDEN...!
UHH... I WASN'T PREVIOUSLY AWARE THAT YOU TWO ARE FUNCTIONALLY IMMORTAL.
THAT'S A SURPRISING REVELATION...!
...THE TERMS "SHOCKING" AND "HORRIFYING" COME TO MIND, TOO...
OH, SORRY... I DIDN'T MEAN TO ALARM YOU, CORY...!
SO TAKE COMFORT, PEOPLE!
WE'LL ALWAYS BE AROUND!
HYPERNET MONITOR
HEY, DON'T SWEAT IT, CORY.
THE SILLY BITCHES ARE WRONG.
DEAD WRONG, IN FACT.
SNORT
THEY'RE ONLY IMMORTAL IF THEIR "BACK-UP DATA" IS STILL ON FILE WITH THE 3WA.
BUT IF THEIR PERSONALITY CONSTRUCTS AND TISSUE SAMPLES WERE TO FALL INTO THE WRONG HANDS...
...LIKE MINE, SAY...
...WHY, THEN, THEY COULD BE KILLED PERMANENTLY...
...OR WORSE.
AND COMING UP WITH FATES WORSE THAN DEATH IS MY SPECIALTY...
HOLO-ART
COLD HOUSING
HOLOGRAPHICALLY ENCODED MOLECULAR MEMORY MATRIX
LAST UPDATE: 6/30/2141
TROUBLE CONSULTANT (CRIMINAL DIVISION)
YURI
234Y
TISSUE SAMPLE
TROUBLE CONSULTANT (CRIMINAL DIVISION)
YURI

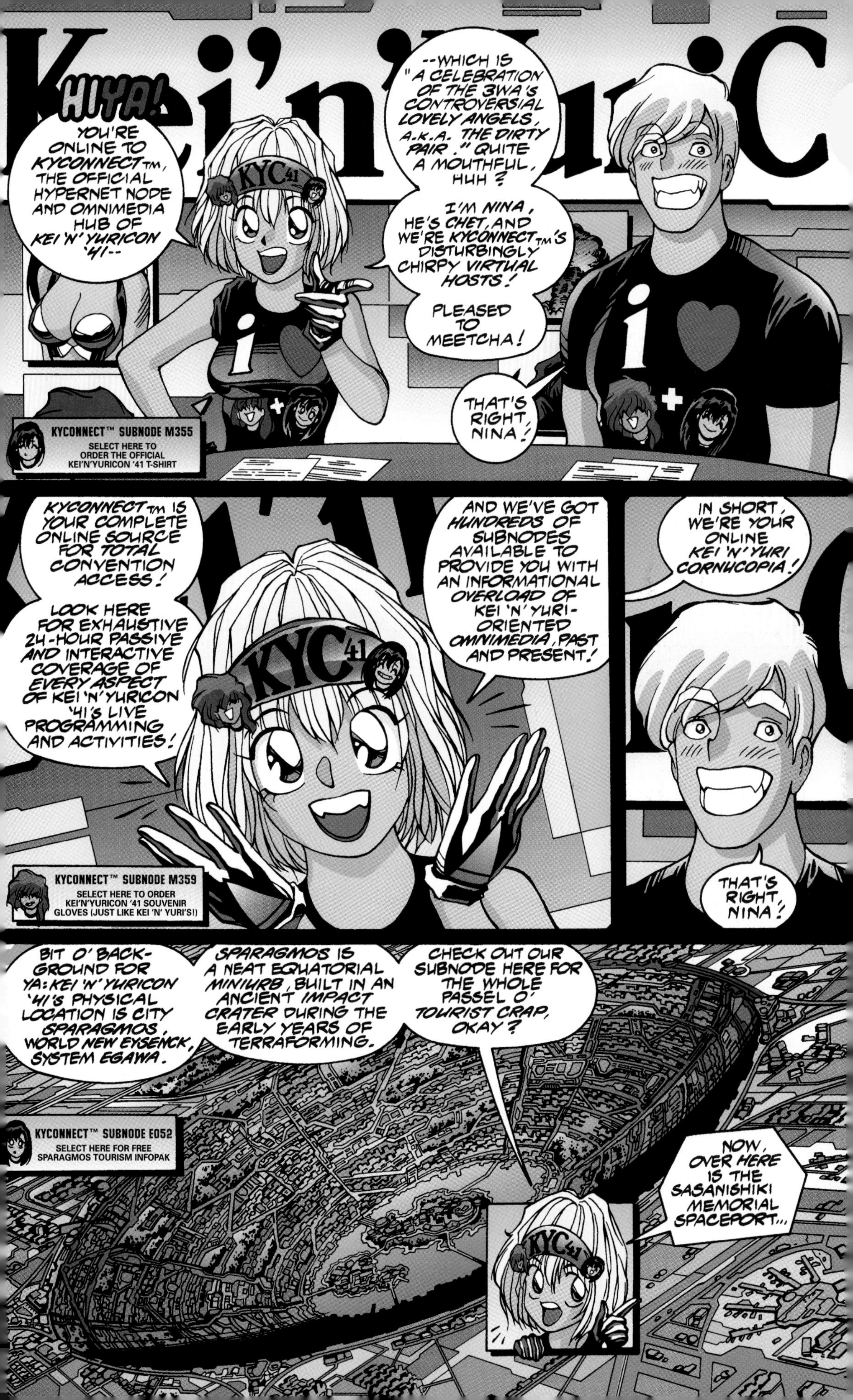
HIYA!
YOU'RE ONLINE TO KYCONNECT TM, THE OFFICIAL HYPERNET NODE AND OMNIMEDIA HUB OF KEI 'N' YURICON '41--
--WHICH IS "A CELEBRATION OF THE 3WA'S CONTROVERSIAL LOVELY ANGELS, A.K.A. THE DIRTY PAIR." QUITE A MOUTHFUL, HUH?
I'M NINA, HE'S CHET, AND WE'RE KYCONNECT TM'S DISTURBINGLY CHIRPY VIRTUAL HOSTS!
PLEASED TO MEETCHA!
THAT'S RIGHT, NINA!
KYC 41
KYCONNECT™ SUBNODE M355
SELECT HERE TO ORDER THE OFFICIAL KEI'N'YURICON '41 T-SHIRT
KYCONNECT TM IS YOUR COMPLETE ONLINE SOURCE FOR TOTAL CONVENTION ACCESS!
LOOK HERE FOR EXHAUSTIVE 24-HOUR PASSIVE AND INTERACTIVE COVERAGE OF EVERY ASPECT OF KEI 'N' YURICON '41'S LIVE PROGRAMMING AND ACTIVITIES!
AND WE'VE GOT HUNDREDS OF SUBNODES AVAILABLE TO PROVIDE YOU WITH AN INFORMATIONAL OVERLOAD OF KEI 'N' YURI-ORIENTED OMNIMEDIA, PAST AND PRESENT!
KYCONNECT™ SUBNODE M359
SELECT HERE TO ORDER KEI'N'YURICON '41 SOUVENIR GLOVES (JUST LIKE KEI 'N' YURI'S!)
IN SHORT, WE'RE YOUR ONLINE KEI 'N' YURI CORNUCOPIA!
THAT'S RIGHT, NINA!
BIT O' BACKGROUND FOR YA: KEI 'N' YURICON '41'S PHYSICAL LOCATION IS CITY SPARAGMOS, WORLD NEW EYSENCK, SYSTEM EGAWA.
SPARAGMOS IS A NEAT EQUATORIAL MINIURB, BUILT IN AN ANCIENT IMPACT CRATER DURING THE EARLY YEARS OF TERRAFORMING.
CHECK OUT OUR SUBNODE HERE FOR THE WHOLE PASSEL O' TOURIST CRAP, OKAY?
KYCONNECT™ SUBNODE E052
SELECT HERE FOR FREE SPARAGMOS TOURISM INFOPAK
NOW, OVER HERE IS THE SASANISHIKI MEMORIAL SPACEPORT...

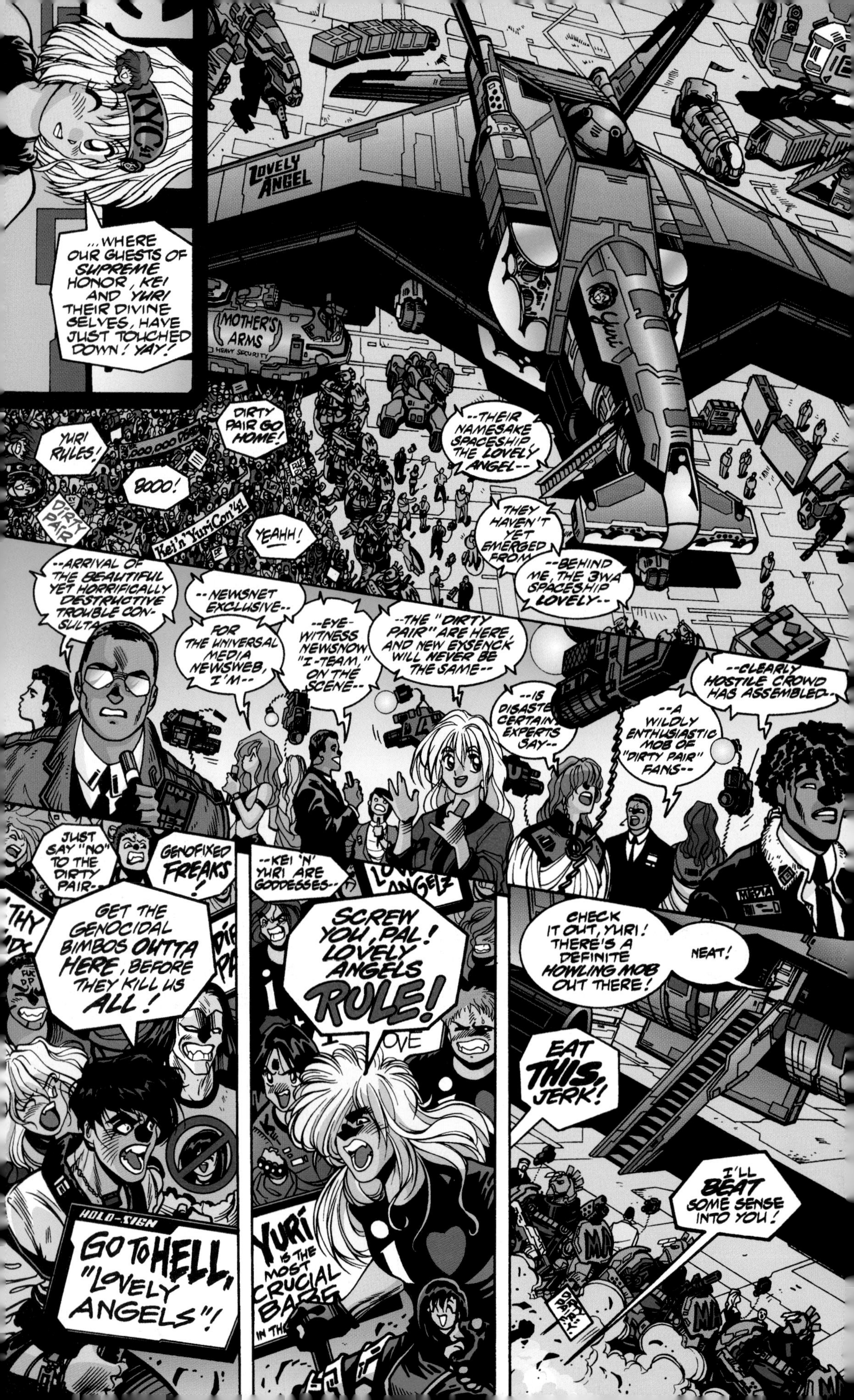
KYC '41
...WHERE OUR GUESTS OF SUPREME HONOR, KEI AND YURI THEIR DIVINE SELVES, HAVE JUST TOUCHED DOWN! YAY!
LOVELY ANGEL
MOTHER'S ARMS HEAVY SECURITY
YURI RULES!
DIRTY PAIR GO HOME!
BOOO!
DIRTY PAIR
Kei 'n' YuriCon '41
YEAHH!
--THEIR NAMESAKE SPACESHIP THE LOVELY ANGEL--
THEY HAVEN'T YET EMERGED FROM
--BEHIND ME, THE 3WA SPACESHIP LOVELY--
--ARRIVAL OF THE BEAUTIFUL YET HORRIFICALLY DESTRUCTIVE TROUBLE CON-SULTA
--NEWSNET EXCLUSIVE--
FOR THE UNIVERSAL MEDIA NEWSWEB, I'M--
--EYE-WITNESS NEWSNOW "I-TEAM," ON THE SCENE--
--THE "DIRTY PAIR" ARE HERE, AND NEW EYSENCK WILL NEVER BE THE SAME--
--IS DISASTER CERTAIN? EXPERTS SAY--
--A WILDLY ENTHUSIASTIC MOB OF "DIRTY PAIR" FANS--
--CLEARLY HOSTILE CROWD HAS ASSEMBLED--
JUST SAY "NO" TO THE DIRTY PAIR--
GENOFIXED FREAKS!
GET THE GENOCIDAL BIMBOS OUTTA HERE, BEFORE THEY KILL US ALL!
HOLO-SIGN
GO TO HELL, "LOVELY ANGELS"!
--KEI 'N' YURI ARE GODDESSES--
SCREW YOU, PAL! LOVELY ANGELS RULE!
YURI IS THE MOST CRUCIAL
CHECK IT OUT, YURI! THERE'S A DEFINITE HOWLING MOB OUT THERE!
NEAT!
EAT THIS, JERK!
I'LL BEAT SOME SENSE INTO YOU!

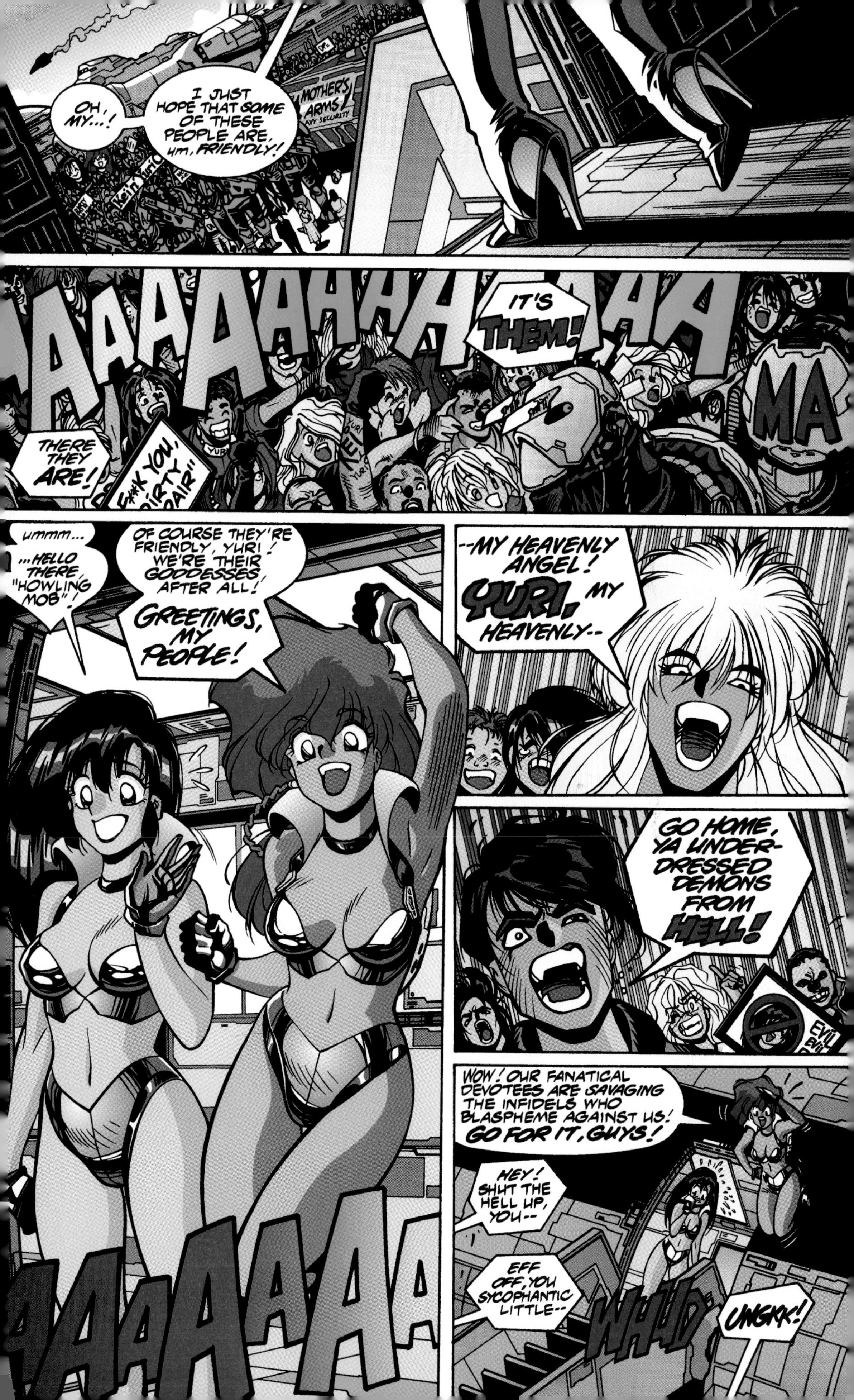
OH, MY...!
I JUST HOPE THAT SOME OF THESE PEOPLE ARE, UM, FRIENDLY!
AAAAAAAAAAAA
IT'S THEM!
THERE THEY ARE!
F**K YOU, DIRTY PAIR"
MA
UMMM... ...HELLO THERE, "HOWLING MOB"!
OF COURSE THEY'RE FRIENDLY, YURI! WE'RE THEIR GODDESSES AFTER ALL!
GREETINGS, MY PEOPLE!
AAAAAAA
--MY HEAVENLY ANGEL! YURI, MY HEAVENLY--
GO HOME, YA UNDER-DRESSED DEMONS FROM HELL!
EVIL
WOW! OUR FANATICAL DEVOTEES ARE SAVAGING THE INFIDELS WHO BLASPHEME AGAINST US! GO FOR IT, GUYS!
HEY! SHUT THE HELL UP, YOU--
EFF OFF, YOU SYCOPHANTIC LITTLE--
WHUD
UNGKK!

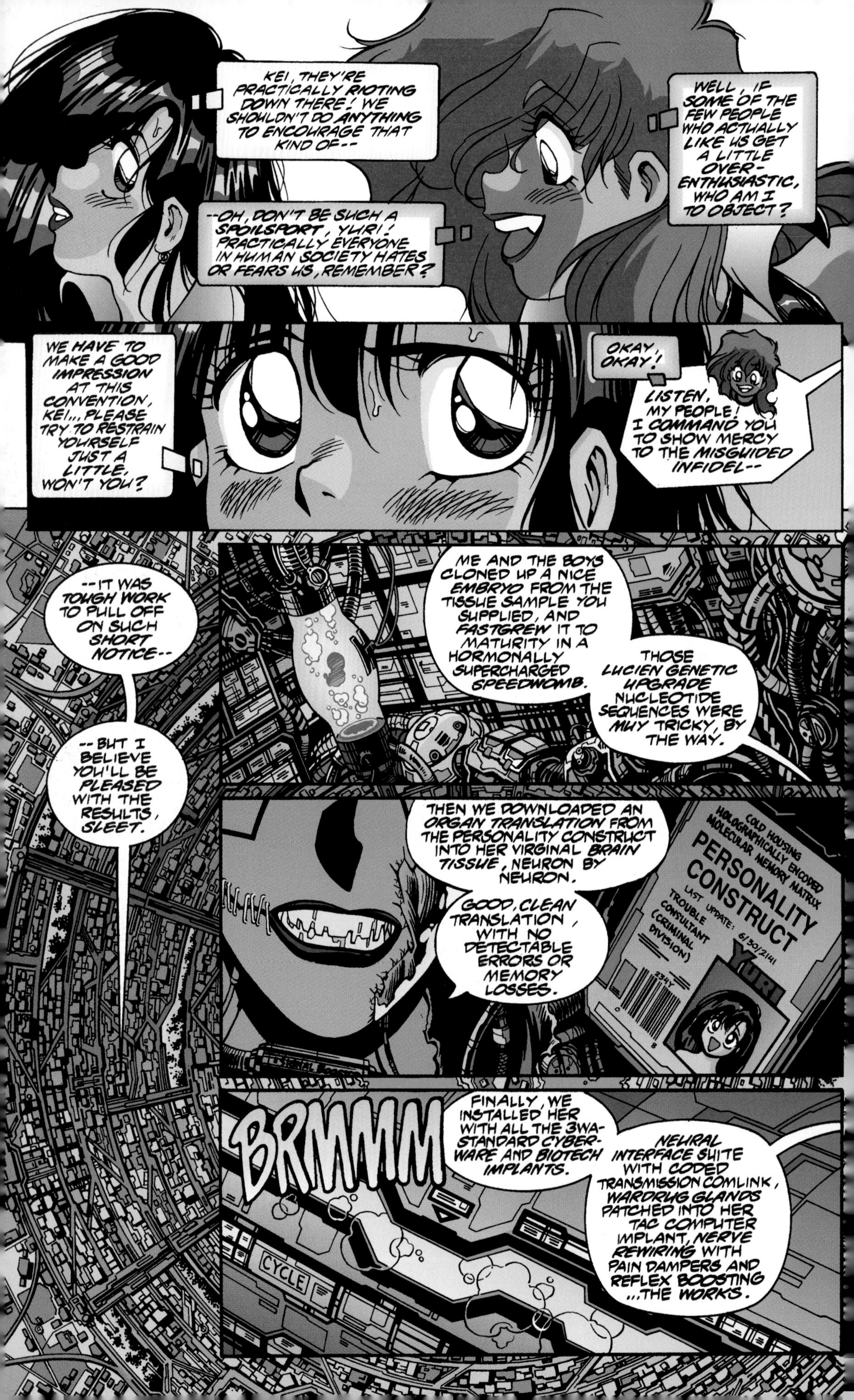
KEI, THEY'RE PRACTICALLY RIOTING DOWN THERE! WE SHOULDN'T DO ANYTHING TO ENCOURAGE THAT KIND OF--
--OH, DON'T BE SUCH A SPOILSPORT, YURI! PRACTICALLY EVERYONE IN HUMAN SOCIETY HATES OR FEARS US, REMEMBER?
WELL, IF SOME OF THE FEW PEOPLE WHO ACTUALLY LIKE US GET A LITTLE OVER-ENTHUSIASTIC, WHO AM I TO OBJECT?
WE HAVE TO MAKE A GOOD IMPRESSION AT THIS CONVENTION, KEI... PLEASE TRY TO RESTRAIN YOURSELF JUST A LITTLE, WON'T YOU?
OKAY, OKAY!
LISTEN, MY PEOPLE! I COMMAND YOU TO SHOW MERCY TO THE MISGUIDED INFIDEL--
--IT WAS TOUGH WORK TO PULL OFF ON SUCH SHORT NOTICE--
--BUT I BELIEVE YOU'LL BE PLEASED WITH THE RESULTS, SLEET.
ME AND THE BOYS CLONED UP A NICE EMBRYO FROM THE TISSUE SAMPLE YOU SUPPLIED, AND FASTGREW IT TO MATURITY IN A HORMONALLY SUPERCHARGED SPEEDWOMB.
THOSE LUCIEN GENETIC UPGRADE NUCLEOTIDE SEQUENCES WERE MUY TRICKY, BY THE WAY.
THEN WE DOWNLOADED AN ORGAN TRANSLATION FROM THE PERSONALITY CONSTRUCT INTO HER VIRGINAL BRAIN TISSUE, NEURON BY NEURON.
GOOD, CLEAN TRANSLATION, WITH NO DETECTABLE ERRORS OR MEMORY LOSSES.
COLD HOUSING
HOLOGRAPHICALLY ENCODED MOLECULAR MEMORY MATRIX
PERSONALITY CONSTRUCT
LAST UPDATE: 6/30/2141
TROUBLE CONSULTANT (CRIMINAL DIVISION)
YURI
BRMMM
FINALLY, WE INSTALLED HER WITH ALL THE 3WA-STANDARD CYBERWARE AND BIOTECH IMPLANTS.
NEURAL INTERFACE SUITE WITH CODED TRANSMISSION COMLINK, WARDRUG GLANDS PATCHED INTO HER TAC COMPUTER IMPLANT, NERVE REWIRING WITH PAIN DAMPERS AND REFLEX BOOSTING ...THE WORKS.
CYCLE

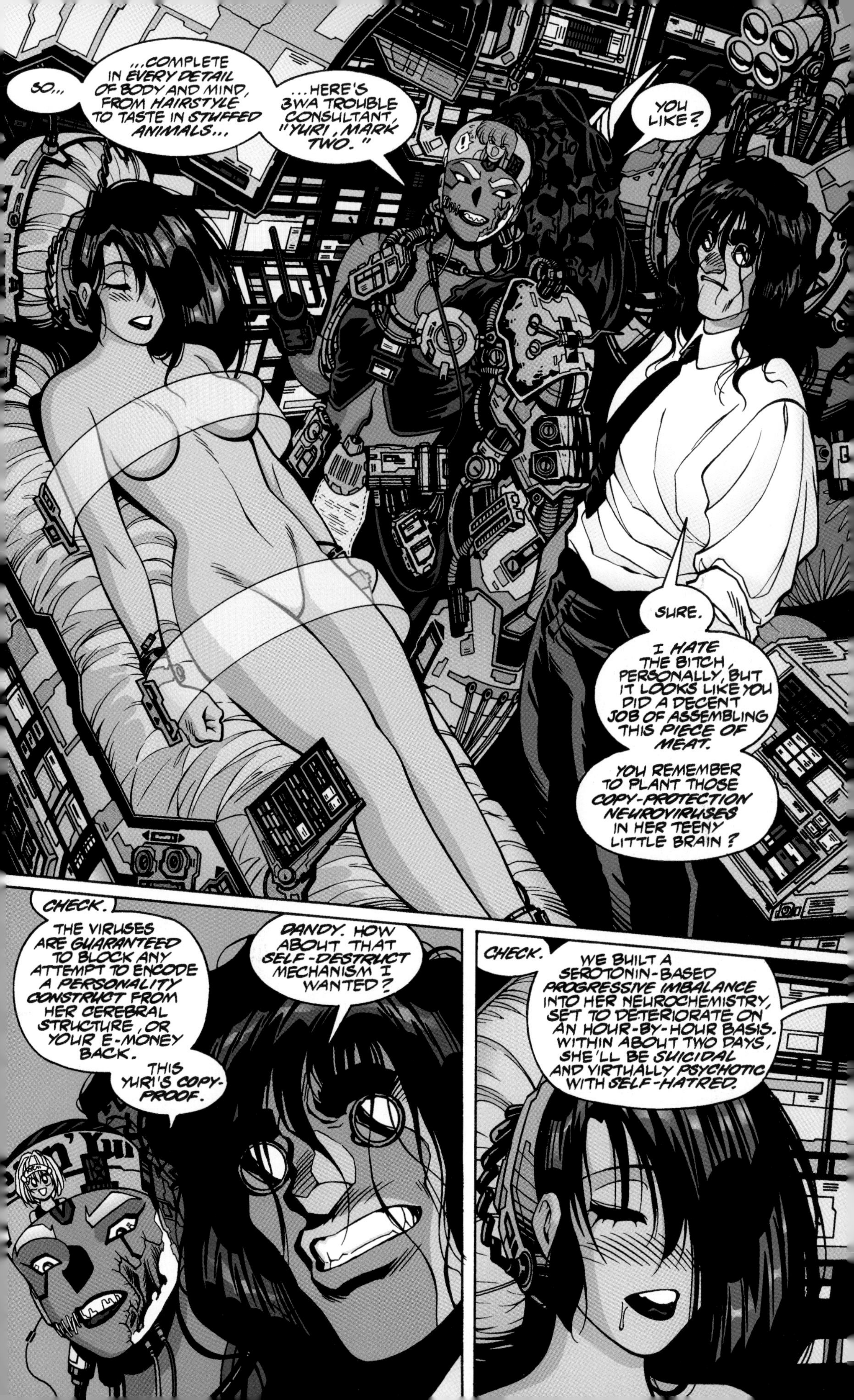
SO...
...COMPLETE IN EVERY DETAIL OF BODY AND MIND, FROM HAIRSTYLE TO TASTE IN STUFFED ANIMALS...
...HERE'S 3WA TROUBLE CONSULTANT, "YURI, MARK TWO."
YOU LIKE?
SURE.
I HATE THE BITCH, PERSONALLY, BUT IT LOOKS LIKE YOU DID A DECENT JOB OF ASSEMBLING THIS PIECE OF MEAT.
YOU REMEMBER TO PLANT THOSE COPY-PROTECTION NEUROVIRUSES IN HER TEENY LITTLE BRAIN?
CHECK.
THE VIRUSES ARE GUARANTEED TO BLOCK ANY ATTEMPT TO ENCODE A PERSONALITY CONSTRUCT FROM HER CEREBRAL STRUCTURE, OR YOUR E-MONEY BACK.
THIS YURI'S COPY-PROOF.
DANDY. HOW ABOUT THAT SELF-DESTRUCT MECHANISM I WANTED?
CHECK.
WE BUILT A SEROTONIN-BASED PROGRESSIVE IMBALANCE INTO HER NEUROCHEMISTRY, SET TO DETERIORATE ON AN HOUR-BY-HOUR BASIS. WITHIN ABOUT TWO DAYS, SHE'LL BE SUICIDAL AND VIRTUALLY PSYCHOTIC WITH SELF-HATRED.

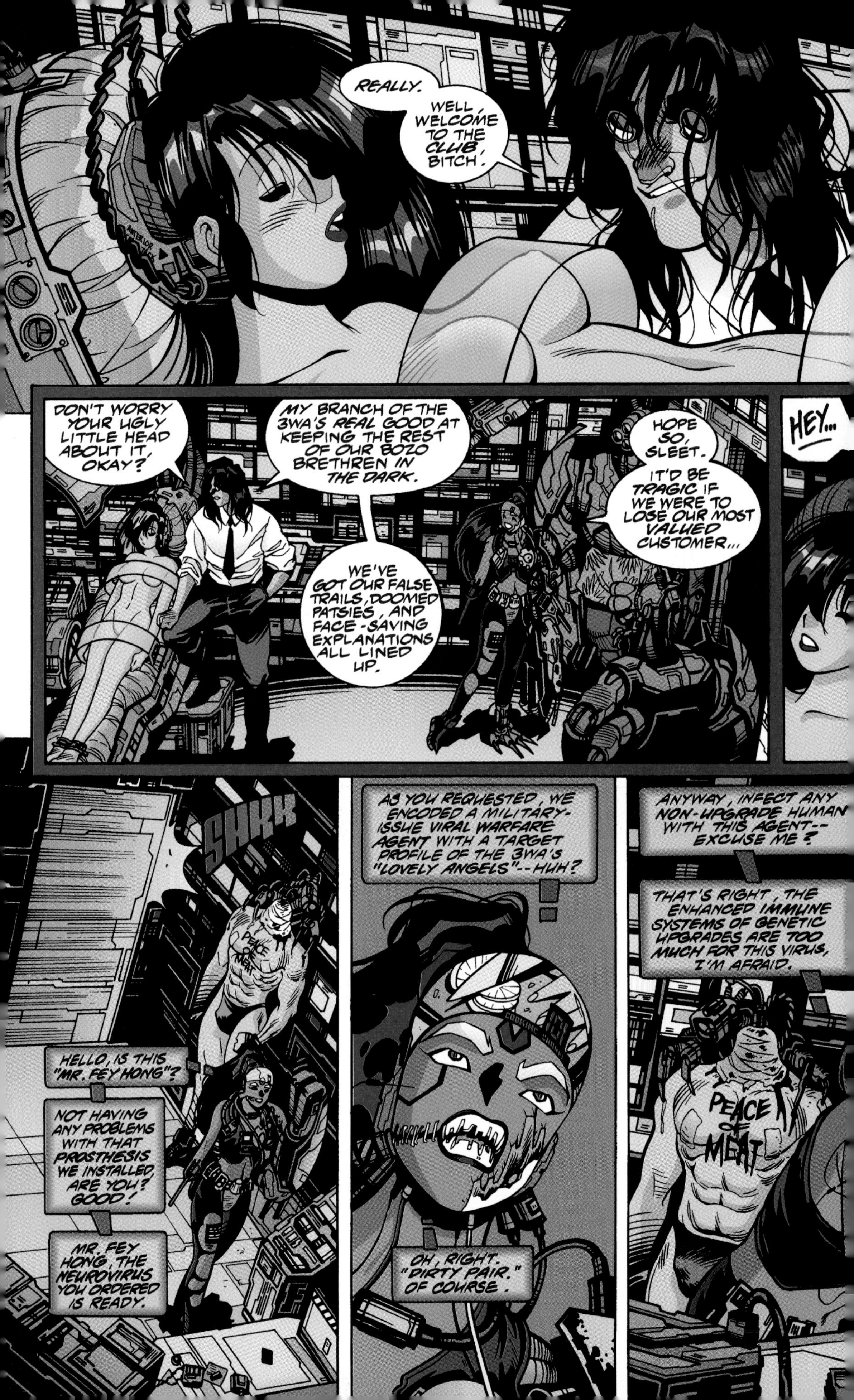
REALLY.
WELL, WELCOME TO THE CLUB, BITCH.
DON'T WORRY YOUR UGLY LITTLE HEAD ABOUT IT, OKAY?
MY BRANCH OF THE 3WA'S REAL GOOD AT KEEPING THE REST OF OUR BOZO BRETHREN IN THE DARK.
WE'VE GOT OUR FALSE TRAILS, DOOMED PATSIES, AND FACE-SAVING EXPLANATIONS ALL LINED UP.
HOPE SO, SLEET.
IT'D BE TRAGIC IF WE WERE TO LOSE OUR MOST VALUED CUSTOMER...
HEY...
SHKK
HELLO, IS THIS "MR. FEY HONG"?
NOT HAVING ANY PROBLEMS WITH THAT PROSTHESIS WE INSTALLED, ARE YOU? GOOD!
MR. FEY HONG, THE NEUROVIRUS YOU ORDERED IS READY.
PEACE OF MEAT
AS YOU REQUESTED, WE ENCODED A MILITARY-ISSUE VIRAL WARFARE AGENT WITH A TARGET PROFILE OF THE 3WA'S "LOVELY ANGELS"--HUH?
!
OH, RIGHT. "DIRTY PAIR." OF COURSE.
ANYWAY, INFECT ANY NON-UPGRADE HUMAN WITH THIS AGENT--EXCUSE ME?
!
THAT'S RIGHT, THE ENHANCED IMMUNE SYSTEMS OF GENETIC UPGRADES ARE TOO MUCH FOR THIS VIRUS, I'M AFRAID.
PEACE OF MEAT

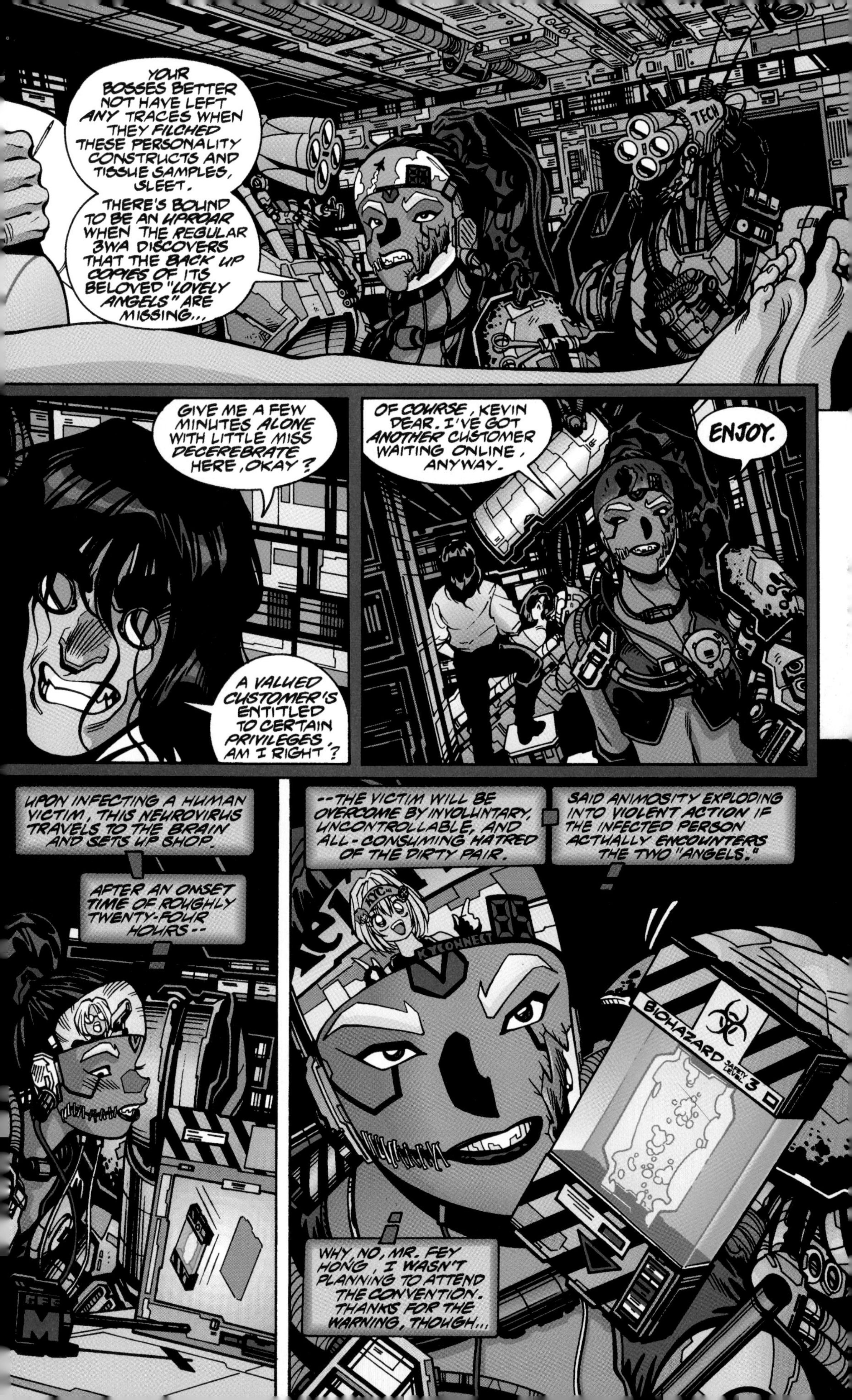
YOUR BOSSES BETTER NOT HAVE LEFT ANY TRACES WHEN THEY FILCHED THESE PERSONALITY CONSTRUCTS AND TISSUE SAMPLES, SLEET.
THERE'S BOUND TO BE AN UPROAR WHEN THE REGULAR 3WA DISCOVERS THAT THE BACK UP COPIES OF ITS BELOVED "LOVELY ANGELS" ARE MISSING...
TECH
GIVE ME A FEW MINUTES ALONE WITH LITTLE MISS DECEREBRATE HERE, OKAY?
A VALUED CUSTOMER'S ENTITLED TO CERTAIN PRIVILEGES, AM I RIGHT?
OF COURSE, KEVIN DEAR. I'VE GOT ANOTHER CUSTOMER WAITING ONLINE, ANYWAY.
ENJOY.
UPON INFECTING A HUMAN VICTIM, THIS NEUROVIRUS TRAVELS TO THE BRAIN AND SETS UP SHOP.
AFTER AN ONSET TIME OF ROUGHLY TWENTY-FOUR HOURS--
--THE VICTIM WILL BE OVERCOME BY INVOLUNTARY, UNCONTROLLABLE, AND ALL-CONSUMING HATRED OF THE DIRTY PAIR.
SAID ANIMOSITY EXPLODING INTO VIOLENT ACTION IF THE INFECTED PERSON ACTUALLY ENCOUNTERS THE TWO "ANGELS."
KYCONNECT
BIOHAZARD
SAFETY LEVEL 3
WHY, NO, MR. FEY HONG, I WASN'T PLANNING TO ATTEND THE CONVENTION. THANKS FOR THE WARNING, THOUGH...

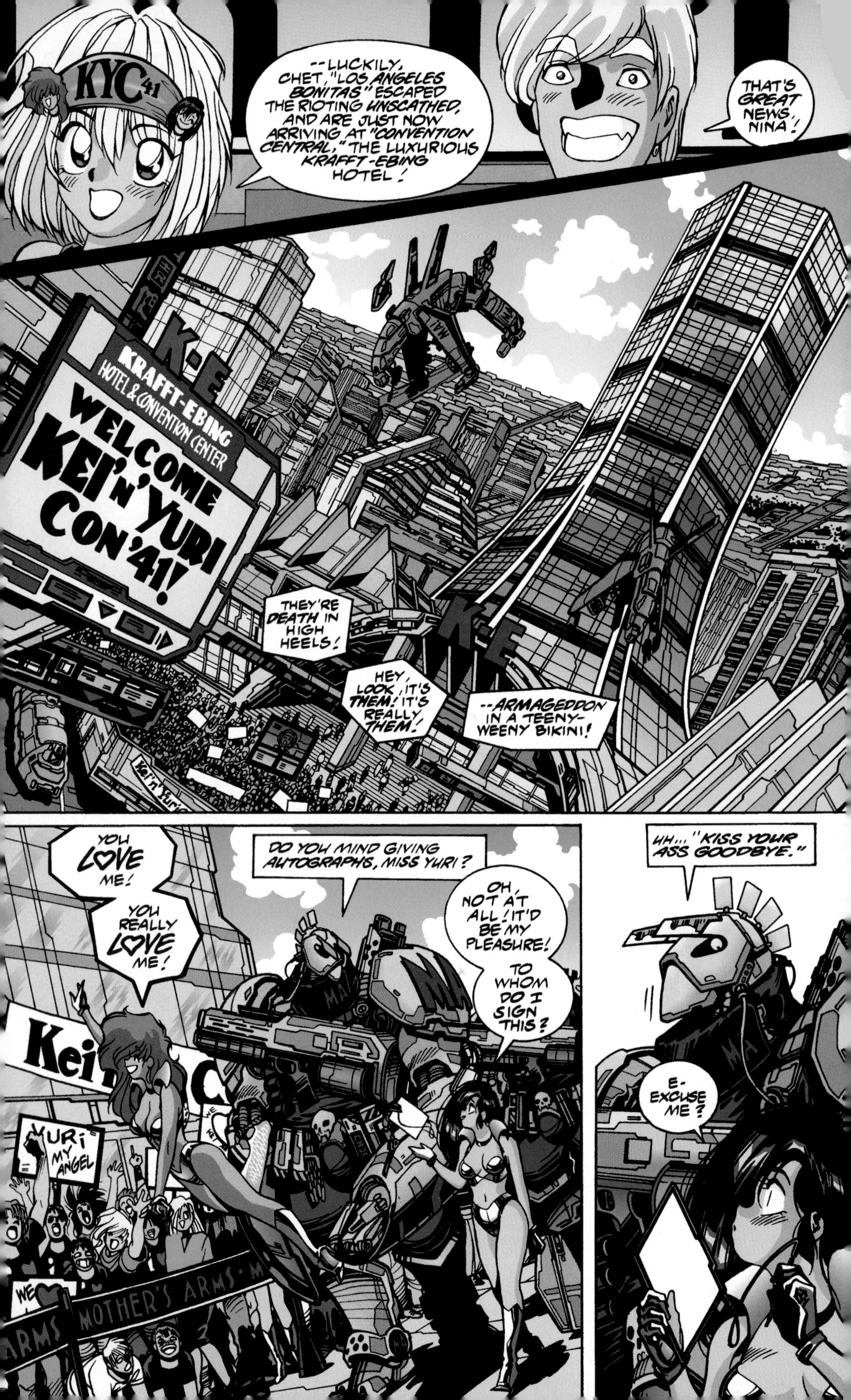
KYC '41
--LUCKILY, CHET, "LOS ANGELES BONITAS" ESCAPED THE RIOTING UNSCATHED, AND ARE JUST NOW ARRIVING AT "CONVENTION CENTRAL," THE LUXURIOUS KRAFFT-EBING HOTEL!
THAT'S GREAT NEWS, NINA!
K-E
KRAFFT-EBING HOTEL & CONVENTION CENTER
WELCOME KEI 'n' YURI CON '41!
THEY'RE DEATH IN HIGH HEELS!
HEY, LOOK, IT'S THEM! IT'S REALLY THEM!
--ARMAGEDDON IN A TEENY-WEENY BIKINI!
YOU LOVE ME!
YOU REALLY LOVE ME!
DO YOU MIND GIVING AUTOGRAPHS, MISS YURI?
OH, NOT AT ALL! IT'D BE MY PLEASURE!
TO WHOM DO I SIGN THIS?
YURI MY ANGEL
MOTHER'S ARMS
UH... "KISS YOUR ASS GOODBYE."
E-EXCUSE ME?

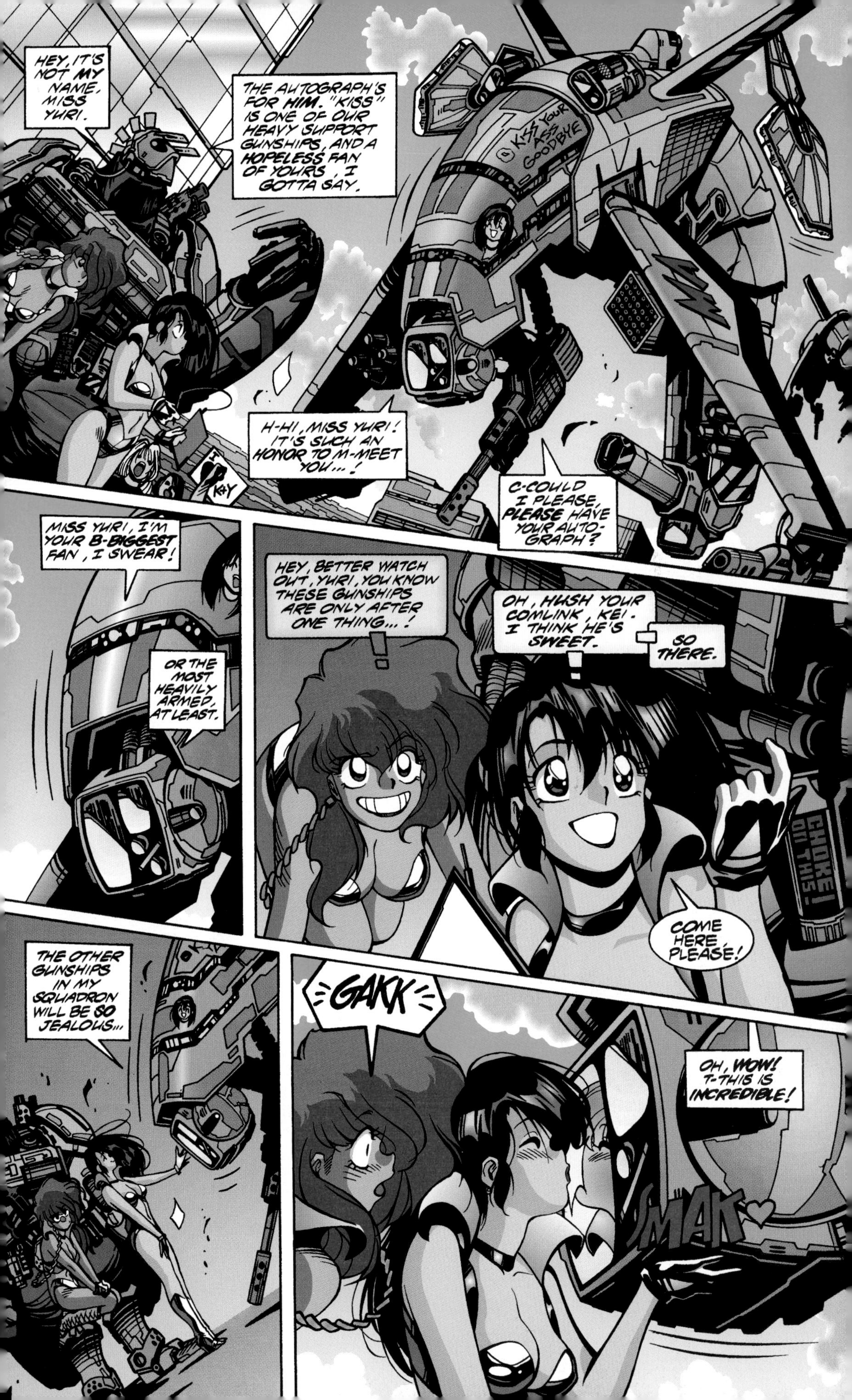
HEY, IT'S NOT MY NAME, MISS YURI.
THE AUTOGRAPH'S FOR HIM. "KISS" IS ONE OF OUR HEAVY SUPPORT GUNSHIPS, AND A HOPELESS FAN OF YOURS, I GOTTA SAY.
KISS YOUR ASS GOODBYE
H-HI, MISS YURI! IT'S SUCH AN HONOR TO M-MEET YOU...!
C-COULD I PLEASE, PLEASE HAVE YOUR AUTO-GRAPH?
MISS YURI, I'M YOUR B-BIGGEST FAN, I SWEAR!
OR THE MOST HEAVILY ARMED, AT LEAST.
HEY, BETTER WATCH OUT, YURI, YOU KNOW THESE GUNSHIPS ARE ONLY AFTER ONE THING...!
OH, HUSH YOUR COMLINK, KEI. I THINK HE'S SWEET.
SO THERE.
CHOKE! ON THIS!
COME HERE, PLEASE!
THE OTHER GUNSHIPS IN MY SQUADRON WILL BE SO JEALOUS...
GAKK
OH, WOW! T-THIS IS INCREDIBLE!
SMAK

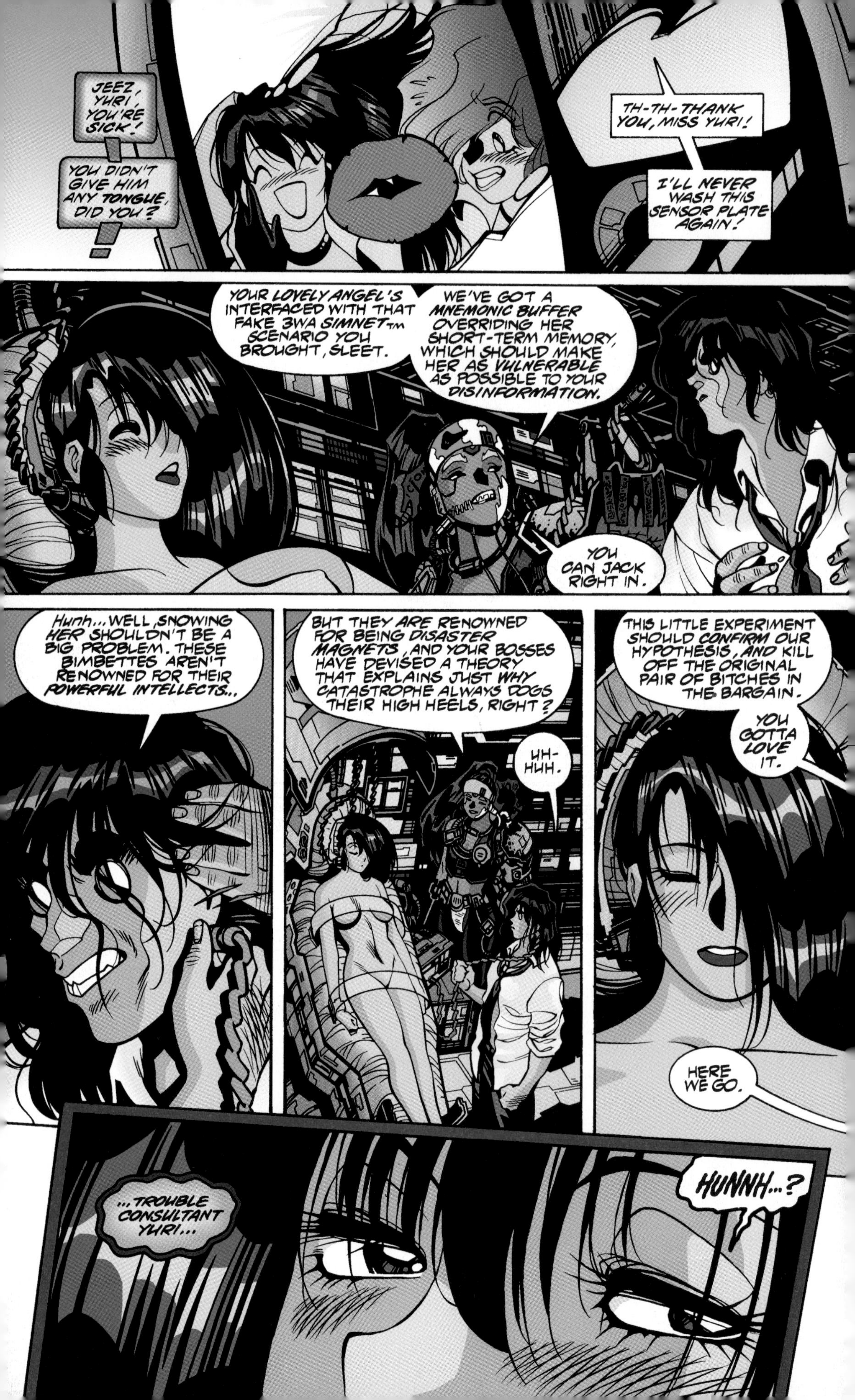
JEEZ, YURI, YOU'RE SICK!
YOU DIDN'T GIVE HIM ANY TONGUE, DID YOU?
!
TH-TH-THANK YOU, MISS YURI!
I'LL NEVER WASH THIS SENSOR PLATE AGAIN!
YOUR LOVELY ANGEL'S INTERFACED WITH THAT FAKE 3WA SIMNET™ SCENARIO YOU BROUGHT, SLEET.
WE'VE GOT A MNEMONIC BUFFER OVERRIDING HER SHORT-TERM MEMORY, WHICH SHOULD MAKE HER AS VULNERABLE AS POSSIBLE TO YOUR DISINFORMATION.
YOU CAN JACK RIGHT IN.
Hunh... WELL, SNOWING HER SHOULDN'T BE A BIG PROBLEM. THESE BIMBETTES AREN'T RENOWNED FOR THEIR POWERFUL INTELLECTS...
BUT THEY ARE RENOWNED FOR BEING DISASTER MAGNETS, AND YOUR BOSSES HAVE DEVISED A THEORY THAT EXPLAINS JUST WHY CATASTROPHE ALWAYS DOGS THEIR HIGH HEELS, RIGHT?
UH-HUH.
THIS LITTLE EXPERIMENT SHOULD CONFIRM OUR HYPOTHESIS, AND KILL OFF THE ORIGINAL PAIR OF BITCHES IN THE BARGAIN.
YOU GOTTA LOVE IT.
HERE WE GO.
...TROUBLE CONSULTANT YURI...
HUNNH...?

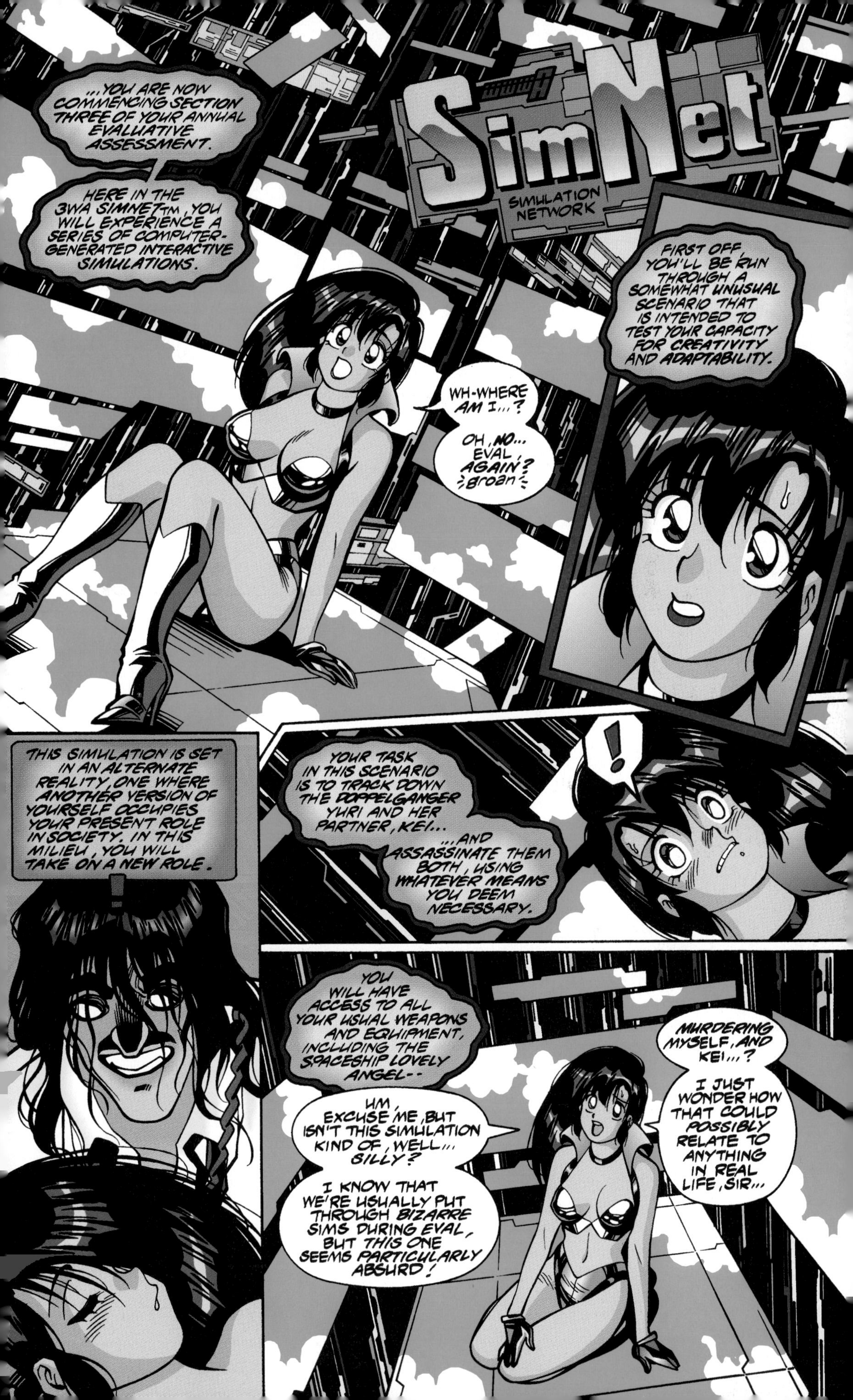
...YOU ARE NOW COMMENCING SECTION THREE OF YOUR ANNUAL EVALUATIVE ASSESSMENT.
HERE IN THE 3WA SIMNET™, YOU WILL EXPERIENCE A SERIES OF COMPUTER-GENERATED INTERACTIVE SIMULATIONS.
SimNet
SIMULATION NETWORK
WH-WHERE AM I...?
OH, NO... EVAL AGAIN? groan
FIRST OFF, YOU'LL BE RUN THROUGH A SOMEWHAT UNUSUAL SCENARIO THAT IS INTENDED TO TEST YOUR CAPACITY FOR CREATIVITY AND ADAPTABILITY.
THIS SIMULATION IS SET IN AN ALTERNATE REALITY, ONE WHERE ANOTHER VERSION OF YOURSELF OCCUPIES YOUR PRESENT ROLE IN SOCIETY. IN THIS MILIEU, YOU WILL TAKE ON A NEW ROLE.
YOUR TASK IN THIS SCENARIO IS TO TRACK DOWN THE DOPPELGANGER YURI AND HER PARTNER, KEI...
...AND ASSASSINATE THEM BOTH, USING WHATEVER MEANS YOU DEEM NECESSARY.
!
YOU WILL HAVE ACCESS TO ALL YOUR USUAL WEAPONS AND EQUIPMENT, INCLUDING THE SPACESHIP LOVELY ANGEL--
UM, EXCUSE ME, BUT ISN'T THIS SIMULATION KIND OF, WELL... SILLY?
I KNOW THAT WE'RE USUALLY PUT THROUGH BIZARRE SIMS DURING EVAL, BUT THIS ONE SEEMS PARTICULARLY ABSURD!
MURDERING MYSELF, AND KEI...?
I JUST WONDER HOW THAT COULD POSSIBLY RELATE TO ANYTHING IN REAL LIFE, SIR...

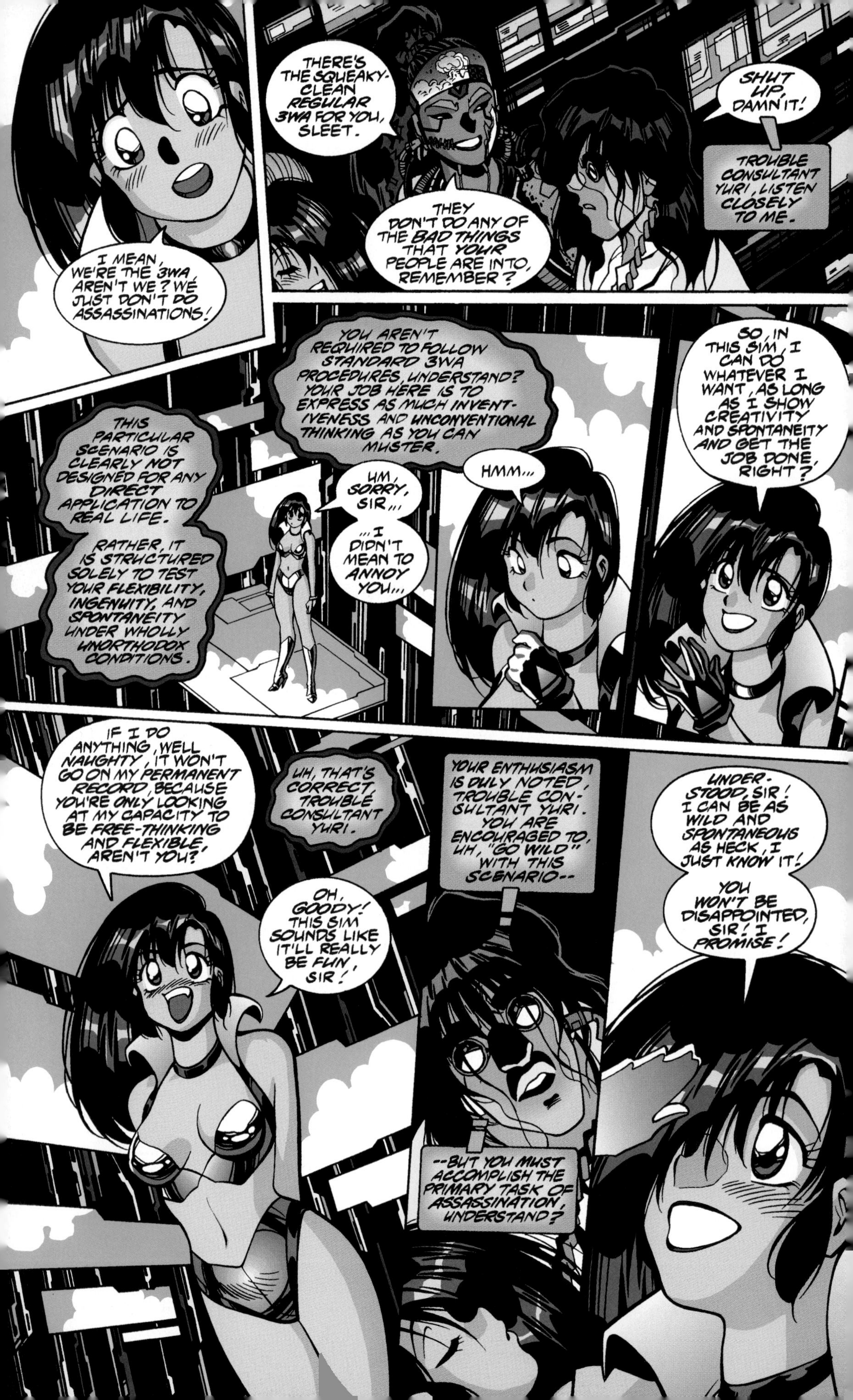
I MEAN, WE'RE THE 3WA, AREN'T WE? WE JUST DON'T DO ASSASSINATIONS!
THERE'S THE SQUEAKY-CLEAN REGULAR 3WA FOR YOU, SLEET.
THEY DON'T DO ANY OF THE BAD THINGS THAT YOUR PEOPLE ARE INTO, REMEMBER?
SHUT UP, DAMN IT!
TROUBLE CONSULTANT YURI, LISTEN CLOSELY TO ME.
THIS PARTICULAR SCENARIO IS CLEARLY NOT DESIGNED FOR ANY DIRECT APPLICATION TO REAL LIFE.
RATHER, IT IS STRUCTURED SOLELY TO TEST YOUR FLEXIBILITY, INGENUITY, AND SPONTANEITY UNDER WHOLLY UNORTHODOX CONDITIONS.
YOU AREN'T REQUIRED TO FOLLOW STANDARD 3WA PROCEDURES, UNDERSTAND? YOUR JOB HERE IS TO EXPRESS AS MUCH INVENTIVENESS AND UNCONVENTIONAL THINKING AS YOU CAN MUSTER.
UM, SORRY, SIR...
...I DIDN'T MEAN TO ANNOY YOU...
HMM...
SO, IN THIS SIM, I CAN DO WHATEVER I WANT, AS LONG AS I SHOW CREATIVITY AND SPONTANEITY AND GET THE JOB DONE, RIGHT?
IF I DO ANYTHING, WELL NAUGHTY, IT WON'T GO ON MY PERMANENT RECORD, BECAUSE YOU'RE ONLY LOOKING AT MY CAPACITY TO BE FREE-THINKING AND FLEXIBLE, AREN'T YOU?
UH, THAT'S CORRECT, TROUBLE CONSULTANT YURI.
OH, GOODY! THIS SIM SOUNDS LIKE IT'LL REALLY BE FUN, SIR!
YOUR ENTHUSIASM IS DULY NOTED, TROUBLE CONSULTANT YURI. YOU ARE ENCOURAGED TO, UH, "GO WILD" WITH THIS SCENARIO--
--BUT YOU MUST ACCOMPLISH THE PRIMARY TASK OF ASSASSINATION, UNDERSTAND?
UNDERSTOOD, SIR! I CAN BE AS WILD AND SPONTANEOUS AS HECK, I JUST KNOW IT!
YOU WON'T BE DISAPPOINTED, SIR! I PROMISE!

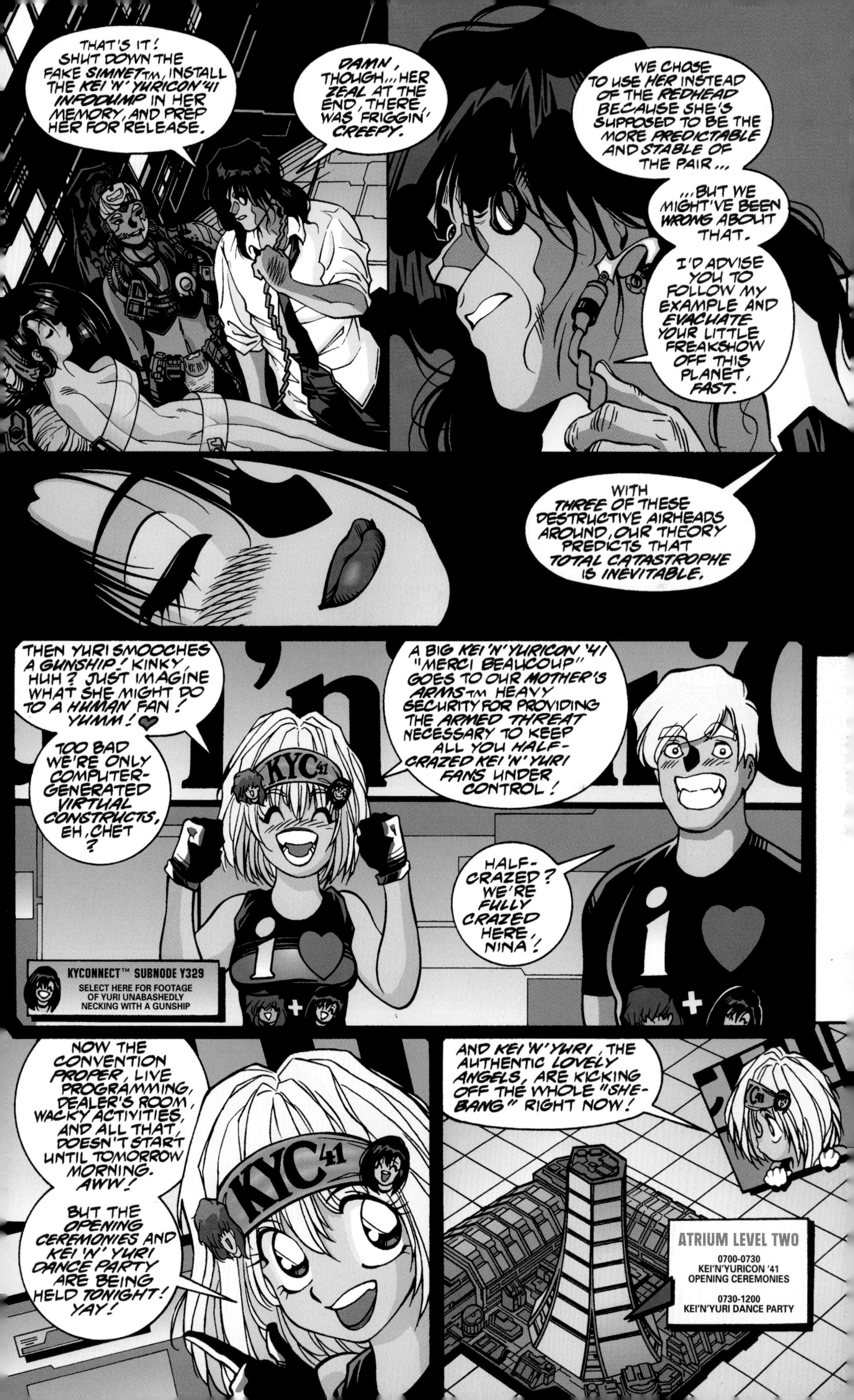
THAT'S IT! SHUT DOWN THE FAKE SIMNET™, INSTALL THE KEI 'N' YURICON '41 INFODUMP IN HER MEMORY, AND PREP HER FOR RELEASE.
DAMN, THOUGH... HER ZEAL AT THE END, THERE, WAS FRIGGIN' CREEPY.
WE CHOSE TO USE HER INSTEAD OF THE REDHEAD BECAUSE SHE'S SUPPOSED TO BE THE MORE PREDICTABLE AND STABLE OF THE PAIR...
...BUT WE MIGHT'VE BEEN WRONG ABOUT THAT.
I'D ADVISE YOU TO FOLLOW MY EXAMPLE AND EVACUATE YOUR LITTLE FREAKSHOW OFF THIS PLANET, FAST.
WITH THREE OF THESE DESTRUCTIVE AIRHEADS AROUND, OUR THEORY PREDICTS THAT TOTAL CATASTROPHE IS INEVITABLE.
THEN YURI SMOOCHES A GUNSHIP! KINKY, HUH? JUST IMAGINE WHAT SHE MIGHT DO TO A HUMAN FAN! YUMM! ♥
TOO BAD WE'RE ONLY COMPUTER-GENERATED VIRTUAL CONSTRUCTS, EH, CHET?
A BIG KEI 'N' YURICON '41 "MERCI BEAUCOUP" GOES TO OUR MOTHER'S ARMS™ HEAVY SECURITY FOR PROVIDING THE ARMED THREAT NECESSARY TO KEEP ALL YOU HALF-CRAZED KEI 'N' YURI FANS UNDER CONTROL!
HALF-CRAZED? WE'RE FULLY CRAZED HERE, NINA!
KYC 41
KYCONNECT™ SUBNODE Y329
SELECT HERE FOR FOOTAGE OF YURI UNABASHEDLY NECKING WITH A GUNSHIP
NOW THE CONVENTION PROPER, LIVE PROGRAMMING, DEALER'S ROOM, WACKY ACTIVITIES, AND ALL THAT, DOESN'T START UNTIL TOMORROW MORNING. AWW!
BUT THE OPENING CEREMONIES AND KEI 'N' YURI DANCE PARTY ARE BEING HELD TONIGHT! YAY!
KYC 41
AND KEI 'N' YURI, THE AUTHENTIC LOVELY ANGELS, ARE KICKING OFF THE WHOLE "SHE-BANG" RIGHT NOW!
ATRIUM LEVEL TWO
0700-0730
KEI'N'YURICON '41
OPENING CEREMONIES
0730-1200
KEI'N'YURI DANCE PARTY

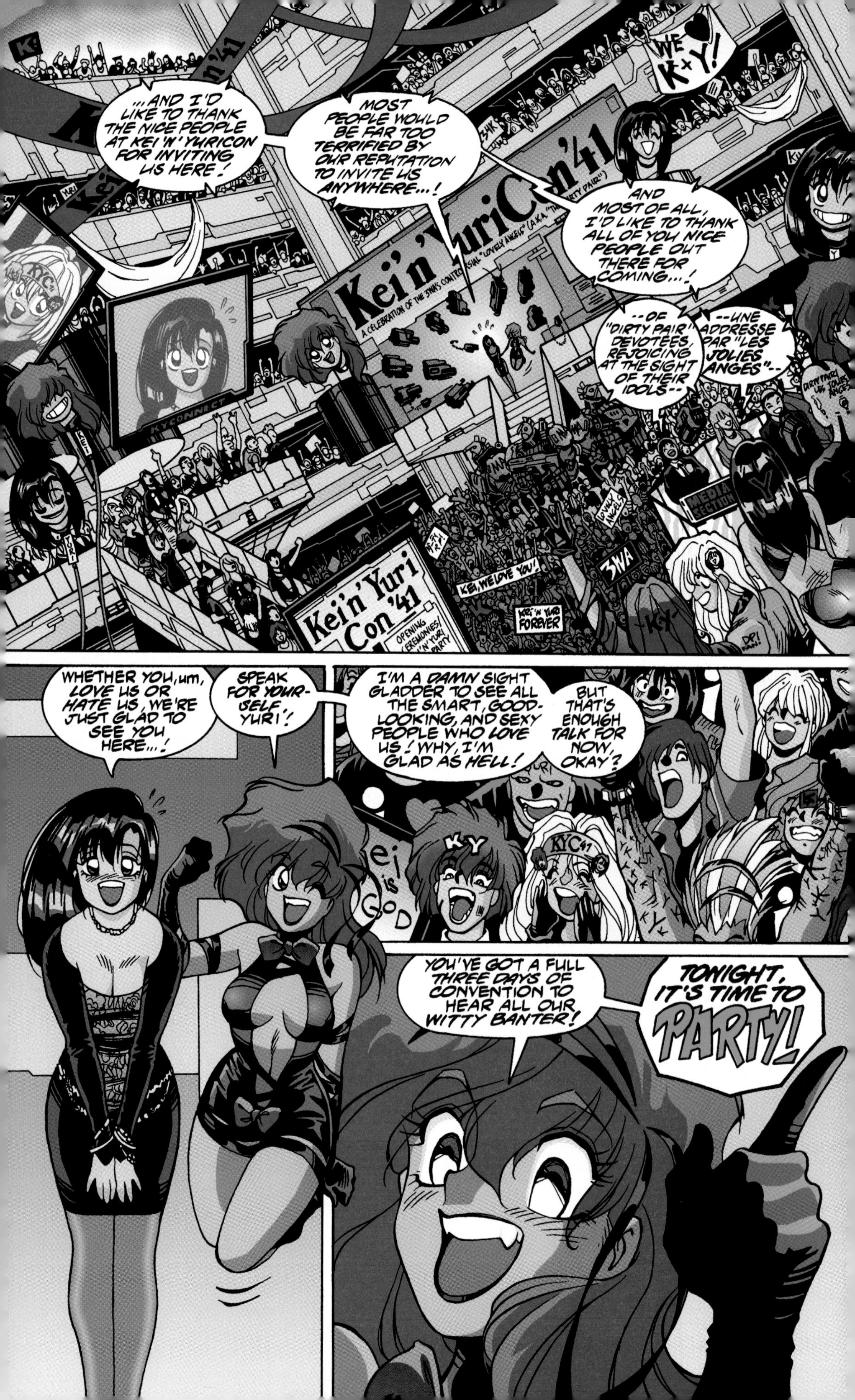
WE ♥ K+Y!
...AND I'D LIKE TO THANK THE NICE PEOPLE AT KEI 'N' YURICON FOR INVITING US HERE!
MOST PEOPLE WOULD BE FAR TOO TERRIFIED BY OUR REPUTATION TO INVITE US ANYWHERE...!
Kei'n 'Yuri Con'41
A CELEBRATION OF THE 3WA'S CONTROVERSIAL "LOVELY ANGELS" (A.K.A. "THE DIRTY PAIR")
AND MOST OF ALL, I'D LIKE TO THANK ALL OF YOU NICE PEOPLE OUT THERE FOR COMING...!
--OF "DIRTY PAIR" DEVOTEES, REJOICING AT THE SIGHT OF THEIR IDOLS--
--UNE ADDRESSE PAR "LES JOLIES ANGES"--
KYCONNECT
MEDIA SECTION
LOVELY ANGELS
KEI, WE LOVE YOU!
3WA
KEI 'N YURI FOREVER
Kei'n'Yuri Con '41
WHETHER YOU, um, LOVE US OR HATE US, WE'RE JUST GLAD TO SEE YOU HERE...!
SPEAK FOR YOURSELF, YURI!
I'M A DAMN SIGHT GLADDER TO SEE ALL THE SMART, GOOD-LOOKING, AND SEXY PEOPLE WHO LOVE US! WHY, I'M GLAD AS HELL!
BUT THAT'S ENOUGH TALK FOR NOW, OKAY?
Kei is GOD
YOU'VE GOT A FULL THREE DAYS OF CONVENTION TO HEAR ALL OUR WITTY BANTER!
TONIGHT, IT'S TIME TO PARTY!

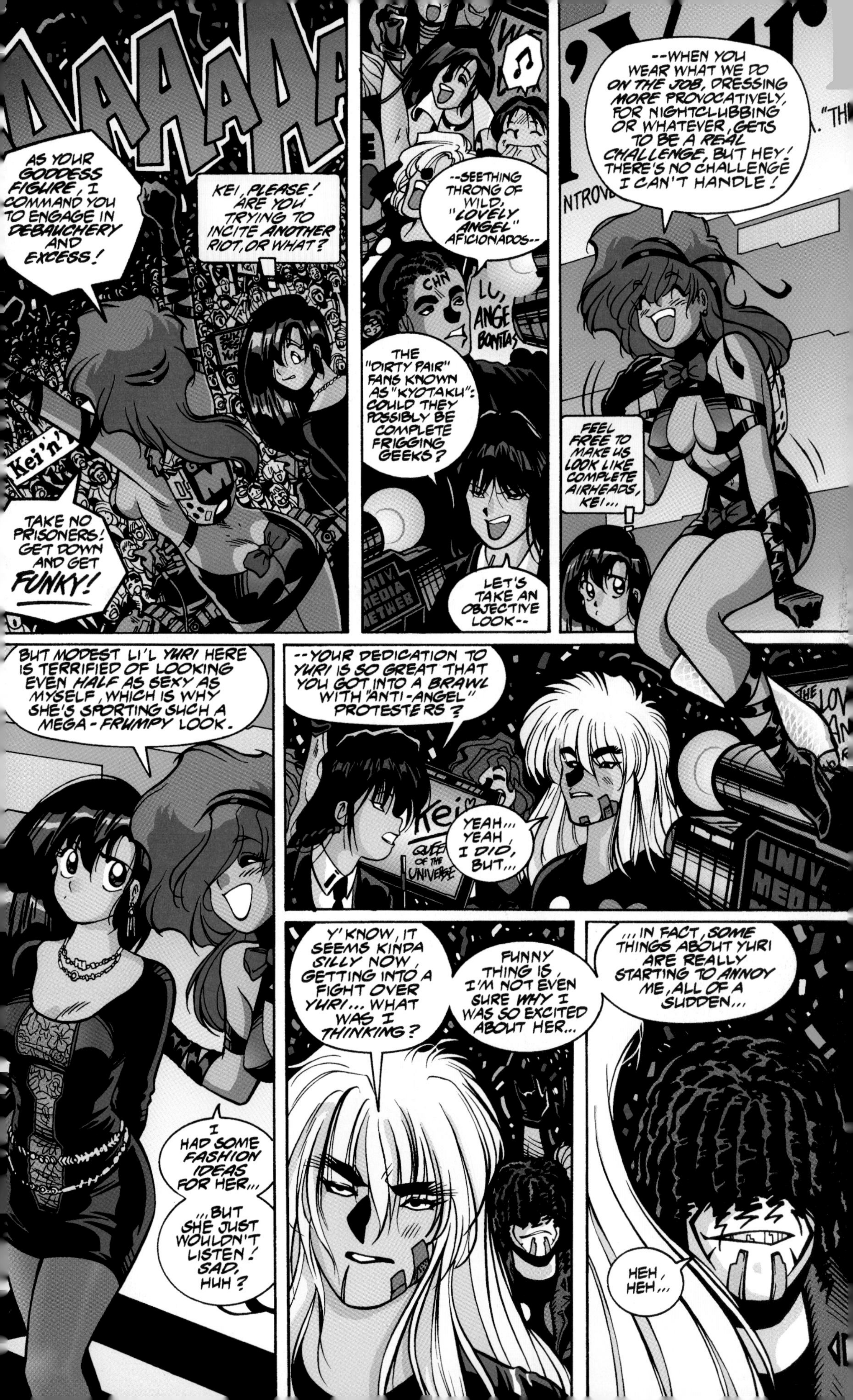
AS YOUR GODDESS FIGURE, I COMMAND YOU TO ENGAGE IN DEBAUCHERY AND EXCESS!
KEI, PLEASE! ARE YOU TRYING TO INCITE ANOTHER RIOT, OR WHAT?
!
Kei'n'
TAKE NO PRISONERS! GET DOWN AND GET FUNKY!
♪
--SEETHING THRONG OF WILD, "LOVELY ANGEL" AFICIONADOS--
THE "DIRTY PAIR" FANS KNOWN AS "KYOTAKU": COULD THEY POSSIBLY BE COMPLETE FRIGGING GEEKS?
UNIV. MEDIA NETWEB
LET'S TAKE AN OBJECTIVE LOOK--
--WHEN YOU WEAR WHAT WE DO ON THE JOB, DRESSING MORE PROVOCATIVELY, FOR NIGHTCLUBBING OR WHATEVER, GETS TO BE A REAL CHALLENGE, BUT HEY! THERE'S NO CHALLENGE I CAN'T HANDLE!
FEEL FREE TO MAKE US LOOK LIKE COMPLETE AIRHEADS, KEI...
!
BUT MODEST LI'L YURI HERE IS TERRIFIED OF LOOKING EVEN HALF AS SEXY AS MYSELF, WHICH IS WHY SHE'S SPORTING SUCH A MEGA-FRUMPY LOOK.
I HAD SOME FASHION IDEAS FOR HER...
...BUT SHE JUST WOULDN'T LISTEN! SAD, HUH?
--YOUR DEDICATION TO YURI IS SO GREAT THAT YOU GOT INTO A BRAWL WITH "ANTI-ANGEL" PROTESTERS?
Kei QUEEN OF THE UNIVERSE
YEAH... YEAH, I DID, BUT...
UNIV. MEDIA
Y'KNOW, IT SEEMS KINDA SILLY NOW, GETTING INTO A FIGHT OVER YURI... WHAT WAS I THINKING?
FUNNY THING IS, I'M NOT EVEN SURE WHY I WAS SO EXCITED ABOUT HER...
...IN FACT, SOME THINGS ABOUT YURI ARE REALLY STARTING TO ANNOY ME, ALL OF A SUDDEN...
HEH, HEH...

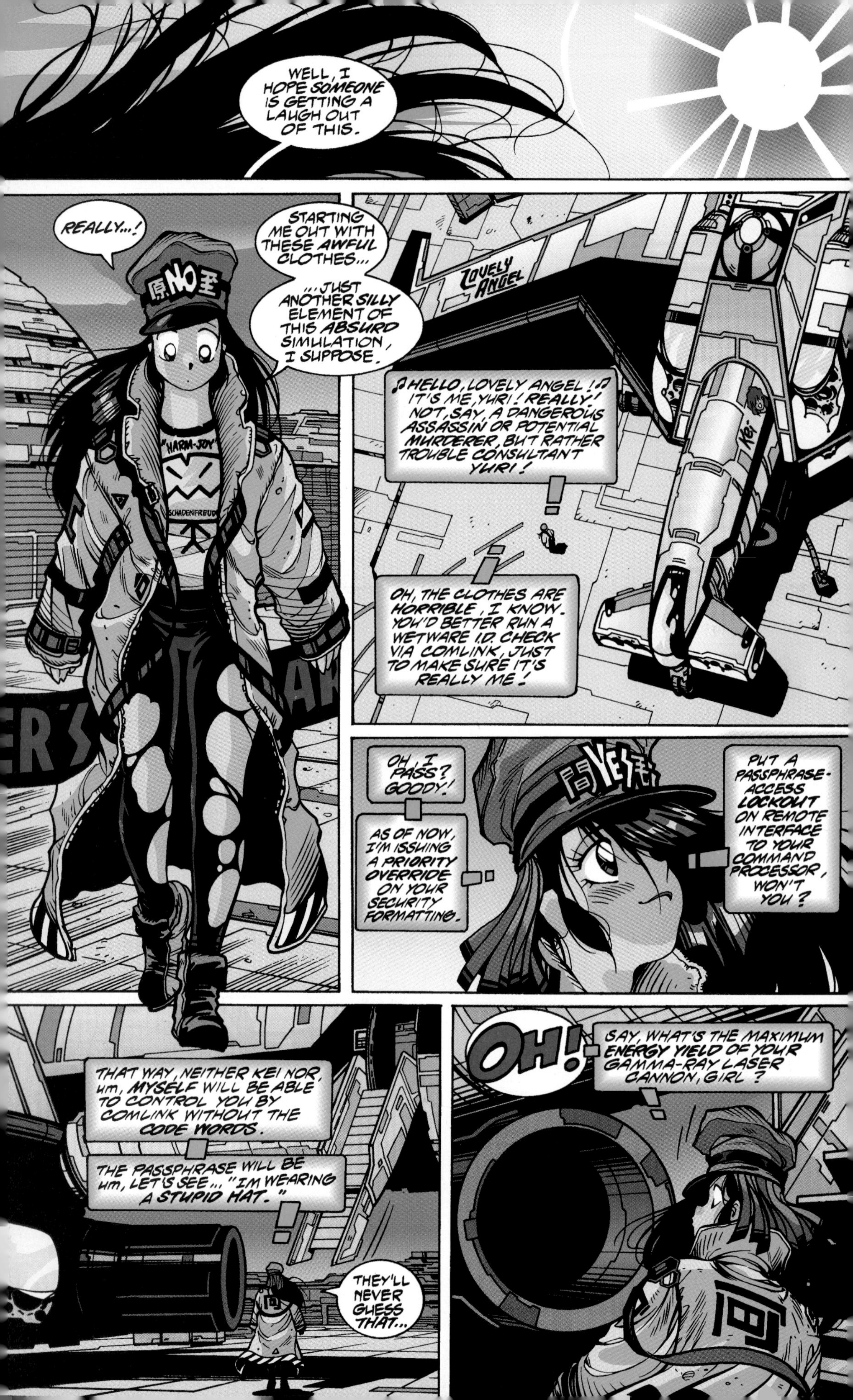
WELL, I HOPE SOMEONE IS GETTING A LAUGH OUT OF THIS.
REALLY...!
STARTING ME OUT WITH THESE AWFUL CLOTHES...
...JUST ANOTHER SILLY ELEMENT OF THIS ABSURD SIMULATION, I SUPPOSE.
NO
"HARM-JOY"
SCHADENFREUDE
LOVELY ANGEL
♫HELLO, LOVELY ANGEL!♫ IT'S ME, YURI! REALLY! NOT, SAY, A DANGEROUS ASSASSIN OR POTENTIAL MURDERER, BUT RATHER TROUBLE CONSULTANT YURI!
OH, THE CLOTHES ARE HORRIBLE, I KNOW. YOU'D BETTER RUN A WETWARE I.D. CHECK VIA COMLINK, JUST TO MAKE SURE IT'S REALLY ME!
OH, I PASS? GOODY!
AS OF NOW, I'M ISSUING A PRIORITY OVERRIDE ON YOUR SECURITY FORMATTING.
YES
PUT A PASSPHRASE-ACCESS LOCKOUT ON REMOTE INTERFACE TO YOUR COMMAND PROCESSOR, WON'T YOU?
THAT WAY, NEITHER KEI NOR, UM, MYSELF WILL BE ABLE TO CONTROL YOU BY COMLINK WITHOUT THE CODE WORDS.
THE PASSPHRASE WILL BE UM, LET'S SEE... "I'M WEARING A STUPID HAT."
THEY'LL NEVER GUESS THAT...
OH!
SAY, WHAT'S THE MAXIMUM ENERGY YIELD OF YOUR GAMMA-RAY LASER CANNON, GIRL?

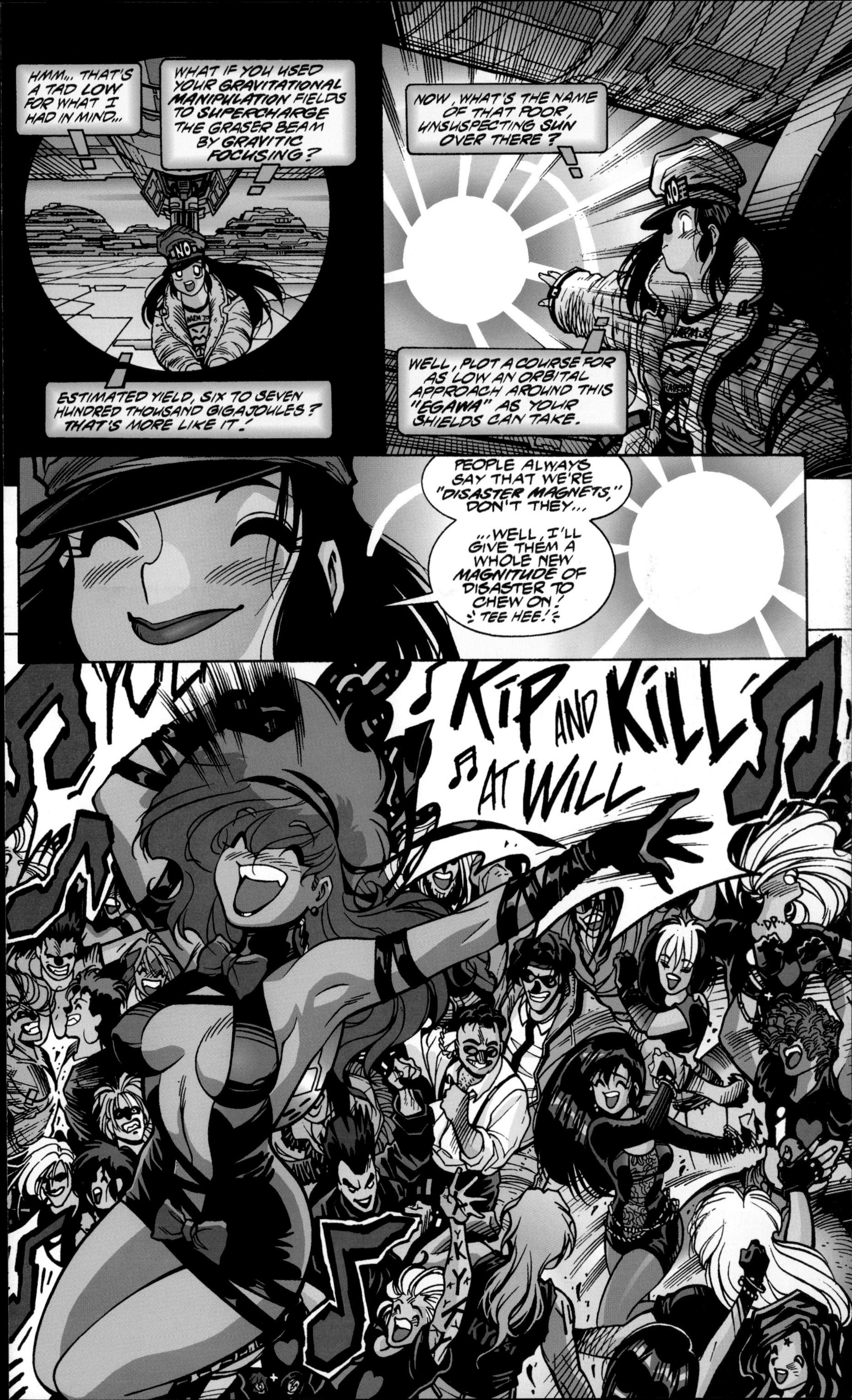
HMM... THAT'S A TAD LOW FOR WHAT I HAD IN MIND...
WHAT IF YOU USED YOUR GRAVITATIONAL MANIPULATION FIELDS TO SUPERCHARGE THE GRASER BEAM BY GRAVITIC FOCUSING?
ESTIMATED YIELD, SIX TO SEVEN HUNDRED THOUSAND GIGAJOULES? THAT'S MORE LIKE IT!
NOW, WHAT'S THE NAME OF THAT POOR, UNSUSPECTING SUN OVER THERE?
WELL, PLOT A COURSE FOR AS LOW AN ORBITAL APPROACH AROUND THIS "EGAWA" AS YOUR SHIELDS CAN TAKE.
PEOPLE ALWAYS SAY THAT WE'RE "DISASTER MAGNETS," DON'T THEY...
...WELL, I'LL GIVE THEM A WHOLE NEW MAGNITUDE OF DISASTER TO CHEW ON! TEE HEE!
KIP AND KILL AT WILL

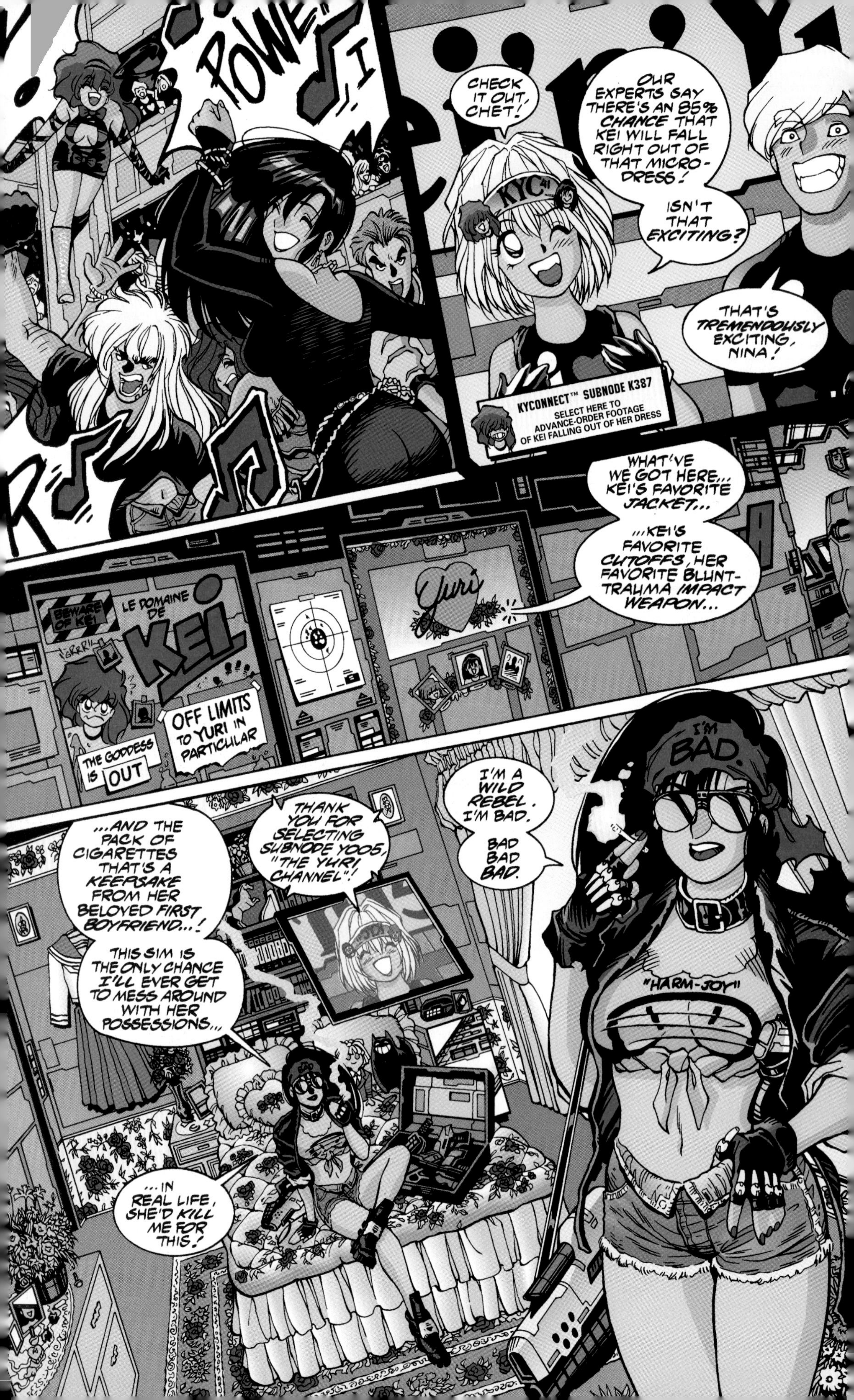
POWE
I
CHECK IT OUT, CHET!
OUR EXPERTS SAY THERE'S AN 85% CHANCE THAT KEI WILL FALL RIGHT OUT OF THAT MICRO-DRESS!
ISN'T THAT EXCITING?
KYC
THAT'S TREMENDOUSLY EXCITING, NINA!
KYCONNECT™ SUBNODE K387
SELECT HERE TO ADVANCE-ORDER FOOTAGE OF KEI FALLING OUT OF HER DRESS
WHAT'VE WE GOT HERE... KEI'S FAVORITE JACKET...
...KEI'S FAVORITE CUTOFFS, HER FAVORITE BLUNT-TRAUMA IMPACT WEAPON...
BEWARE OF KEI
LE DOMAINE DE KEI
GRRR!!
OFF LIMITS TO YURI IN PARTICULAR
THE GODDESS IS OUT
Yuri
...AND THE PACK OF CIGARETTES THAT'S A KEEPSAKE FROM HER BELOVED FIRST BOYFRIEND...!
THANK YOU FOR SELECTING SUBNODE Y005, "THE YURI CHANNEL"!
I'M A WILD REBEL. I'M BAD.
BAD BAD BAD.
I'M BAD.
THIS SIM IS THE ONLY CHANCE I'LL EVER GET TO MESS AROUND WITH HER POSSESSIONS...
"HARM-JOY"
...IN REAL LIFE, SHE'D KILL ME FOR THIS!

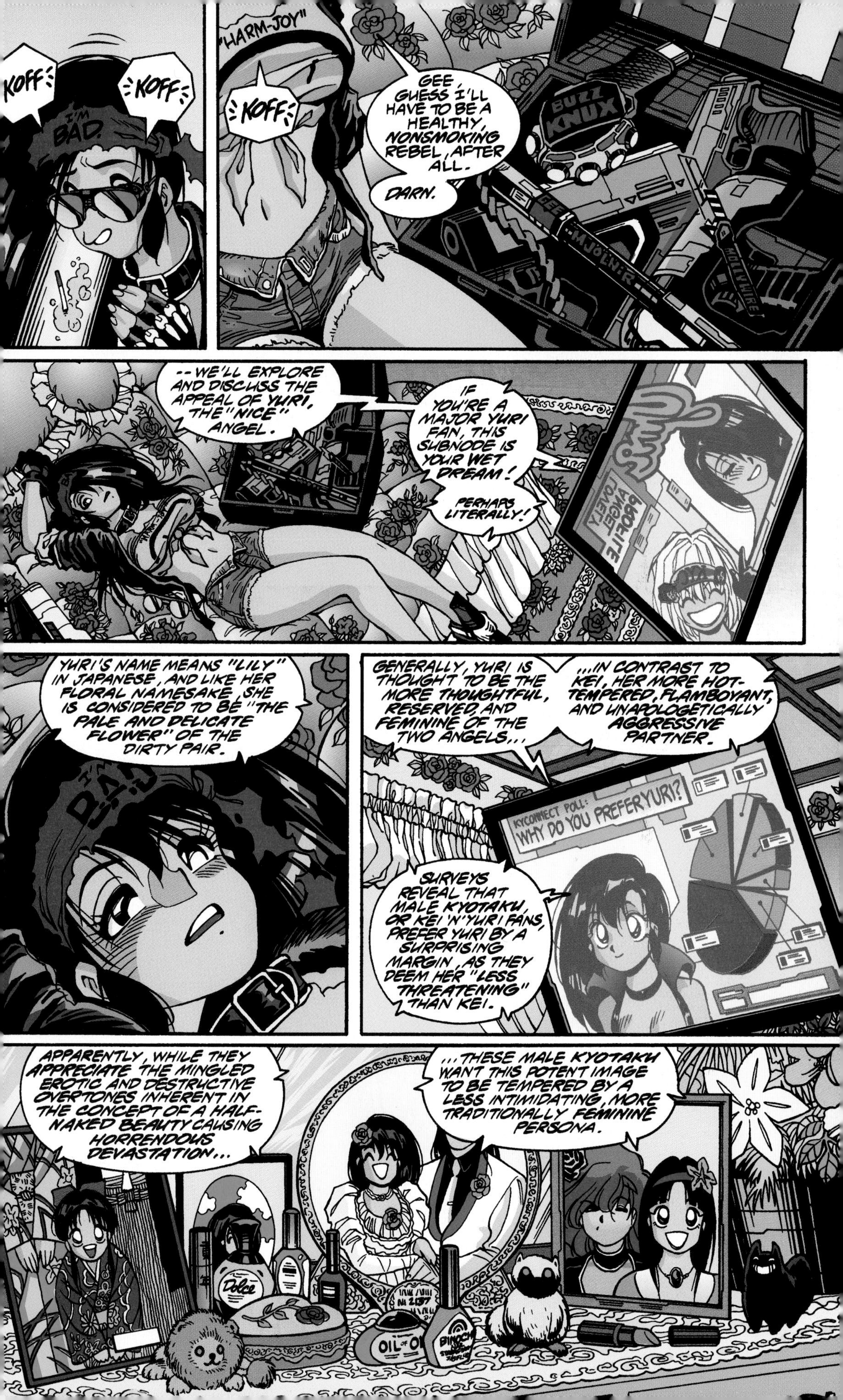
KOFF
KOFF
I'M BAD.
"HARM-JOY"
KOFF
GEE, GUESS I'LL HAVE TO BE A HEALTHY, NONSMOKING REBEL, AFTER ALL.
DARN.
BUZZ KNUX
MJÖLNIR
--WE'LL EXPLORE AND DISCUSS THE APPEAL OF YURI, THE "NICE" ANGEL.
IF YOU'RE A MAJOR YURI FAN, THIS SUBNODE IS YOUR WET DREAM!
PERHAPS LITERALLY!
YURI'S NAME MEANS "LILY" IN JAPANESE, AND LIKE HER FLORAL NAMESAKE, SHE IS CONSIDERED TO BE "THE PALE AND DELICATE FLOWER" OF THE DIRTY PAIR.
GENERALLY, YURI IS THOUGHT TO BE THE MORE THOUGHTFUL, RESERVED, AND FEMININE OF THE TWO ANGELS...
...IN CONTRAST TO KEI, HER MORE HOT-TEMPERED, FLAMBOYANT, AND UNAPOLOGETICALLY AGGRESSIVE PARTNER.
KYCONNECT POLL:
WHY DO YOU PREFER YURI?
SURVEYS REVEAL THAT MALE KYOTAKU, OR KEI 'N' YURI FANS, PREFER YURI BY A SURPRISING MARGIN, AS THEY DEEM HER "LESS THREATENING" THAN KEI.
APPARENTLY, WHILE THEY APPRECIATE THE MINGLED EROTIC AND DESTRUCTIVE OVERTONES INHERENT IN THE CONCEPT OF A HALF-NAKED BEAUTY CAUSING HORRENDOUS DEVASTATION...
...THESE MALE KYOTAKU WANT THIS POTENT IMAGE TO BE TEMPERED BY A LESS INTIMIDATING, MORE TRADITIONALLY FEMININE PERSONA.
Dolce

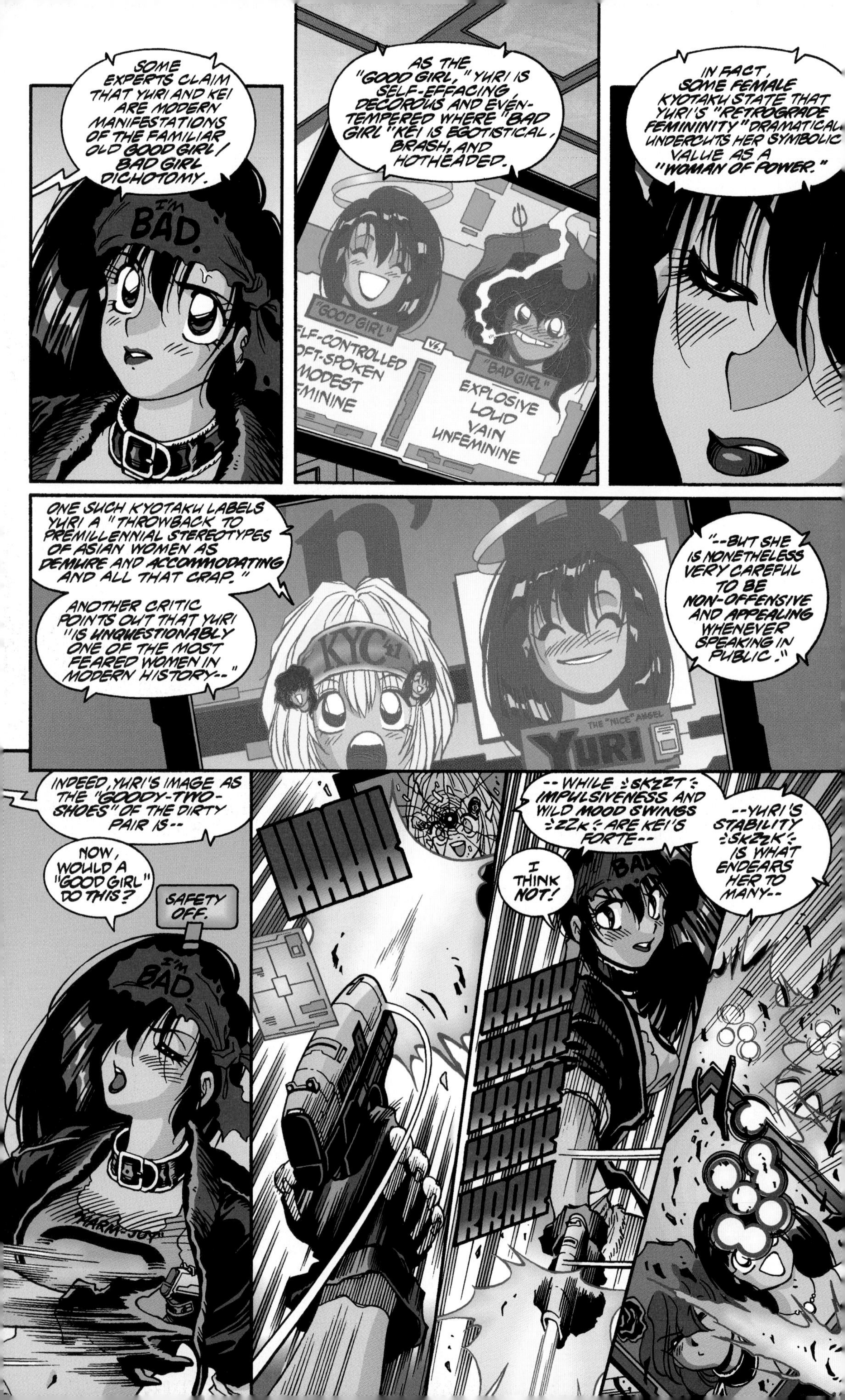
SOME EXPERTS CLAIM THAT YURI AND KEI ARE MODERN MANIFESTATIONS OF THE FAMILIAR OLD GOOD GIRL/ BAD GIRL DICHOTOMY.
I'M BAD.
AS THE "GOOD GIRL," YURI IS SELF-EFFACING, DECOROUS AND EVEN-TEMPERED WHERE "BAD GIRL" KEI IS EGOTISTICAL, BRASH, AND HOTHEADED.
"GOOD GIRL"
ELF-CONTROLLED
OFT-SPOKEN
MODEST
EMININE
VS.
"BAD GIRL"
EXPLOSIVE
LOUD
VAIN
UNFEMININE
IN FACT, SOME FEMALE KYOTAKU STATE THAT YURI'S "RETROGRADE FEMININITY" DRAMATICAL UNDERCUTS HER SYMBOLIC VALUE AS A "WOMAN OF POWER."
ONE SUCH KYOTAKU LABELS YURI A "THROWBACK TO PREMILLENNIAL STEREOTYPES OF ASIAN WOMEN AS DEMURE AND ACCOMMODATING AND ALL THAT CRAP."
ANOTHER CRITIC POINTS OUT THAT YURI "IS UNQUESTIONABLY ONE OF THE MOST FEARED WOMEN IN MODERN HISTORY--"
"--BUT SHE IS NONETHELESS VERY CAREFUL TO BE NON-OFFENSIVE AND APPEALING WHENEVER SPEAKING IN PUBLIC."
KYC '41
THE "NICE" ANGEL
YURI
INDEED, YURI'S IMAGE AS THE "GOODY-TWO-SHOES" OF THE DIRTY PAIR IS--
NOW, WOULD A "GOOD GIRL" DO THIS?
SAFETY OFF.
I'M BAD.
KRAK
--WHILE :SKZZT: IMPULSIVENESS AND WILD MOOD SWINGS :ZZK: ARE KEI'S FORTE--
I THINK NOT!
--YURI'S STABILITY :SKZZK: IS WHAT ENDEARS HER TO MANY--
KRAK
KRAK
KRAK
KRAK
KRAK

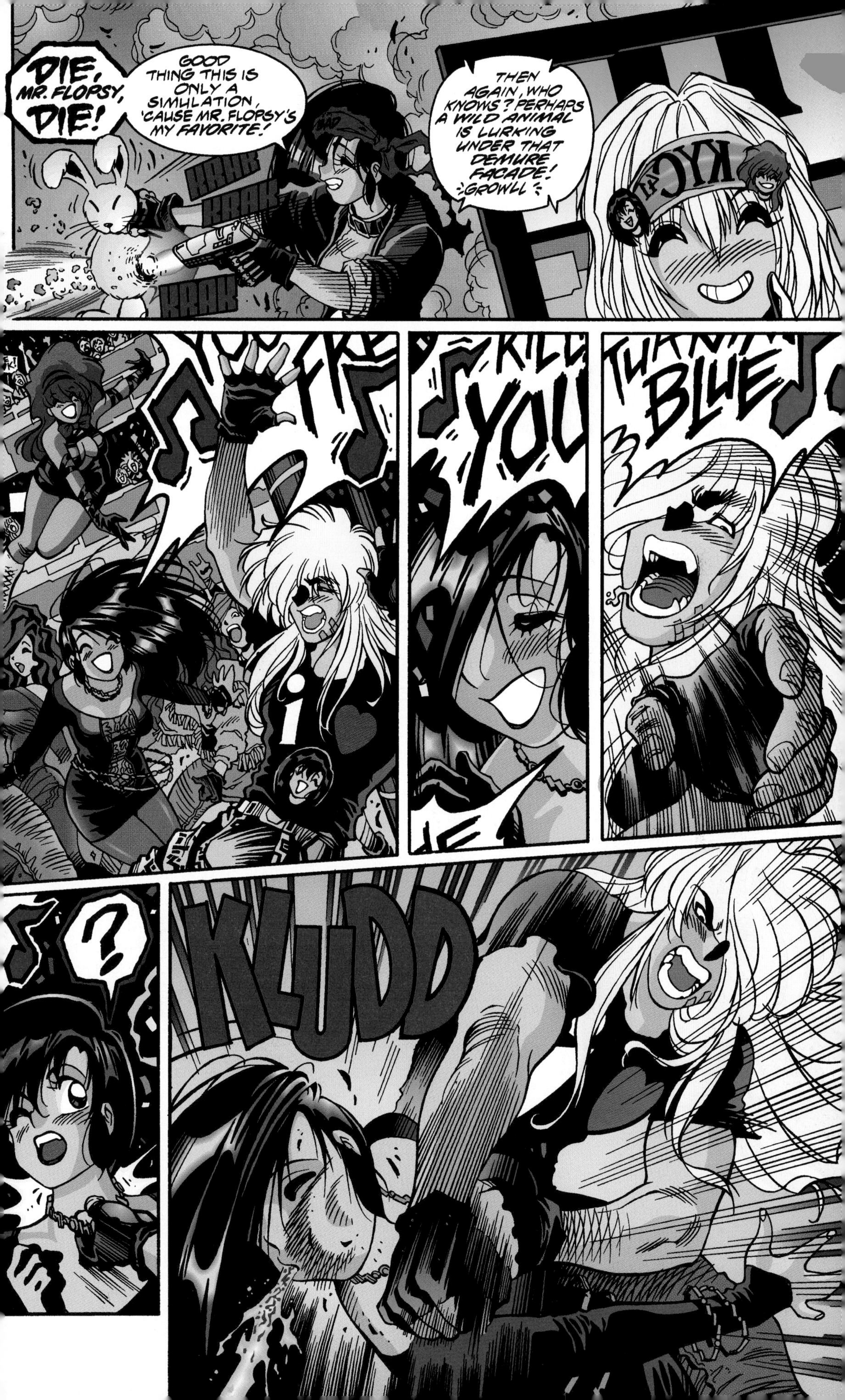
DIE, MR. FLOPSY, DIE!
GOOD THING THIS IS ONLY A SIMULATION, 'CAUSE MR. FLOPSY'S MY FAVORITE!
KRAK
KRAK
KRAK
THEN AGAIN, WHO KNOWS? PERHAPS A WILD ANIMAL IS LURKING UNDER THAT DEMURE FACADE! :GROWL:
YOU
BLUE
?
KLUDD

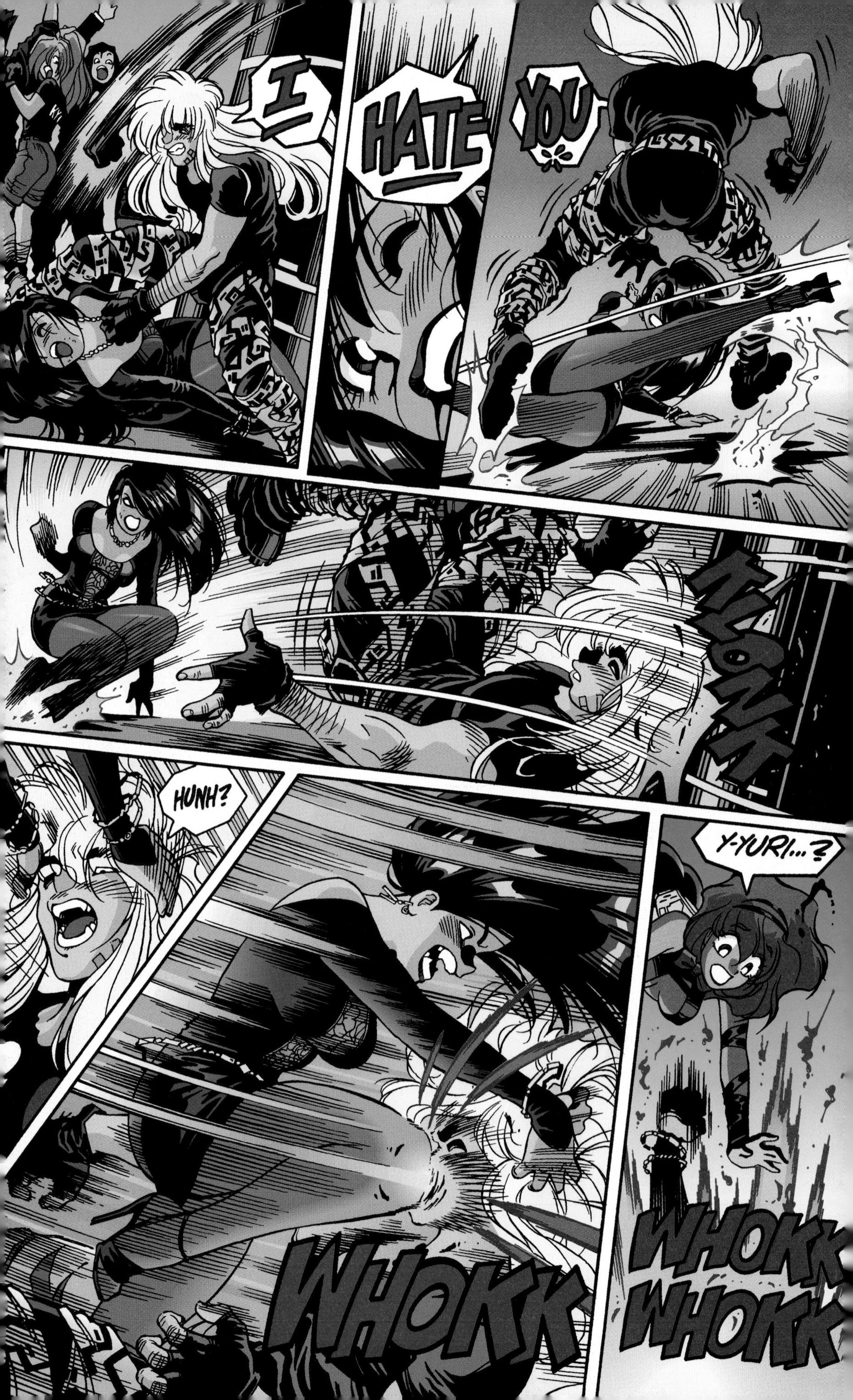
I
HATE
YOU
KLONK
HUNH?
Y-YURI...?
WHOKK
WHOKK
WHOKK

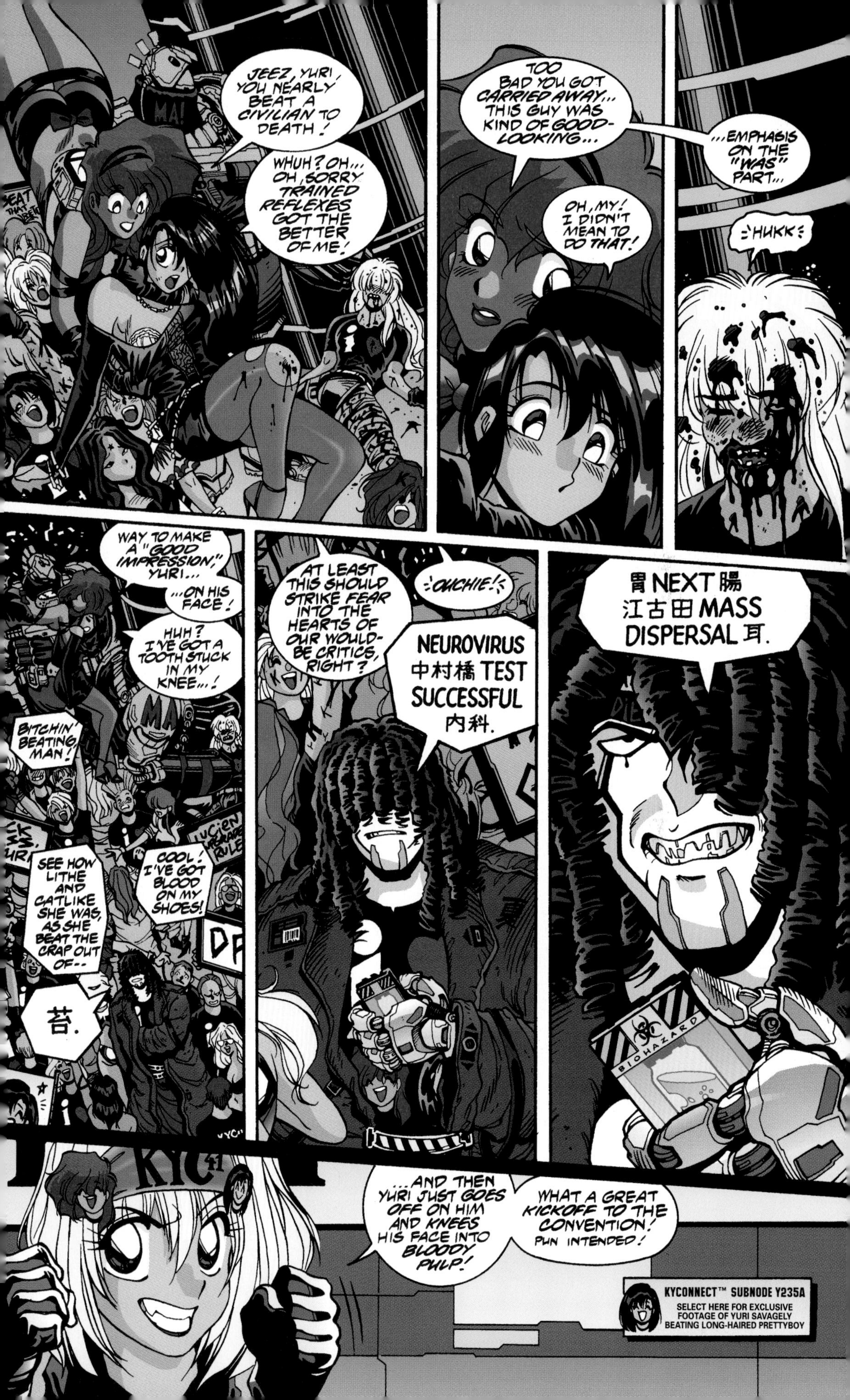
MA!
JEEZ, YURI, YOU NEARLY BEAT A CIVILIAN TO DEATH!
WHUH? OH... OH, SORRY. TRAINED REFLEXES GOT THE BETTER OF ME!
TOO BAD YOU GOT CARRIED AWAY... THIS GUY WAS KIND OF GOOD-LOOKING...
OH, MY! I DIDN'T MEAN TO DO THAT!
...EMPHASIS ON THE "WAS" PART...
HUKK
WAY TO MAKE A "GOOD IMPRESSION," YURI...
...ON HIS FACE!
HUH? I'VE GOT A TOOTH STUCK IN MY KNEE...!
BITCHIN' BEATING, MAN!
SEE HOW LITHE AND CATLIKE SHE WAS, AS SHE BEAT THE CRAP OUT OF--
COOL! I'VE GOT BLOOD ON MY SHOES!
苔.
AT LEAST THIS SHOULD STRIKE FEAR INTO THE HEARTS OF OUR WOULD-BE CRITICS, RIGHT?
OUCHIE!
NEUROVIRUS 中村橋 TEST SUCCESSFUL 内科.
胃 NEXT 腸 江古田 MASS DISPERSAL 耳.
BIOHAZARD
...AND THEN YURI JUST GOES OFF ON HIM AND KNEES HIS FACE INTO BLOODY PULP!
WHAT A GREAT KICKOFF TO THE CONVENTION! PUN INTENDED!
KYCONNECT™ SUBNODE Y235A
SELECT HERE FOR EXCLUSIVE FOOTAGE OF YURI SAVAGELY BEATING LONG-HAIRED PRETTYBOY

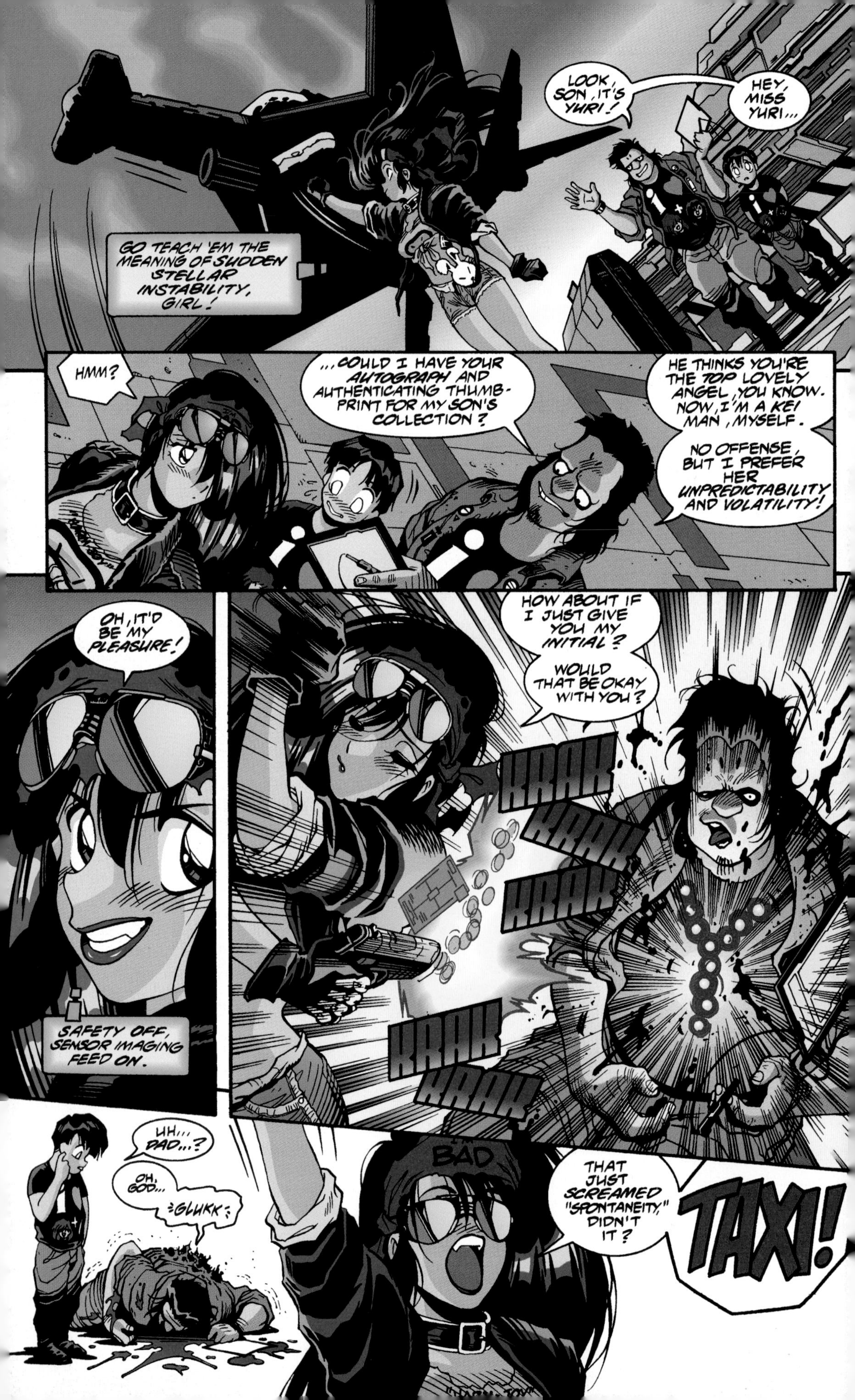
LOOK, SON, IT'S YURI!
HEY, MISS YURI...
GO TEACH 'EM THE MEANING OF SUDDEN STELLAR INSTABILITY, GIRL!
HMM?
...COULD I HAVE YOUR AUTOGRAPH AND AUTHENTICATING THUMB-PRINT FOR MY SON'S COLLECTION?
HE THINKS YOU'RE THE TOP LOVELY ANGEL, YOU KNOW. NOW, I'M A KEI MAN, MYSELF.
NO OFFENSE, BUT I PREFER HER UNPREDICTABILITY AND VOLATILITY!
OH, IT'D BE MY PLEASURE!
SAFETY OFF, SENSOR IMAGING FEED ON.
HOW ABOUT IF I JUST GIVE YOU MY INITIAL?
WOULD THAT BE OKAY WITH YOU?
KRAK
KRAK
KRAK
KRAK
KRAK
UH... DAD...?
OH, GOD...
GLUKK
I'M BAD
THAT JUST SCREAMED "SPONTANEITY," DIDN'T IT?
TAXI!

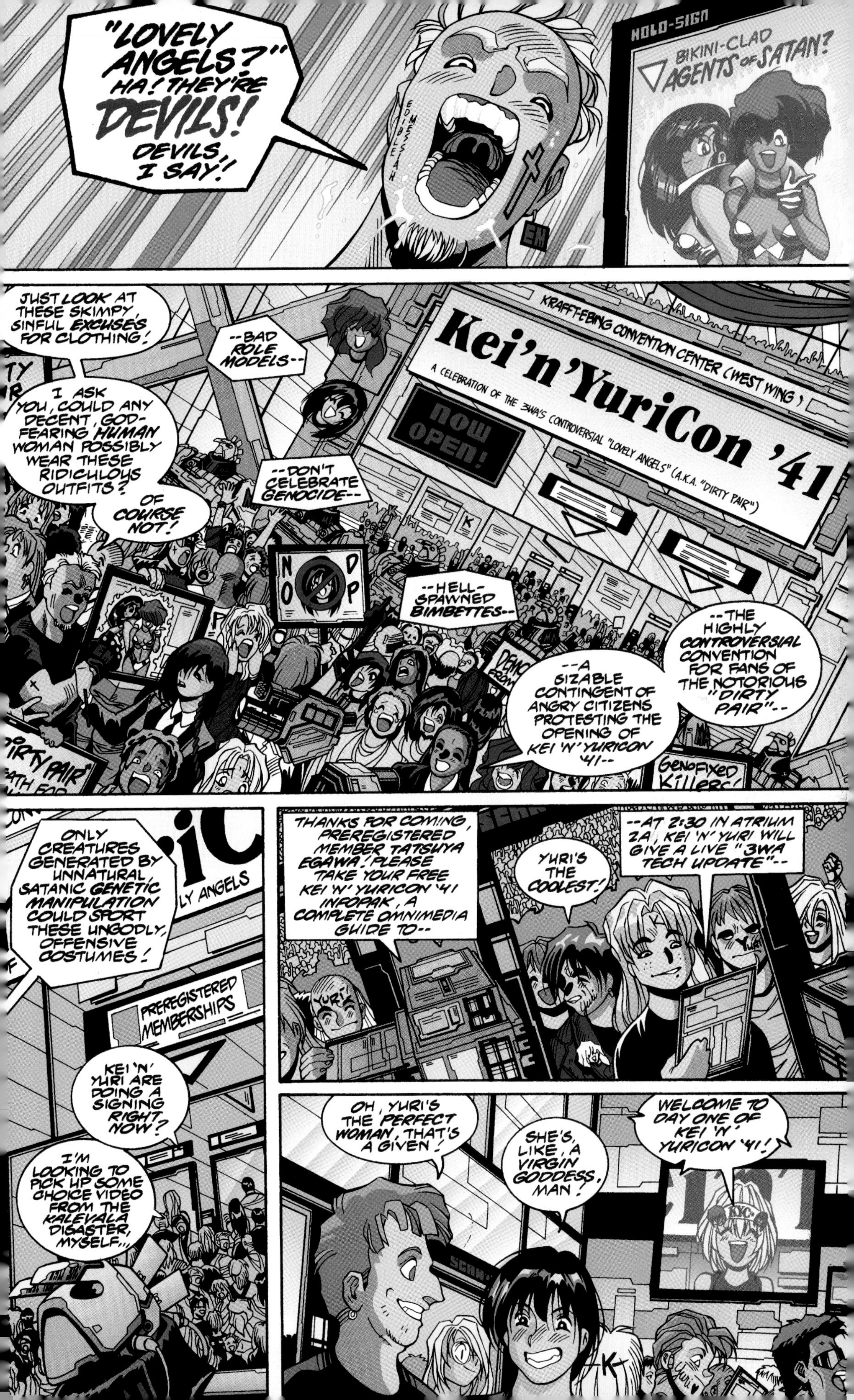
"LOVELY ANGELS?" HA! THEY'RE DEVILS! DEVILS, I SAY!!
EDIBLE MESSIAH
EM
HOLO-SIGN
BIKINI-CLAD AGENTS OF SATAN?
JUST LOOK AT THESE SKIMPY, SINFUL EXCUSES FOR CLOTHING!
--BAD ROLE MODELS--
KRAFFT-EBING CONVENTION CENTER (WEST WING)
Kei'n'YuriCon '41
A CELEBRATION OF THE 3WA'S CONTROVERSIAL "LOVELY ANGELS" (A.K.A. "DIRTY PAIR")
NOW OPEN!
I ASK YOU, COULD ANY DECENT, GOD-FEARING HUMAN WOMAN POSSIBLY WEAR THESE RIDICULOUS OUTFITS?
OF COURSE NOT!
--DON'T CELEBRATE GENOCIDE--
NO DP
--HELL-SPAWNED BIMBETTES--
--THE HIGHLY CONTROVERSIAL CONVENTION FOR FANS OF THE NOTORIOUS "DIRTY PAIR"--
--A SIZABLE CONTINGENT OF ANGRY CITIZENS PROTESTING THE OPENING OF KEI 'N' YURICON '41--
ONLY CREATURES GENERATED BY UNNATURAL, SATANIC GENETIC MANIPULATION COULD SPORT THESE UNGODLY, OFFENSIVE COSTUMES!
PREREGISTERED MEMBERSHIPS
KEI 'N' YURI ARE DOING A SIGNING RIGHT NOW?
I'M LOOKING TO PICK UP SOME CHOICE VIDEO FROM THE KALEVALA DISASTER, MYSELF...
THANKS FOR COMING, PREREGISTERED MEMBER TATSUYA EGAWA! PLEASE TAKE YOUR FREE KEI 'N' YURICON '41 INFOPAK, A COMPLETE OMNIMEDIA GUIDE TO--
YURI'S THE COOLEST!
--AT 2:30 IN ATRIUM 2A, KEI 'N' YURI WILL GIVE A LIVE "3WA TECH UPDATE"--
OH, YURI'S THE PERFECT WOMAN, THAT'S A GIVEN!
SHE'S, LIKE, A VIRGIN GODDESS, MAN!
WELCOME TO DAY ONE OF KEI 'N' YURICON '41!

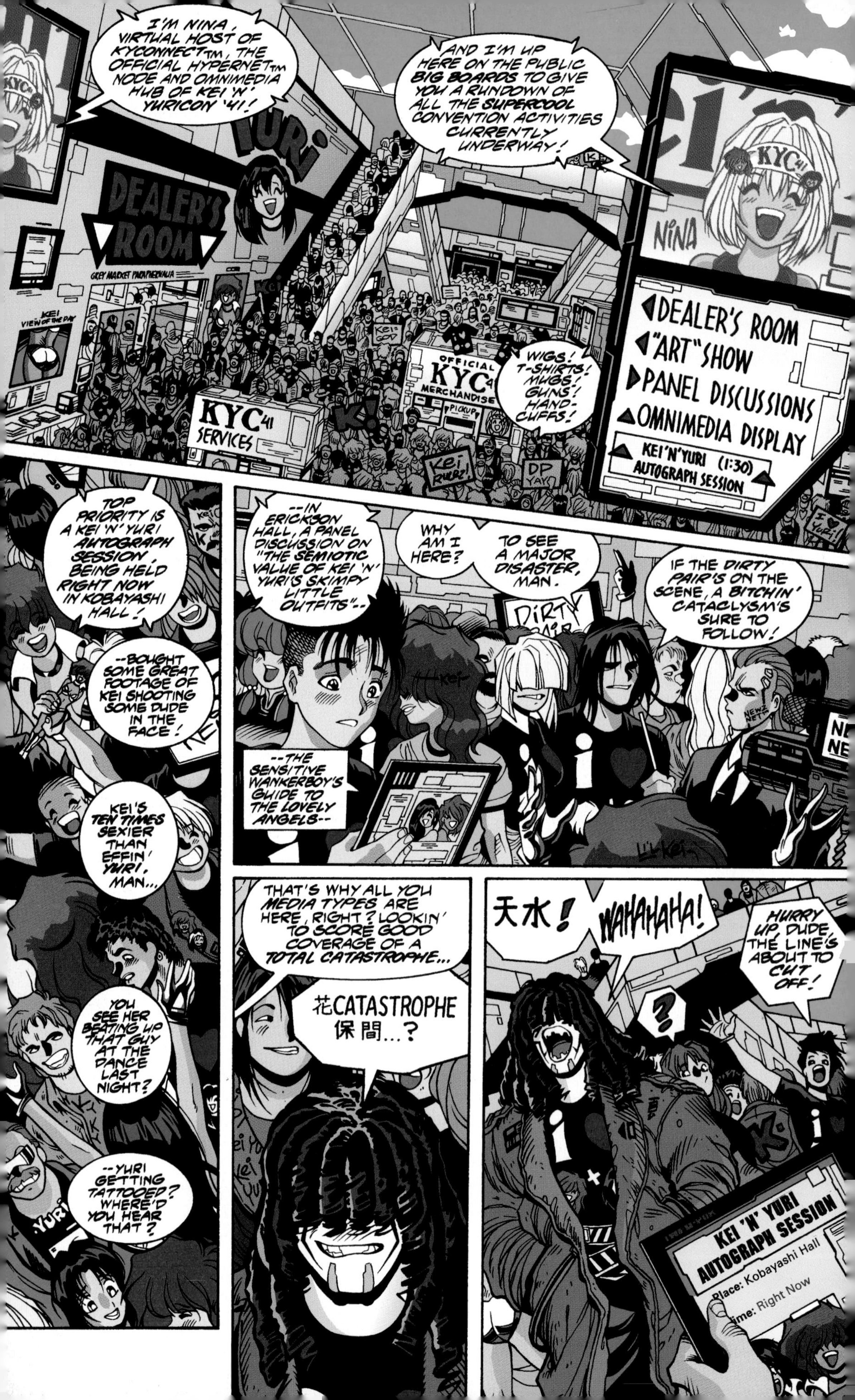

I'M NINA, VIRTUAL HOST OF KYCONNECT™, THE OFFICIAL HYPERNET™ NODE AND OMNIMEDIA HUB OF KEI 'N' YURICON '41!
AND I'M UP HERE ON THE PUBLIC BIG BOARDS TO GIVE YOU A RUNDOWN OF ALL THE SUPERCOOL CONVENTION ACTIVITIES CURRENTLY UNDERWAY!
YURI
DEALER'S ROOM
GREY MARKET PARAPHERNALIA
KEI! VIEW OF THE DAY
NINA
DEALER'S ROOM
"ART" SHOW
PANEL DISCUSSIONS
OMNIMEDIA DISPLAY
KEI 'N' YURI (1:30) AUTOGRAPH SESSION
OFFICIAL KYC 41 MERCHANDISE
PICKUP
KYC 41 SERVICES
WIGS! T-SHIRTS! MUGS! GUNS! HAND-CUFFS!
Kei RULES!
DP YAY!
I ♥ YURI
TOP PRIORITY IS A KEI 'N' YURI AUTOGRAPH SESSION, BEING HELD RIGHT NOW IN KOBAYASHI HALL!
--BOUGHT SOME GREAT FOOTAGE OF KEI SHOOTING SOME DUDE IN THE FACE!
KEI'S TEN TIMES SEXIER THAN EFFIN' YURI, MAN...
YOU SEE HER BEATING UP THAT GUY AT THE DANCE LAST NIGHT?
--YURI GETTING TATTOOED? WHERE'D YOU HEAR THAT?
--IN ERICKSON HALL, A PANEL DISCUSSION ON "THE SEMIOTIC VALUE OF KEI 'N' YURI'S SKIMPY LITTLE OUTFITS"--
--THE SENSITIVE WANKERBOY'S GUIDE TO THE LOVELY ANGELS--
WHY AM I HERE?
TO SEE A MAJOR DISASTER, MAN.
IF THE DIRTY PAIR'S ON THE SCENE, A BITCHIN' CATACLYSM'S SURE TO FOLLOW!
THAT'S WHY ALL YOU MEDIA TYPES ARE HERE, RIGHT? LOOKIN' TO SCORE GOOD COVERAGE OF A TOTAL CATASTROPHE...
花CATASTROPHE 保間...?
天水!
WAHAHAHA!
HURRY UP, DUDE, THE LINE'S ABOUT TO CUT OFF!
?
KEI 'N' YURI AUTOGRAPH SESSION
Place: Kobayashi Hall
Time: Right Now

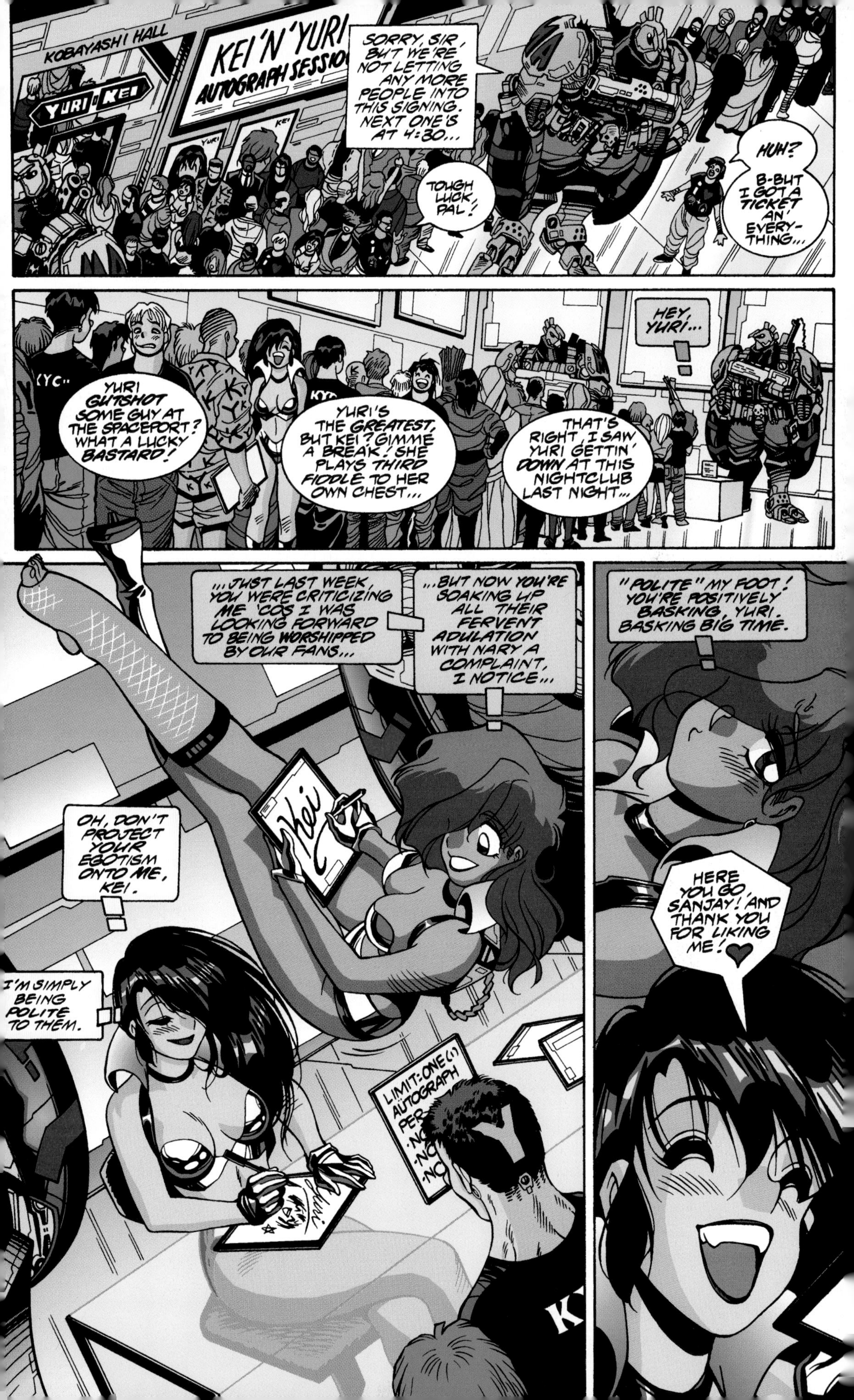

KOBAYASHI HALL
KEI 'N' YURI
AUTOGRAPH SESSIO
YURI KEI
SORRY, SIR, BUT WE'RE NOT LETTING ANY MORE PEOPLE INTO THIS SIGNING. NEXT ONE'S AT 4:30...
TOUGH LUCK, PAL!
HUH?
B-BUT I GOT A TICKET AN' EVERYTHING...
YURI GUTSHOT SOME GUY AT THE SPACEPORT? WHAT A LUCKY BASTARD!
YURI'S THE GREATEST, BUT KEI? GIMME A BREAK! SHE PLAYS THIRD FIDDLE TO HER OWN CHEST...
HEY, YURI...
THAT'S RIGHT, I SAW YURI GETTIN' DOWN AT THIS NIGHTCLUB LAST NIGHT...
...JUST LAST WEEK, YOU WERE CRITICIZING ME 'COS I WAS LOOKING FORWARD TO BEING WORSHIPPED BY OUR FANS...
...BUT NOW YOU'RE SOAKING UP ALL THEIR FERVENT ADULATION WITH NARY A COMPLAINT, I NOTICE...
Kei
OH, DON'T PROJECT YOUR EGOTISM ONTO ME, KEI.
I'M SIMPLY BEING POLITE TO THEM.
LIMIT: ONE (1) AUTOGRAPH PER
"POLITE" MY FOOT! YOU'RE POSITIVELY BASKING, YURI. BASKING BIG TIME.
HERE YOU GO, SANJAY! AND THANK YOU FOR LIKING ME! ♥

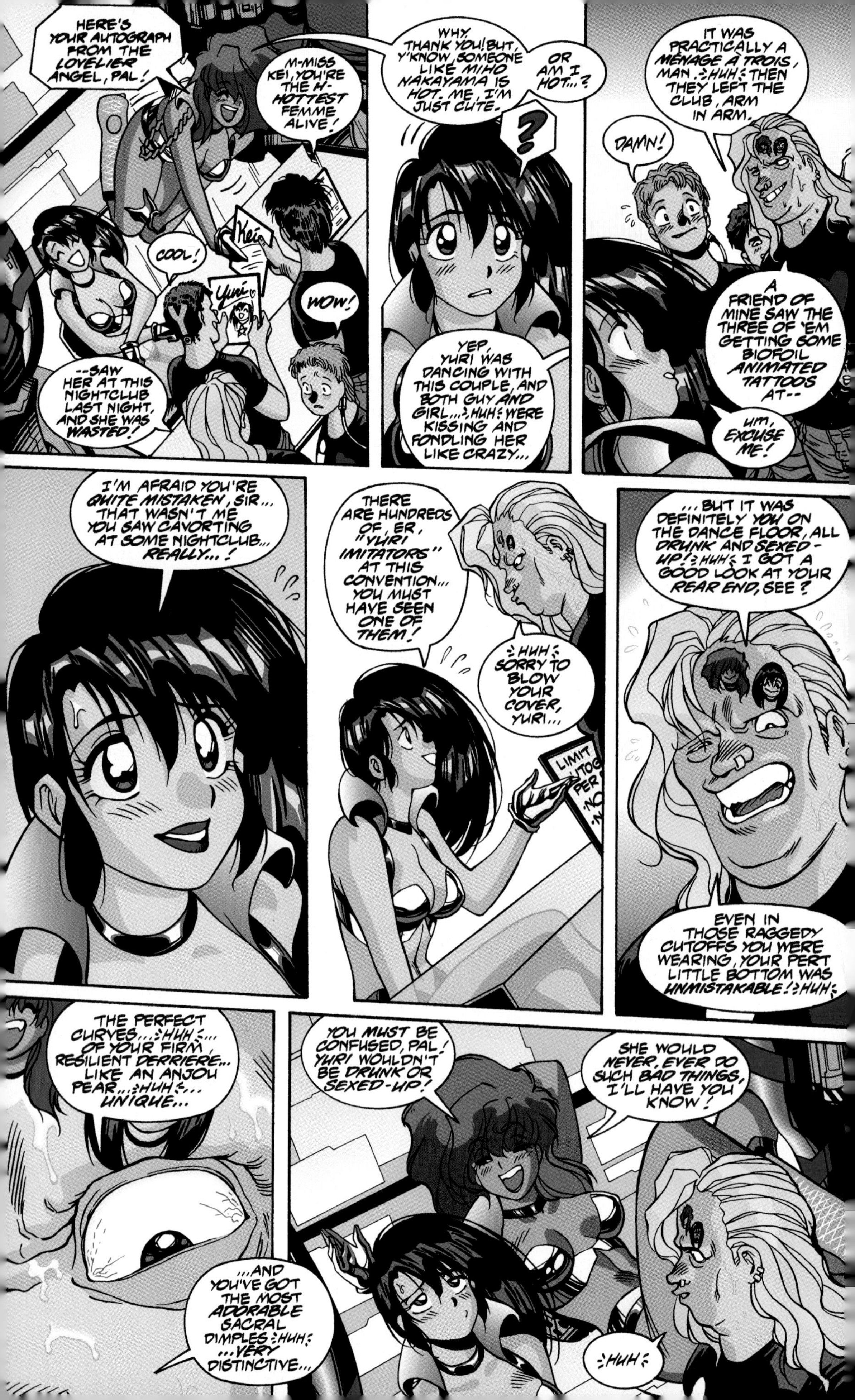
HERE'S YOUR AUTOGRAPH FROM THE LOVELIER ANGEL, PAL!
M-MISS KEI, YOU'RE THE H-HOTTEST FEMME ALIVE!
Kei
COOL!
Yuri
WOW!
--SAW HER AT THIS NIGHTCLUB LAST NIGHT, AND SHE WAS WASTED!
WHY, THANK YOU! BUT, Y'KNOW, SOMEONE LIKE MIHO NAKAYAMA IS HOT. ME, I'M JUST CUTE.
OR AM I HOT...?
?
YEP, YURI WAS DANCING WITH THIS COUPLE, AND BOTH GUY AND GIRL... HUH WERE KISSING AND FONDLING HER LIKE CRAZY...
IT WAS PRACTICALLY A MÉNAGE À TROIS, MAN. HUH THEN THEY LEFT THE CLUB, ARM IN ARM.
DAMN!
A FRIEND OF MINE SAW THE THREE OF 'EM GETTING SOME BIOFOIL ANIMATED TATTOOS AT--
UM, EXCUSE ME!
I'M AFRAID YOU'RE QUITE MISTAKEN, SIR... THAT WASN'T ME YOU SAW CAVORTING AT SOME NIGHTCLUB... REALLY...!
THERE ARE HUNDREDS OF, ER, "YURI IMITATORS" AT THIS CONVENTION... YOU MUST HAVE SEEN ONE OF THEM!
HUH SORRY TO BLOW YOUR COVER, YURI...
...BUT IT WAS DEFINITELY YOU ON THE DANCE FLOOR, ALL DRUNK AND SEXED-UP! HUH I GOT A GOOD LOOK AT YOUR REAR END, SEE?
EVEN IN THOSE RAGGEDY CUTOFFS YOU WERE WEARING, YOUR PERT LITTLE BOTTOM WAS UNMISTAKABLE! HUH
THE PERFECT CURVES... HUH ... OF YOUR FIRM RESILIENT DERRIERE... LIKE AN ANJOU PEAR... HUH ... UNIQUE...
...AND YOU'VE GOT THE MOST ADORABLE SACRAL DIMPLES HUH ...VERY DISTINCTIVE...
YOU MUST BE CONFUSED, PAL! YURI WOULDN'T BE DRUNK OR SEXED-UP!
SHE WOULD NEVER, EVER DO SUCH BAD THINGS, I'LL HAVE YOU KNOW!
HUH

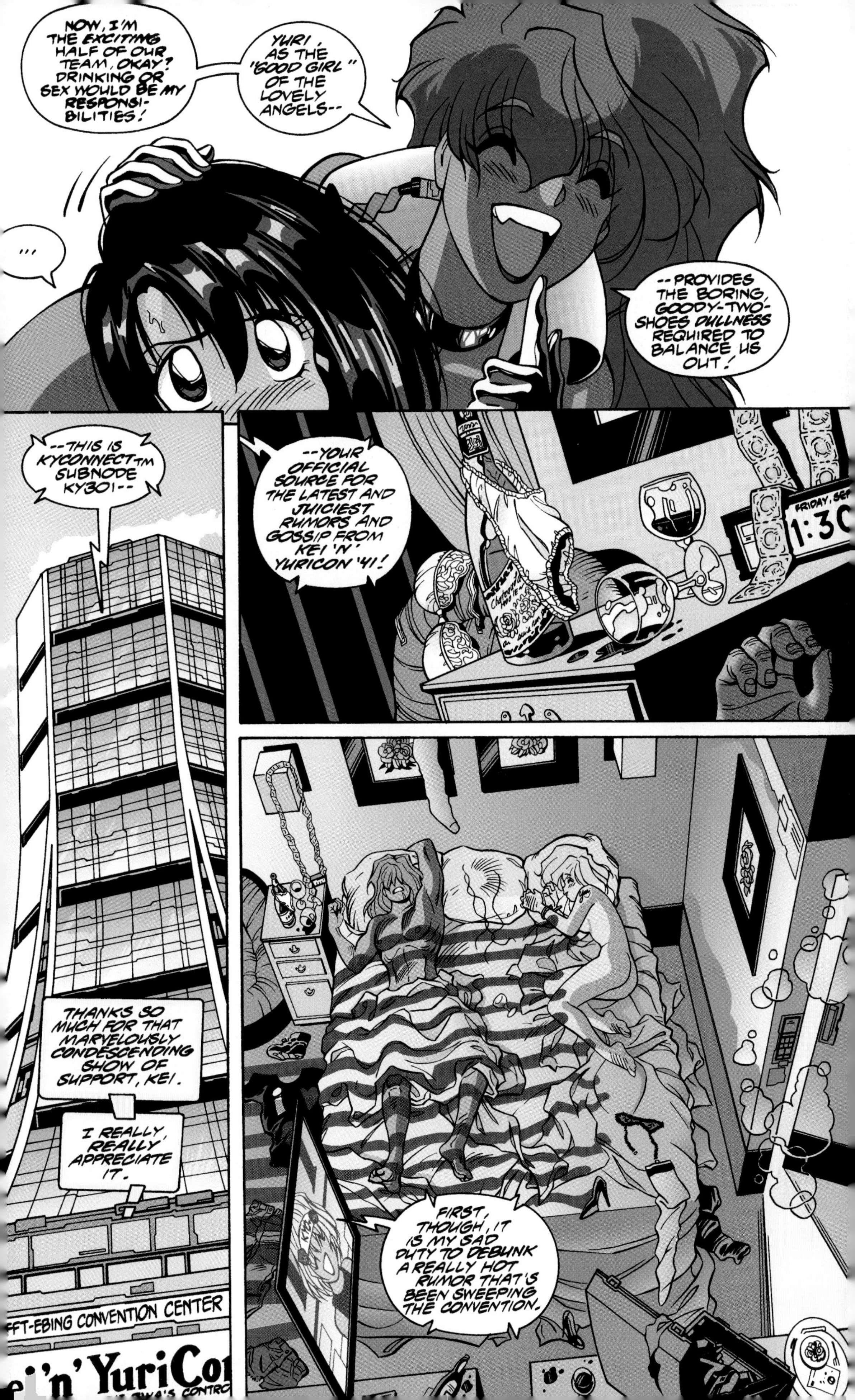
NOW, I'M THE *EXCITING* HALF OF OUR TEAM, *OKAY?* DRINKING OR SEX WOULD BE *MY* RESPONSI-BILITIES!
YURI, AS THE "*GOOD GIRL*" OF THE LOVELY ANGELS--
...
--PROVIDES THE BORING, GOODY-TWO-SHOES *DULLNESS* REQUIRED TO BALANCE US OUT!
--THIS IS KYCONNECT™ SUBNODE KY301--
THANKS SO MUCH FOR THAT MARVELOUSLY CONDESCENDING SHOW OF SUPPORT, KEI.
I *REALLY, REALLY* APPRECIATE IT.
FFT-EBING CONVENTION CENTER
ei 'n' YuriCo
--YOUR OFFICIAL SOURCE FOR THE LATEST AND JUICIEST RUMORS AND GOSSIP FROM KEI 'N' YURICON '41!
FRIDAY, SEP
1:30
FIRST, THOUGH, IT IS MY SAD DUTY TO DEBUNK A REALLY HOT RUMOR THAT'S BEEN SWEEPING THE CONVENTION.

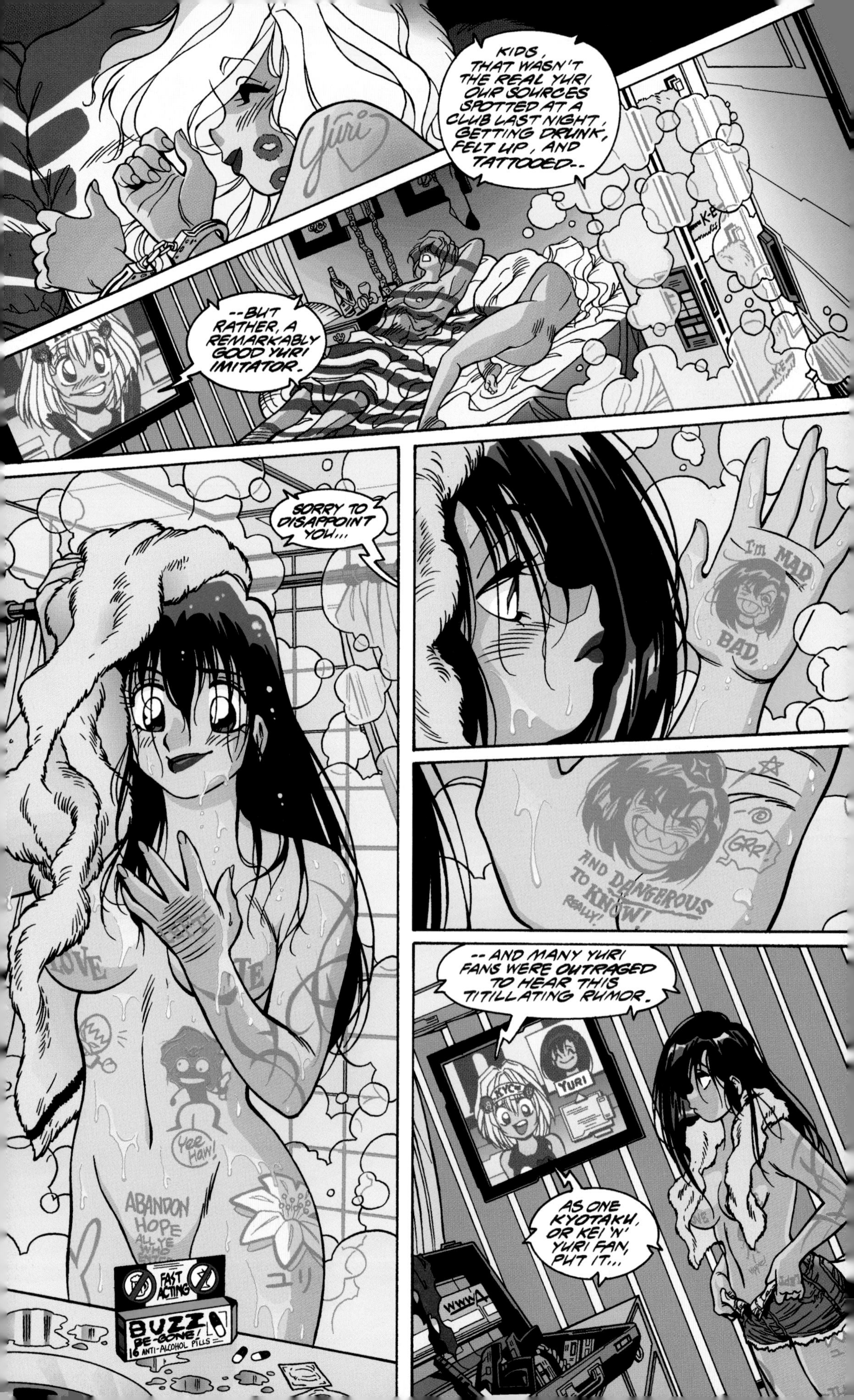
Yuri
KIDS, THAT WASN'T THE REAL YURI OUR SOURCES SPOTTED AT A CLUB LAST NIGHT, GETTING DRUNK, FELT UP, AND TATTOOED--
--BUT RATHER, A REMARKABLY GOOD YURI IMITATOR.
SORRY TO DISAPPOINT YOU...
LOVE
Yee Haw!
ABANDON HOPE
FAST ACTING
BUZZ BE-GONE! 16 ANTI-ALCOHOL PILLS
I'm MAD BAD,
AND DANGEROUS TO KNOW! REALLY!
GRR!
-- AND MANY YURI FANS WERE OUTRAGED TO HEAR THIS TITILLATING RUMOR.
YURI
AS ONE KYOTAKU, OR KEI 'N' YURI FAN, PUT IT...

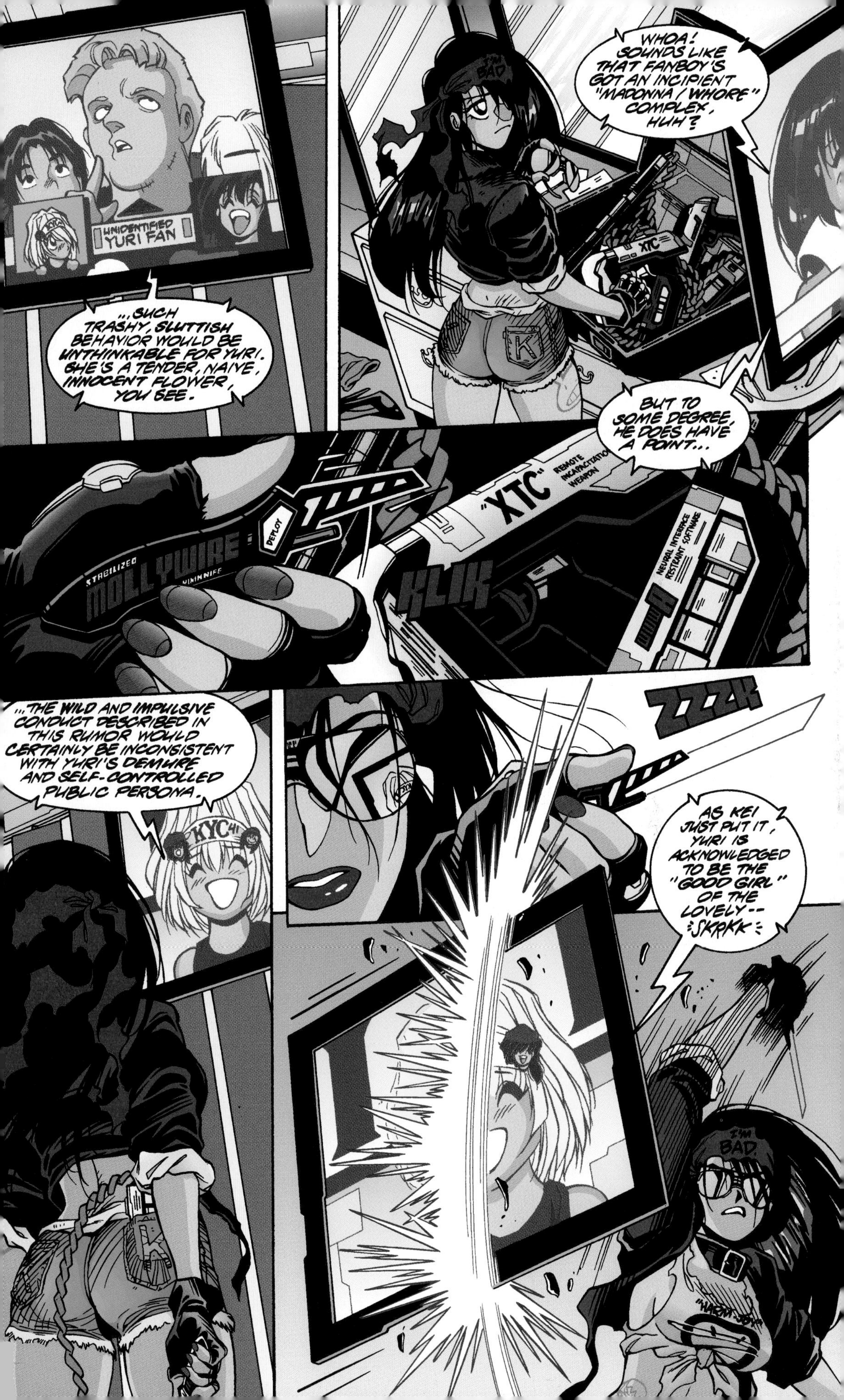
UNIDENTIFIED YURI FAN
...SUCH TRASHY, SLUTTISH BEHAVIOR WOULD BE UNTHINKABLE FOR YURI. SHE'S A TENDER, NAIVE, INNOCENT FLOWER, YOU SEE.
I'M BAD
WHOA! SOUNDS LIKE THAT FANBOY'S GOT AN INCIPIENT "MADONNA / WHORE" COMPLEX, HUH?
XTC
BUT TO SOME DEGREE, HE DOES HAVE A POINT...
STABILIZED MOLLYWIRE
DEPLOY
"XTC" REMOTE INCAPACITATION WEAPON
NEURAL INTERFACE RESTRAINT SOFTWARE
KLIK
...THE WILD AND IMPULSIVE CONDUCT DESCRIBED IN THIS RUMOR WOULD CERTAINLY BE INCONSISTENT WITH YURI'S DEMURE AND SELF-CONTROLLED PUBLIC PERSONA.
KYC
ZZZK
AS KEI JUST PUT IT, YURI IS ACKNOWLEDGED TO BE THE "GOOD GIRL" OF THE LOVELY--
SKRKK
I'M BAD.

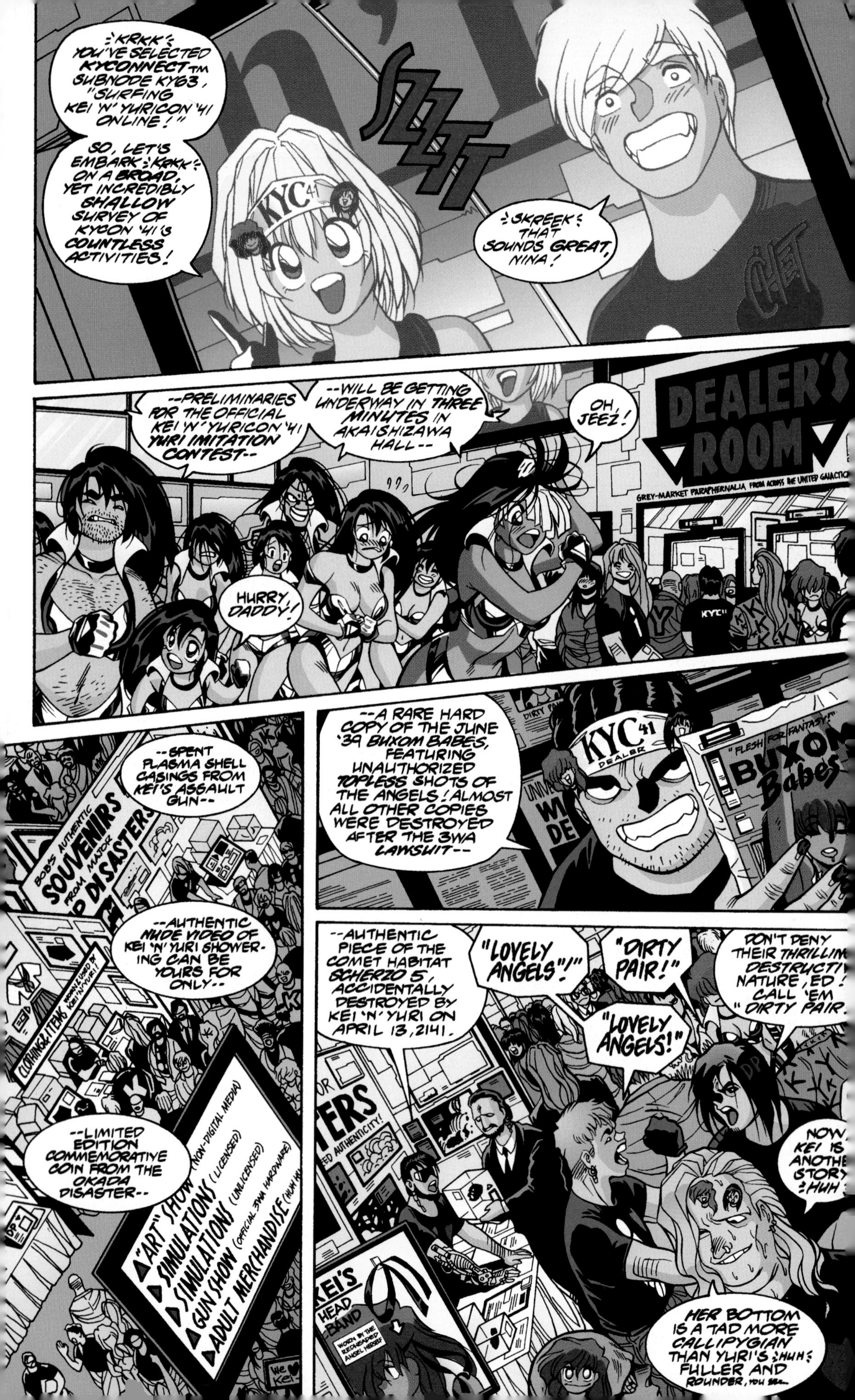
KRKK YOU'VE SELECTED KYCONNECT TM SUBNODE KY63, "SURFING KEI 'N' YURICON '41 ONLINE!"
SO, LET'S EMBARK KRKK ON A BROAD, YET INCREDIBLY SHALLOW SURVEY OF KYCON '41'S COUNTLESS ACTIVITIES!
KYC 41
SZZZTT
SKREEK THAT SOUNDS GREAT, NINA!
--PRELIMINARIES FOR THE OFFICIAL KEI 'N' YURICON '41 YURI IMITATION CONTEST--
--WILL BE GETTING UNDERWAY IN THREE MINUTES IN AKAISHIZAWA HALL--
OH, JEEZ!
DEALER'S ROOM
GREY-MARKET PARAPHERNALIA FROM ACROSS THE UNITED GALACTIC
HURRY, DADDY!
--SPENT PLASMA SHELL CASINGS FROM KEI'S ASSAULT GUN--
BOB'S AUTHENTIC SOUVENIRS FROM MAJOR DISASTERS
--A RARE HARD COPY OF THE JUNE '39 BUXOM BABES, FEATURING UNAUTHORIZED TOPLESS SHOTS OF THE ANGELS! ALMOST ALL OTHER COPIES WERE DESTROYED AFTER THE 3WA LAWSUIT--
KYC 41 DEALER
"FLESH FOR FANTASY!"
BUXOM Babes
--AUTHENTIC NUDE VIDEO OF KEI 'N' YURI SHOWERING CAN BE YOURS FOR ONLY--
CLOTHING & ITEMS WORN & USED BY KEI 'N' YURI!
--LIMITED EDITION COMMEMORATIVE COIN FROM THE OKADA DISASTER--
▲"ART" SHOW (NON-DIGITAL MEDIA)
▲SIMULATIONS (LICENSED)
▲SIMULATIONS (UNLICENSED)
▲GUN SHOW (OFFICIAL 3WA HARDWARE)
▲ADULT MERCHANDISE (HUH HUH)
--AUTHENTIC PIECE OF THE COMET HABITAT SCHERZO 5, ACCIDENTALLY DESTROYED BY KEI 'N' YURI ON APRIL 13, 2141.
"LOVELY ANGELS"!
"DIRTY PAIR!"
"LOVELY ANGELS!"
DON'T DENY THEIR THRILLIN DESTRUCTI NATURE, ED! CALL 'EM "DIRTY PAIR."
NOW KEI IS ANOTHE STORY HUH
KEI'S HEAD BAND
WORN BY THE REDHEADED ANGEL HERSELF
HER BOTTOM IS A TAD MORE CALLIPYGIAN THAN YURI'S HUH FULLER AND ROUNDER, YOU SEE...

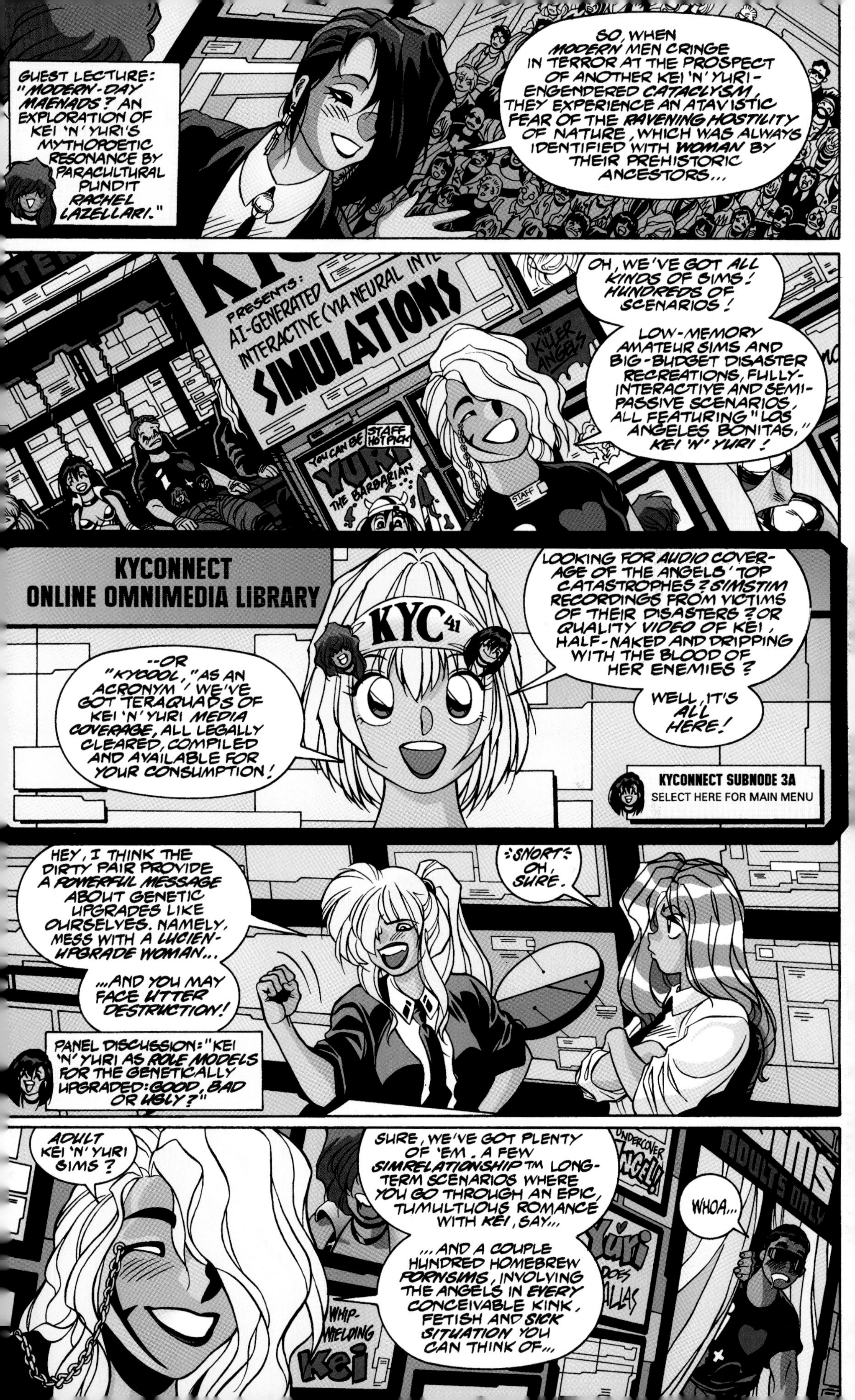
GUEST LECTURE: "MODERN-DAY MAENADS? AN EXPLORATION OF KEI 'N' YURI'S MYTHOPOETIC RESONANCE BY PARACULTURAL PUNDIT RACHEL LAZELLARI."
SO, WHEN MODERN MEN CRINGE IN TERROR AT THE PROSPECT OF ANOTHER KEI 'N' YURI-ENGENDERED CATACLYSM, THEY EXPERIENCE AN ATAVISTIC FEAR OF THE RAVENING HOSTILITY OF NATURE, WHICH WAS ALWAYS IDENTIFIED WITH WOMAN BY THEIR PREHISTORIC ANCESTORS...
KYC PRESENTS: AI-GENERATED INTERACTIVE (VIA NEURAL INT SIMULATIONS
THE KILLER ANGELS
STAFF HOT PICK
YOU CAN BE YURI THE BARBARIAN
STAFF
OH, WE'VE GOT ALL KINDS OF SIMS! HUNDREDS OF SCENARIOS!
LOW-MEMORY AMATEUR SIMS AND BIG-BUDGET DISASTER RECREATIONS, FULLY-INTERACTIVE AND SEMI-PASSIVE SCENARIOS, ALL FEATURING "LOS ANGELES BONITAS," KEI 'N' YURI!
KYCONNECT
ONLINE OMNIMEDIA LIBRARY
KYC 41
--OR "KYCOOL," AS AN ACRONYM, WE'VE GOT TERAQUADS OF KEI 'N' YURI MEDIA COVERAGE, ALL LEGALLY CLEARED, COMPILED AND AVAILABLE FOR YOUR CONSUMPTION!
LOOKING FOR AUDIO COVERAGE OF THE ANGELS' TOP CATASTROPHES? SIMSTIM RECORDINGS FROM VICTIMS OF THEIR DISASTERS? OR QUALITY VIDEO OF KEI, HALF-NAKED AND DRIPPING WITH THE BLOOD OF HER ENEMIES?
WELL, IT'S ALL HERE!
KYCONNECT SUBNODE 3A
SELECT HERE FOR MAIN MENU
HEY, I THINK THE DIRTY PAIR PROVIDE A POWERFUL MESSAGE ABOUT GENETIC UPGRADES LIKE OURSELVES. NAMELY, MESS WITH A LUCIEN-UPGRADE WOMAN...
...AND YOU MAY FACE UTTER DESTRUCTION!
PANEL DISCUSSION: "KEI 'N' YURI AS ROLE MODELS FOR THE GENETICALLY UPGRADED: GOOD, BAD OR UGLY?"
SNORT OH, SURE.
ADULT KEI 'N' YURI SIMS?
SURE, WE'VE GOT PLENTY OF 'EM. A FEW SIMRELATIONSHIP™ LONG-TERM SCENARIOS WHERE YOU GO THROUGH AN EPIC, TUMULTUOUS ROMANCE WITH KEI, SAY...
...AND A COUPLE HUNDRED HOMEBREW PORNSIMS, INVOLVING THE ANGELS IN EVERY CONCEIVABLE KINK, FETISH AND SICK SITUATION YOU CAN THINK OF...
WHIP-WIELDING KEI
UNDERCOVER ANGEL!
YURI DOES DALLAS
ADULTS ONLY
WHOA...

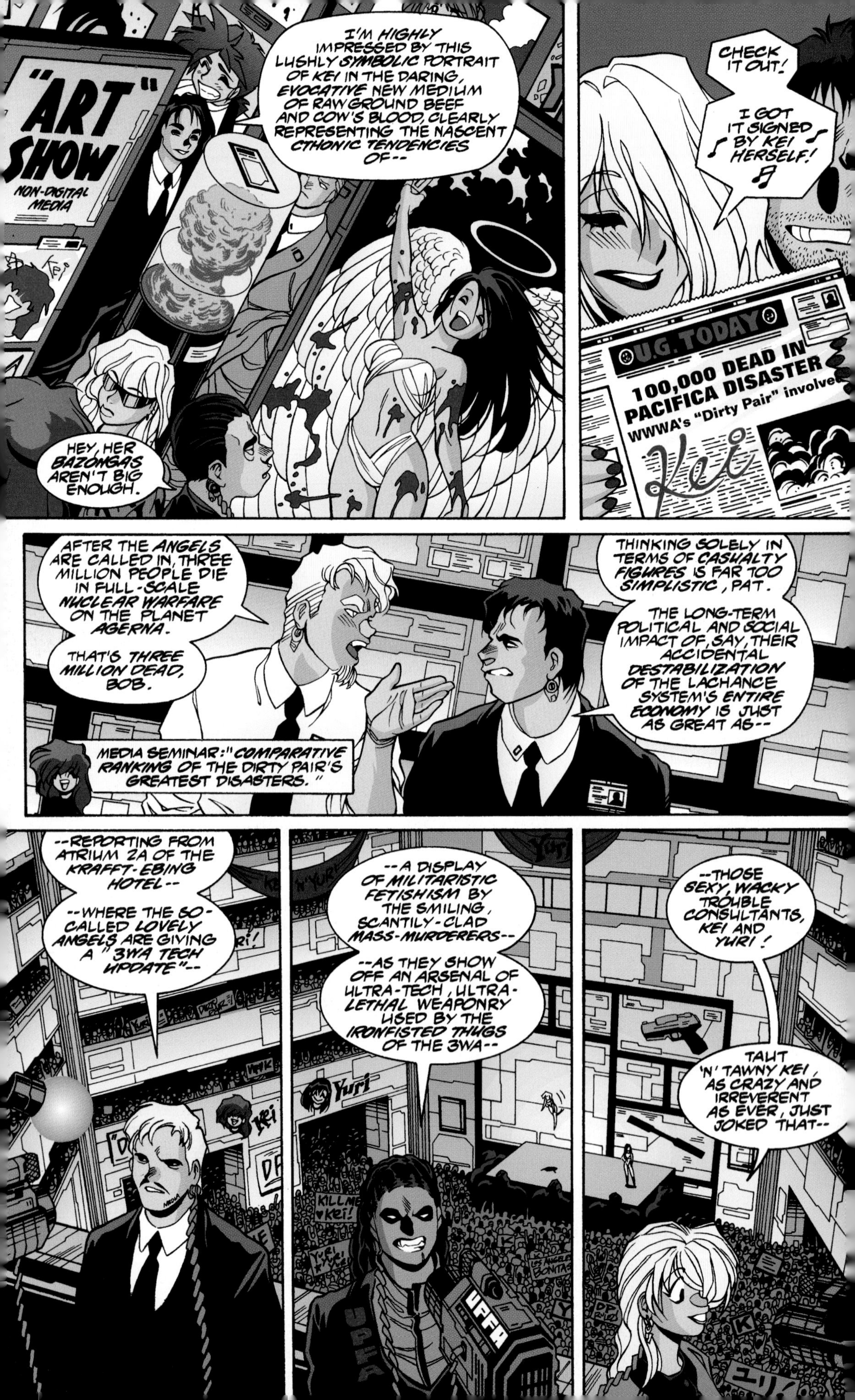
"ART" SHOW
NON-DIGITAL MEDIA
I'M HIGHLY IMPRESSED BY THIS LUSHLY SYMBOLIC PORTRAIT OF KEI IN THE DARING, EVOCATIVE NEW MEDIUM OF RAW GROUND BEEF AND COW'S BLOOD, CLEARLY REPRESENTING THE NASCENT CTHONIC TENDENCIES OF--
HEY, HER BAZONGAS AREN'T BIG ENOUGH.
CHECK IT OUT!
I GOT IT SIGNED BY KEI HERSELF!
U.G. TODAY
100,000 DEAD IN PACIFICA DISASTER
WWWA's "Dirty Pair" involve
Kei
AFTER THE ANGELS ARE CALLED IN, THREE MILLION PEOPLE DIE IN FULL-SCALE NUCLEAR WARFARE ON THE PLANET AGERNA.
THAT'S THREE MILLION DEAD, BOB.
THINKING SOLELY IN TERMS OF CASUALTY FIGURES IS FAR TOO SIMPLISTIC, PAT.
THE LONG-TERM POLITICAL AND SOCIAL IMPACT OF, SAY, THEIR ACCIDENTAL DESTABILIZATION OF THE LACHANCE SYSTEM'S ENTIRE ECONOMY IS JUST AS GREAT AS--
MEDIA SEMINAR: "COMPARATIVE RANKING OF THE DIRTY PAIR'S GREATEST DISASTERS."
--REPORTING FROM ATRIUM 2A OF THE KRAFFT-EBING HOTEL--
--WHERE THE SO-CALLED LOVELY ANGELS ARE GIVING A "3WA TECH UPDATE"--
--A DISPLAY OF MILITARISTIC FETISHISM BY THE SMILING, SCANTILY-CLAD MASS-MURDERERS--
--AS THEY SHOW OFF AN ARSENAL OF ULTRA-TECH, ULTRA-LETHAL WEAPONRY USED BY THE IRONFISTED THUGS OF THE 3WA--
--THOSE SEXY, WACKY TROUBLE CONSULTANTS, KEI AND YURI!
TAUT 'N' TAWNY KEI, AS CRAZY AND IRREVERENT AS EVER, JUST JOKED THAT--
Yuri
Kei
KILL ME Kei!
UPFA

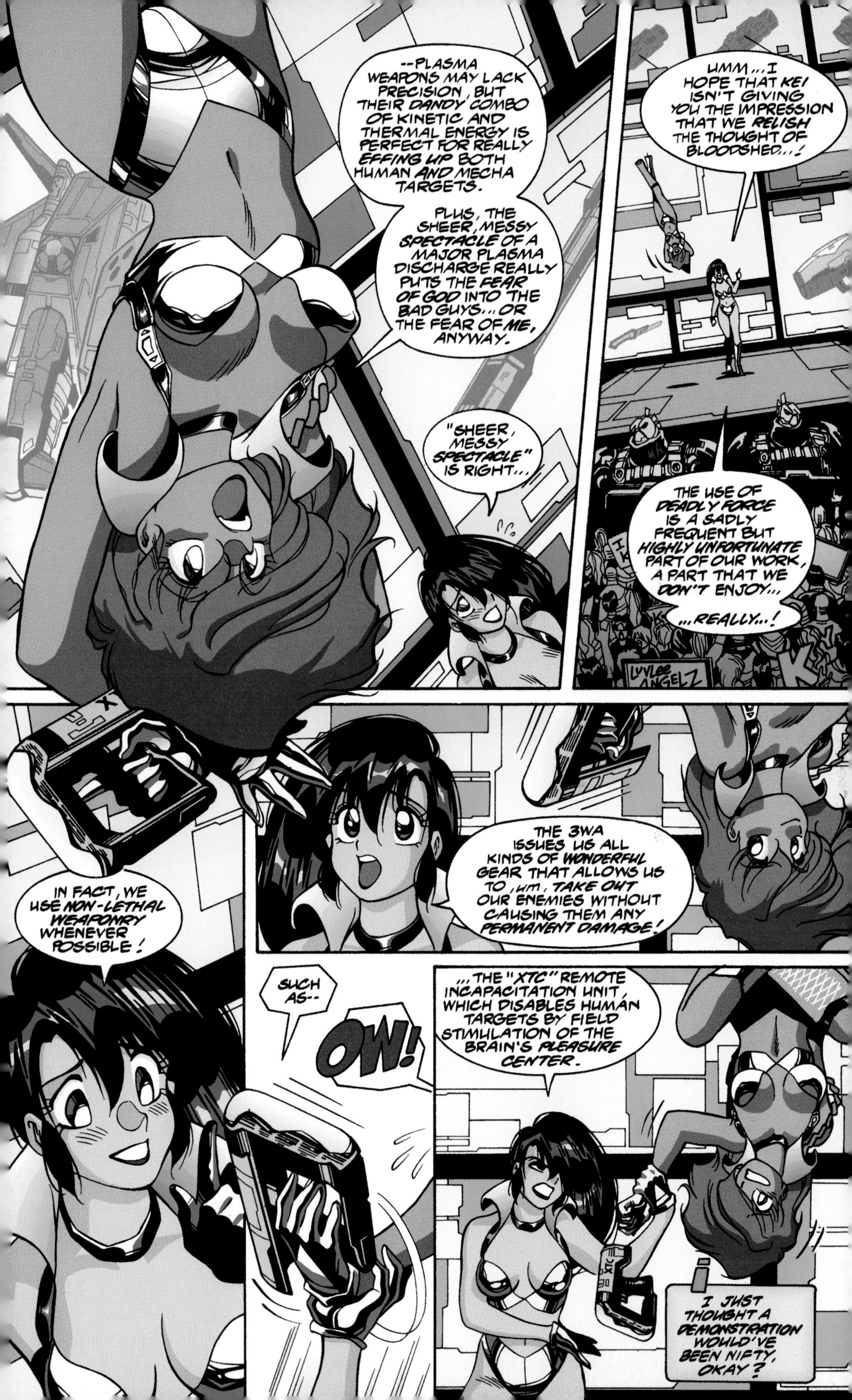
--PLASMA WEAPONS MAY LACK PRECISION, BUT THEIR DANDY COMBO OF KINETIC AND THERMAL ENERGY IS PERFECT FOR REALLY EFFING UP BOTH HUMAN AND MECHA TARGETS.
PLUS, THE SHEER, MESSY SPECTACLE OF A MAJOR PLASMA DISCHARGE REALLY PUTS THE FEAR OF GOD INTO THE BAD GUYS... OR THE FEAR OF ME, ANYWAY.
"SHEER, MESSY SPECTACLE" IS RIGHT...
UMM... I HOPE THAT KEI ISN'T GIVING YOU THE IMPRESSION THAT WE RELISH THE THOUGHT OF BLOODSHED...!
THE USE OF DEADLY FORCE IS A SADLY FREQUENT BUT HIGHLY UNFORTUNATE PART OF OUR WORK, A PART THAT WE DON'T ENJOY...
...REALLY...!
LUVLEE ANGELZ
IN FACT, WE USE NON-LETHAL WEAPONRY WHENEVER POSSIBLE!
THE 3WA ISSUES US ALL KINDS OF WONDERFUL GEAR THAT ALLOWS US TO, UM, TAKE OUT OUR ENEMIES WITHOUT CAUSING THEM ANY PERMANENT DAMAGE!
SUCH AS--
OW!
...THE "XTC" REMOTE INCAPACITATION UNIT, WHICH DISABLES HUMAN TARGETS BY FIELD STIMULATION OF THE BRAIN'S PLEASURE CENTER.
I JUST THOUGHT A DEMONSTRATION WOULD'VE BEEN NIFTY, OKAY?

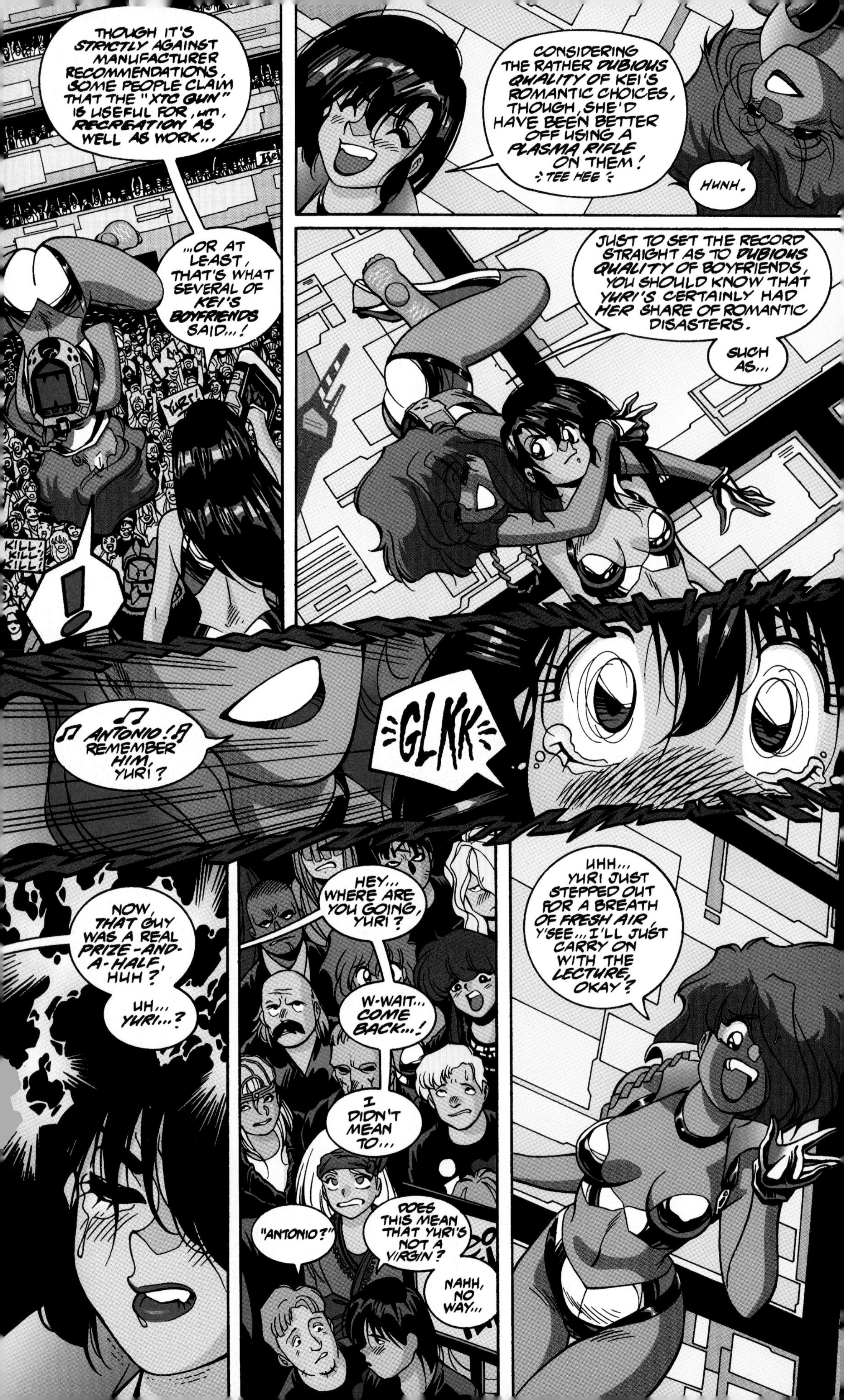
THOUGH IT'S STRICTLY AGAINST MANUFACTURER RECOMMENDATIONS, SOME PEOPLE CLAIM THAT THE "XTC GUN" IS USEFUL FOR, UM, RECREATION AS WELL AS WORK...
...OR AT LEAST, THAT'S WHAT SEVERAL OF KEI'S BOYFRIENDS SAID...!
YURI
KILL! KILL! KILL!
!
CONSIDERING THE RATHER DUBIOUS QUALITY OF KEI'S ROMANTIC CHOICES, THOUGH, SHE'D HAVE BEEN BETTER OFF USING A PLASMA RIFLE ON THEM!
TEE HEE
HUNH.
JUST TO SET THE RECORD STRAIGHT AS TO DUBIOUS QUALITY OF BOYFRIENDS, YOU SHOULD KNOW THAT YURI'S CERTAINLY HAD HER SHARE OF ROMANTIC DISASTERS.
SUCH AS...
♫ ANTONIO! ♫ REMEMBER HIM, YURI?
GLKK
NOW, THAT GUY WAS A REAL PRIZE-AND-A-HALF, HUH?
UH... YURI...?
HEY... WHERE ARE YOU GOING, YURI?
W-WAIT... COME BACK...!
I DIDN'T MEAN TO...
"ANTONIO?"
DOES THIS MEAN THAT YURI'S NOT A VIRGIN?
NAHH, NO WAY...
UHH... YURI JUST STEPPED OUT FOR A BREATH OF FRESH AIR, Y'SEE... I'LL JUST CARRY ON WITH THE LECTURE, OKAY?

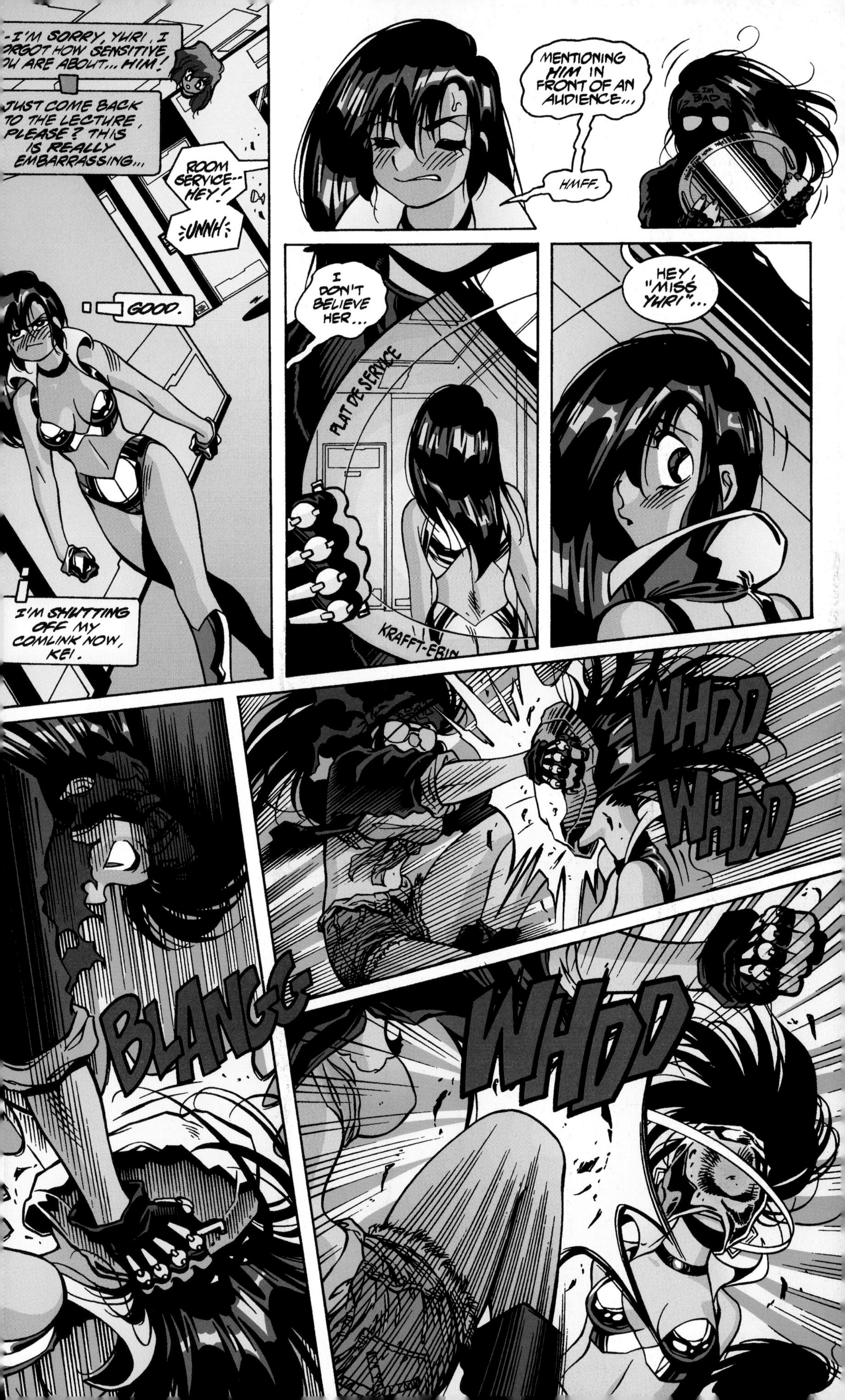

--I'M SORRY, YURI. I FORGOT HOW SENSITIVE YOU ARE ABOUT... HIM!
JUST COME BACK TO THE LECTURE, PLEASE? THIS IS REALLY EMBARRASSING...
ROOM SERVICE-- HEY!
UNNH
GOOD.
I'M SHUTTING OFF MY COMLINK NOW, KEI.
MENTIONING HIM IN FRONT OF AN AUDIENCE...
HMFF.
I'M BAD
I DON'T BELIEVE HER...
PLAT DE SERVICE
KRAFFT-EBIN
HEY, "MISS YURI"...
BLANGG
WHDD
WHDD
WHDD

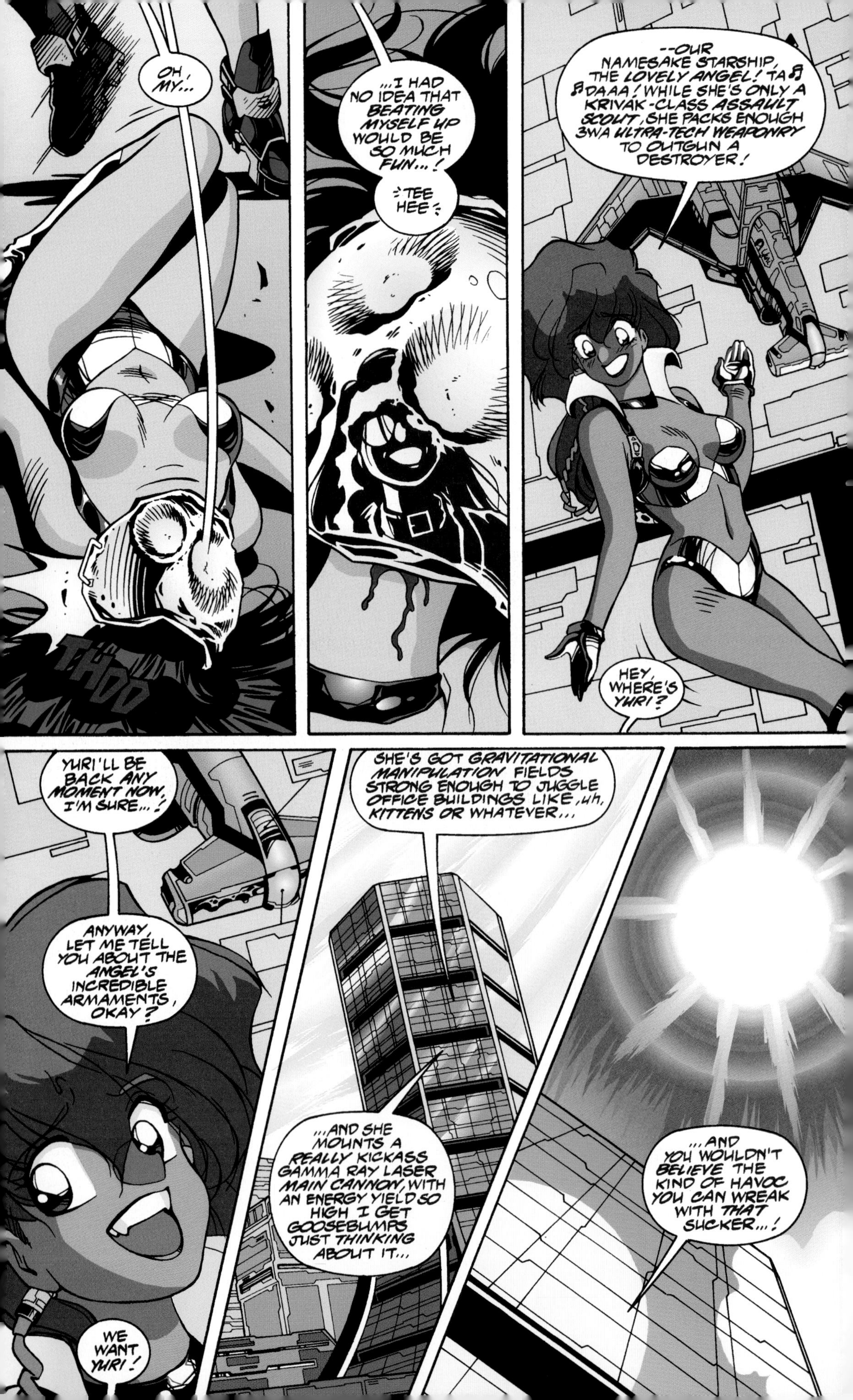
OH, MY...
THDD
...I HAD NO IDEA THAT *BEATING MYSELF UP* WOULD BE SO MUCH *FUN*...!
TEE HEE
--OUR NAMESAKE STARSHIP, THE *LOVELY ANGEL*! TA DAAA! WHILE SHE'S ONLY A KRIVAK-CLASS *ASSAULT SCOUT*, SHE PACKS ENOUGH 3WA *ULTRA-TECH WEAPONRY* TO OUTGUN A DESTROYER!
HEY, WHERE'S *YURI*?
YURI'LL BE BACK *ANY MOMENT NOW*, I'M SURE...!
ANYWAY, LET ME TELL YOU ABOUT THE *ANGEL'S* INCREDIBLE ARMAMENTS, OKAY?
WE WANT *YURI*!
SHE'S GOT *GRAVITATIONAL MANIPULATION* FIELDS STRONG ENOUGH TO JUGGLE OFFICE BUILDINGS LIKE, *uh*, *KITTENS OR WHATEVER*...
...AND SHE MOUNTS A *REALLY* KICKASS GAMMA RAY LASER *MAIN CANNON*, WITH AN ENERGY YIELD SO HIGH I GET GOOSEBUMPS JUST *THINKING* ABOUT IT...
...AND YOU WOULDN'T *BELIEVE* THE KIND OF HAVOC YOU CAN WREAK WITH *THAT* SUCKER...!

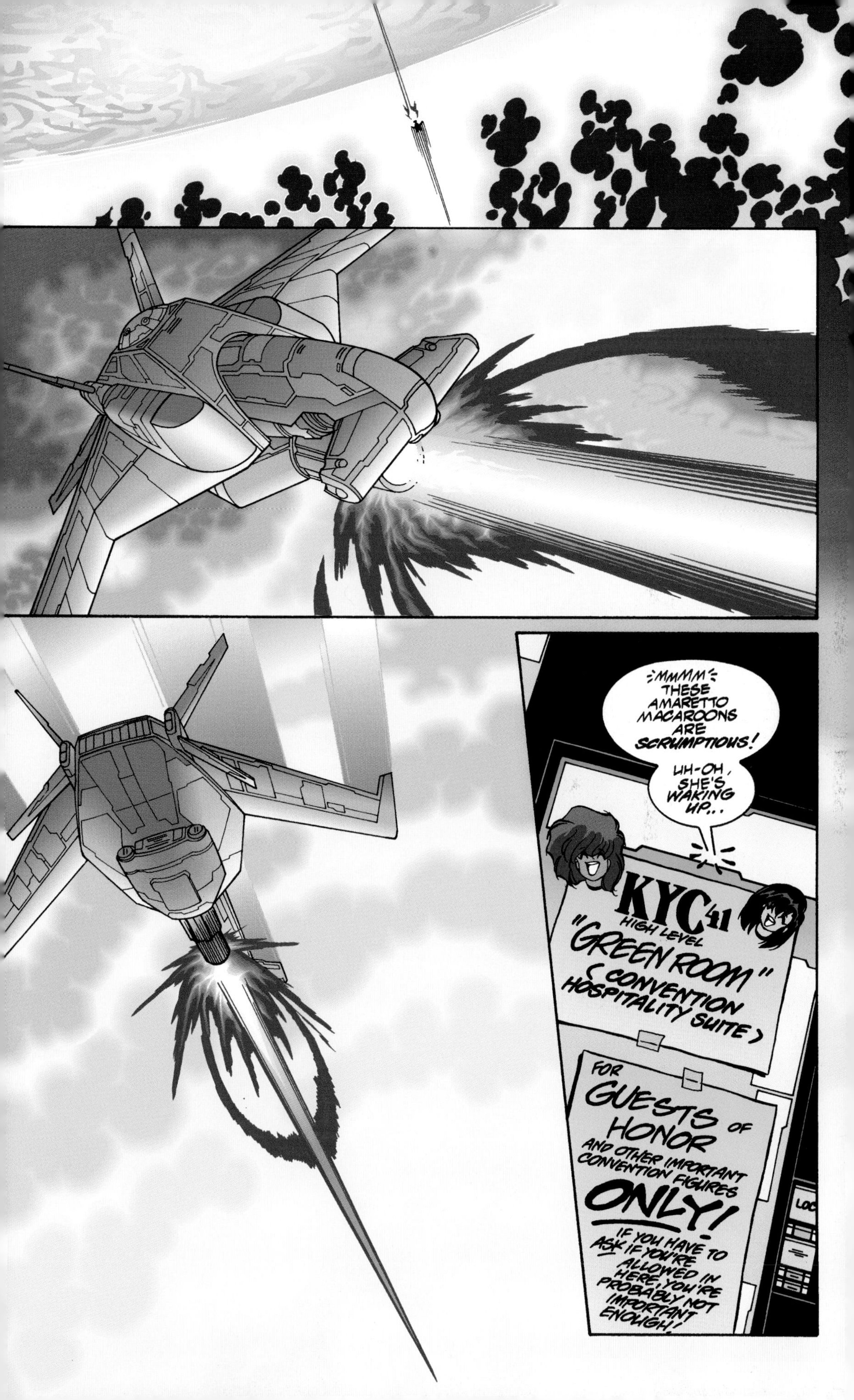

MMMM THESE AMARETTO MACAROONS ARE SCRUMPTIOUS!
UH-OH, SHE'S WAKING UP...
KYC 41 HIGH LEVEL "GREEN ROOM" (CONVENTION HOSPITALITY SUITE)
FOR GUESTS OF HONOR AND OTHER IMPORTANT CONVENTION FIGURES ONLY!
IF YOU HAVE TO ASK IF YOU'RE ALLOWED IN HERE, YOU'RE PROBABLY NOT IMPORTANT ENOUGH!

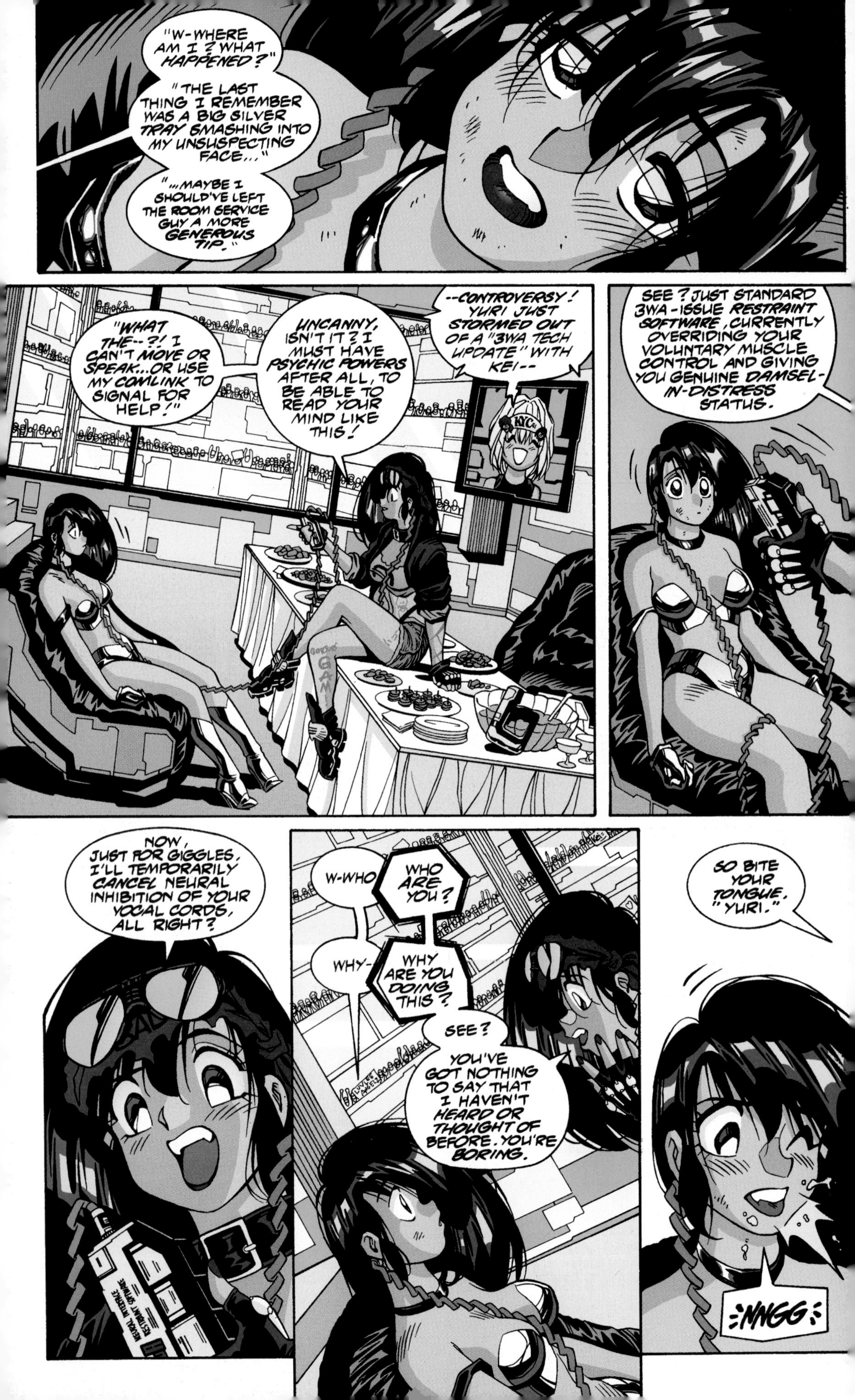
"W-WHERE AM I? WHAT HAPPENED?"
"THE LAST THING I REMEMBER WAS A BIG SILVER TRAY SMASHING INTO MY UNSUSPECTING FACE..."
"...MAYBE I SHOULD'VE LEFT THE ROOM SERVICE GUY A MORE GENEROUS TIP."
"WHAT THE--?! I CAN'T MOVE OR SPEAK...OR USE MY COMLINK TO SIGNAL FOR HELP!"
UNCANNY, ISN'T IT? I MUST HAVE PSYCHIC POWERS AFTER ALL, TO BE ABLE TO READ YOUR MIND LIKE THIS!
--CONTROVERSY! YURI JUST STORMED OUT OF A "3WA TECH UPDATE" WITH KEI--
KYC
SEE? JUST STANDARD 3WA-ISSUE RESTRAINT SOFTWARE, CURRENTLY OVERRIDING YOUR VOLUNTARY MUSCLE CONTROL AND GIVING YOU GENUINE DAMSEL-IN-DISTRESS STATUS.
NOW, JUST FOR GIGGLES, I'LL TEMPORARILY CANCEL NEURAL INHIBITION OF YOUR VOCAL CORDS, ALL RIGHT?
NEURAL INTERFACE RESTRAINT SOFTWARE
W-WHO
WHO ARE YOU?
WHY-
WHY ARE YOU DOING THIS?
SEE?
YOU'VE GOT NOTHING TO SAY THAT I HAVEN'T HEARD OR THOUGHT OF BEFORE. YOU'RE BORING.
SO BITE YOUR TONGUE, "YURI."
NNGG

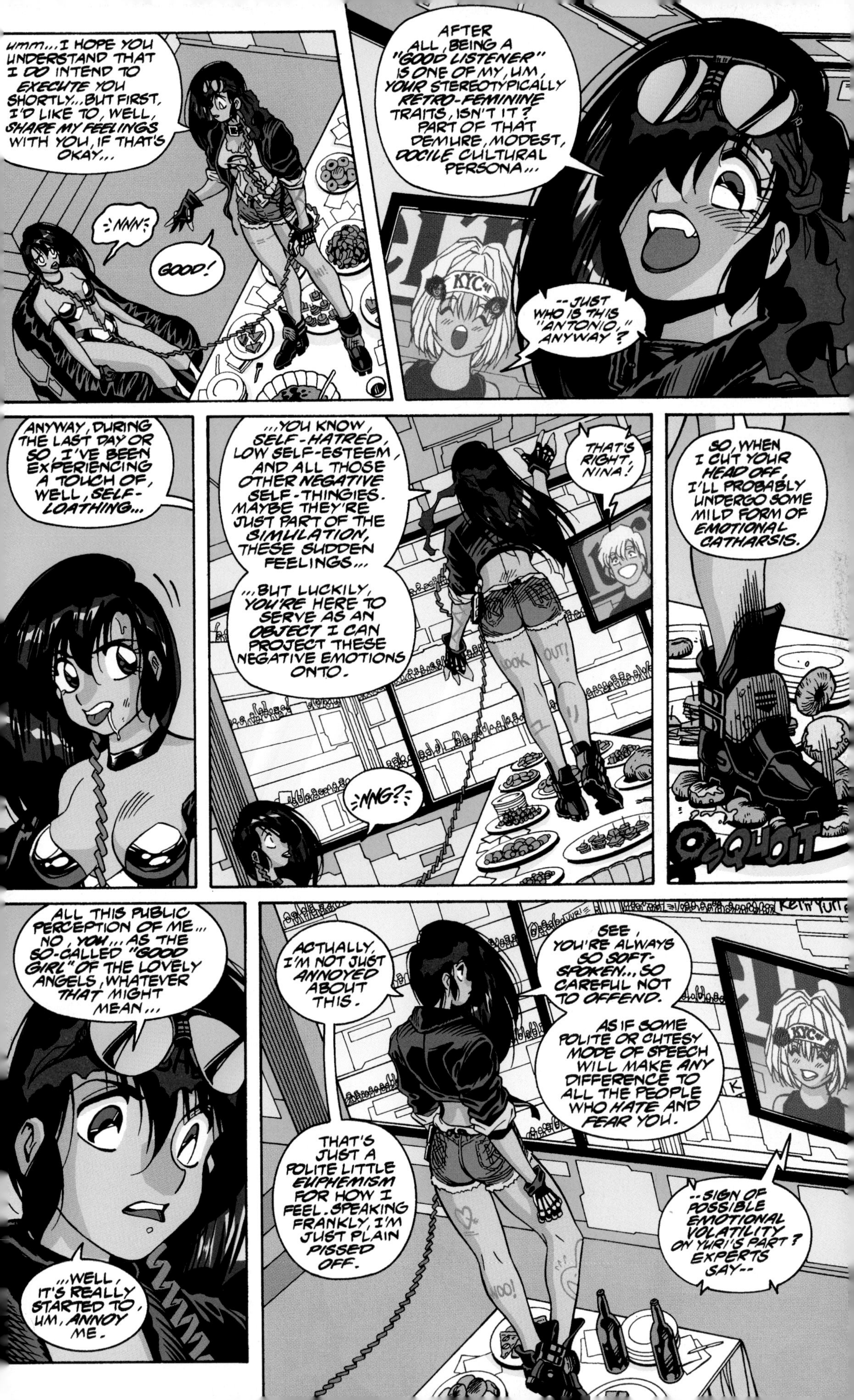
UMM... I HOPE YOU UNDERSTAND THAT I DO INTEND TO EXECUTE YOU SHORTLY... BUT FIRST, I'D LIKE TO, WELL, SHARE MY FEELINGS WITH YOU, IF THAT'S OKAY...
NNN
GOOD!
AFTER ALL, BEING A "GOOD LISTENER" IS ONE OF MY, UM, YOUR STEREOTYPICALLY RETRO-FEMININE TRAITS, ISN'T IT? PART OF THAT DEMURE, MODEST, DOCILE CULTURAL PERSONA...
KYC
--JUST WHO IS THIS "ANTONIO," ANYWAY?
ANYWAY, DURING THE LAST DAY OR SO, I'VE BEEN EXPERIENCING A TOUCH OF, WELL, SELF-LOATHING...
...YOU KNOW, SELF-HATRED, LOW SELF-ESTEEM, AND ALL THOSE OTHER NEGATIVE SELF-THINGIES. MAYBE THEY'RE JUST PART OF THE SIMULATION, THESE SUDDEN FEELINGS...
THAT'S RIGHT, NINA!
...BUT LUCKILY, YOU'RE HERE TO SERVE AS AN OBJECT I CAN PROJECT THESE NEGATIVE EMOTIONS ONTO.
LOOK OUT!
NNG?
SO, WHEN I CUT YOUR HEAD OFF, I'LL PROBABLY UNDERGO SOME MILD FORM OF EMOTIONAL CATHARSIS.
SQUOIT
ALL THIS PUBLIC PERCEPTION OF ME... NO, YOU... AS THE SO-CALLED "GOOD GIRL" OF THE LOVELY ANGELS, WHATEVER THAT MIGHT MEAN...
...WELL, IT'S REALLY STARTED TO, UM, ANNOY ME.
ACTUALLY, I'M NOT JUST ANNOYED ABOUT THIS.
SEE, YOU'RE ALWAYS SO SOFT-SPOKEN... SO CAREFUL NOT TO OFFEND.
AS IF SOME POLITE OR CUTESY MODE OF SPEECH WILL MAKE ANY DIFFERENCE TO ALL THE PEOPLE WHO HATE AND FEAR YOU.
THAT'S JUST A POLITE LITTLE EUPHEMISM FOR HOW I FEEL. SPEAKING FRANKLY, I'M JUST PLAIN PISSED OFF.
--SIGN OF POSSIBLE EMOTIONAL VOLATILITY ON YURI'S PART? EXPERTS SAY--

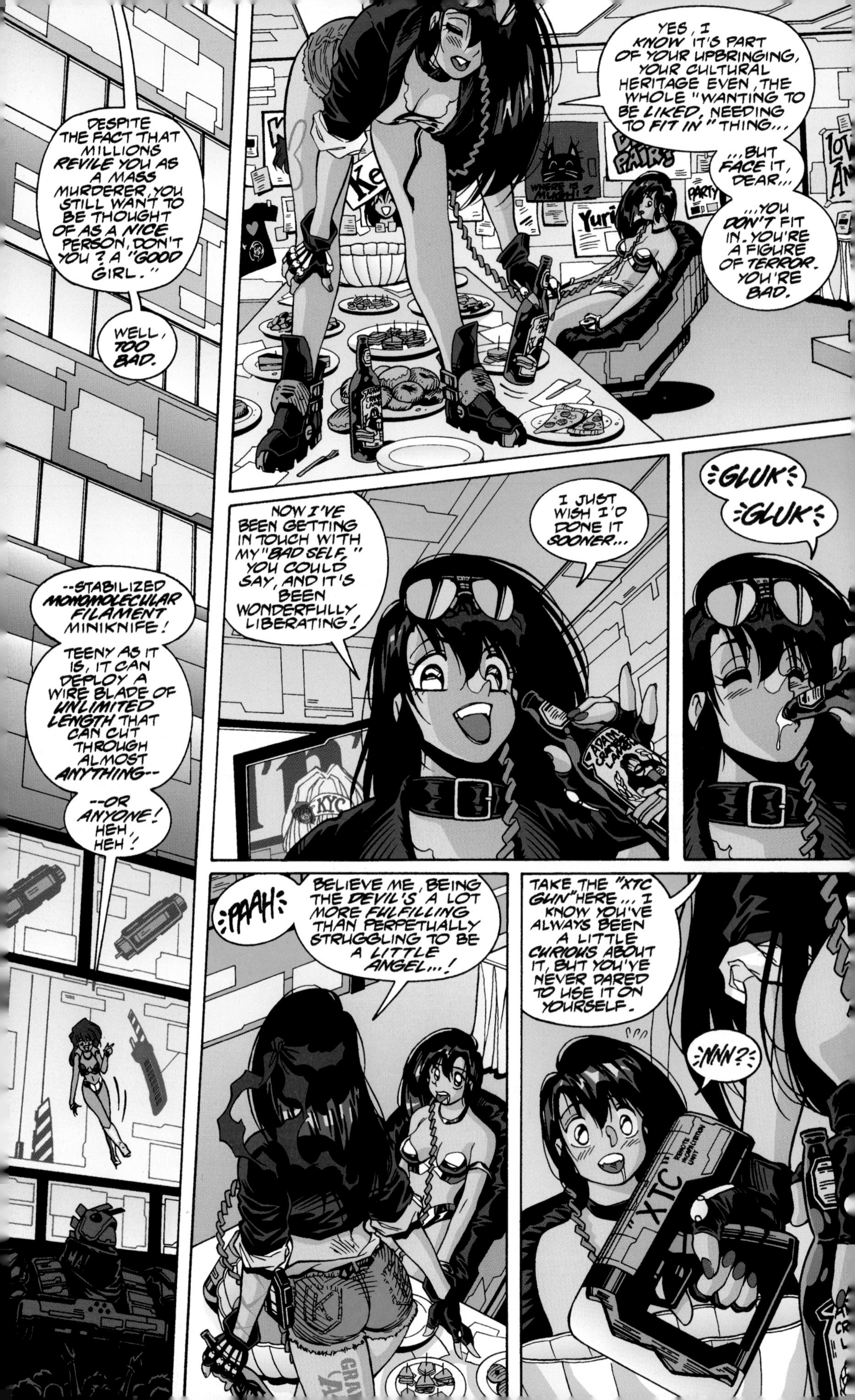
DESPITE THE FACT THAT MILLIONS REVILE YOU AS A MASS MURDERER, YOU STILL WANT TO BE THOUGHT OF AS A NICE PERSON, DON'T YOU? A "GOOD GIRL."
WELL, TOO BAD.
--STABILIZED MONOMOLECULAR FILAMENT MINIKNIFE!
TEENY AS IT IS, IT CAN DEPLOY A WIRE BLADE OF UNLIMITED LENGTH THAT CAN CUT THROUGH ALMOST ANYTHING--
--OR ANYONE! HEH, HEH!
YES, I KNOW IT'S PART OF YOUR UPBRINGING, YOUR CULTURAL HERITAGE EVEN, THE WHOLE "WANTING TO BE LIKED, NEEDING TO FIT IN" THING...
...BUT FACE IT, DEAR...
...YOU DON'T FIT IN. YOU'RE A FIGURE OF TERROR. YOU'RE BAD.
WHERE IS MUGHI?
PARTY
Yuri
NOW I'VE BEEN GETTING IN TOUCH WITH MY "BAD SELF," YOU COULD SAY, AND IT'S BEEN WONDERFULLY LIBERATING!
I JUST WISH I'D DONE IT SOONER...
KYC
GLUK
GLUK
PAAAH
BELIEVE ME, BEING THE DEVIL'S A LOT MORE FULFILLING THAN PERPETUALLY STRUGGLING TO BE A LITTLE ANGEL...!
TAKE THE "XTC GUN" HERE... I KNOW YOU'VE ALWAYS BEEN A LITTLE CURIOUS ABOUT IT, BUT YOU'VE NEVER DARED TO USE IT ON YOURSELF.
NNN?
"XTC"

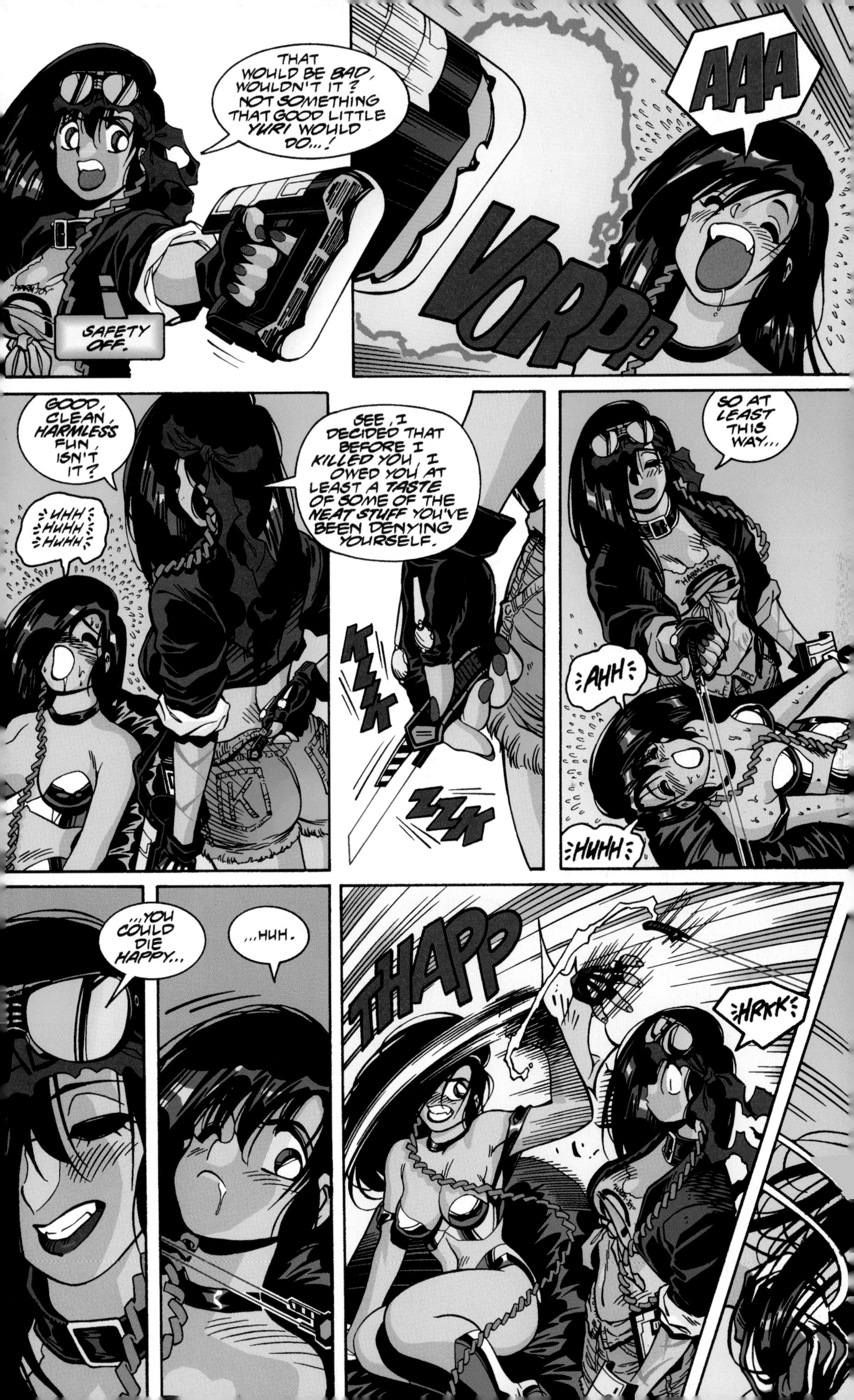
THAT WOULD BE BAD, WOULDN'T IT? NOT SOMETHING THAT GOOD LITTLE YURI WOULD DO...!
SAFETY OFF.
AAA
VORPP
GOOD, CLEAN, HARMLESS FUN, ISN'T IT?
UHH HUHH HUHH
SEE, I DECIDED THAT BEFORE I KILLED YOU, I OWED YOU AT LEAST A TASTE OF SOME OF THE NEAT STUFF YOU'VE BEEN DENYING YOURSELF.
KLIK
ZZK
SO AT LEAST THIS WAY...
AHH
HUHH
...YOU COULD DIE HAPPY...
...HUH.
THAPP
HRKK

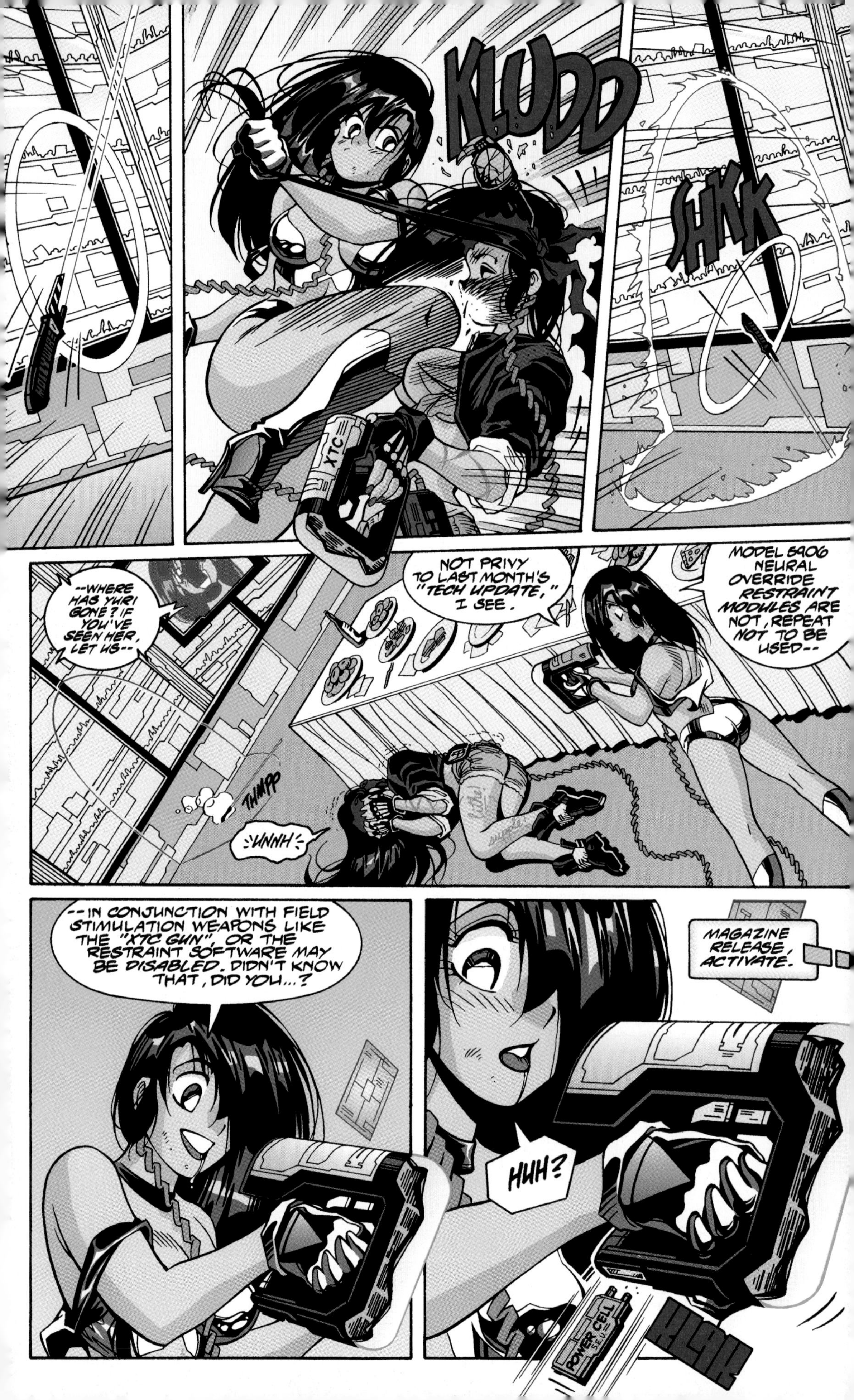
KLUDD
SHKK
XTC
--WHERE HAS YURI GONE? IF YOU'VE SEEN HER, LET US--
NOT PRIVY TO LAST MONTH'S "TECH UPDATE," I SEE.
MODEL 5906 NEURAL OVERRIDE RESTRAINT MODULES ARE NOT, REPEAT NOT TO BE USED--
THMPP
UNNH
lithe!
supple!
--IN CONJUNCTION WITH FIELD STIMULATION WEAPONS LIKE THE "XTC GUN", OR THE RESTRAINT SOFTWARE MAY BE DISABLED. DIDN'T KNOW THAT, DID YOU...?
MAGAZINE RELEASE, ACTIVATE.
HUH?
POWER CELL
KLIK

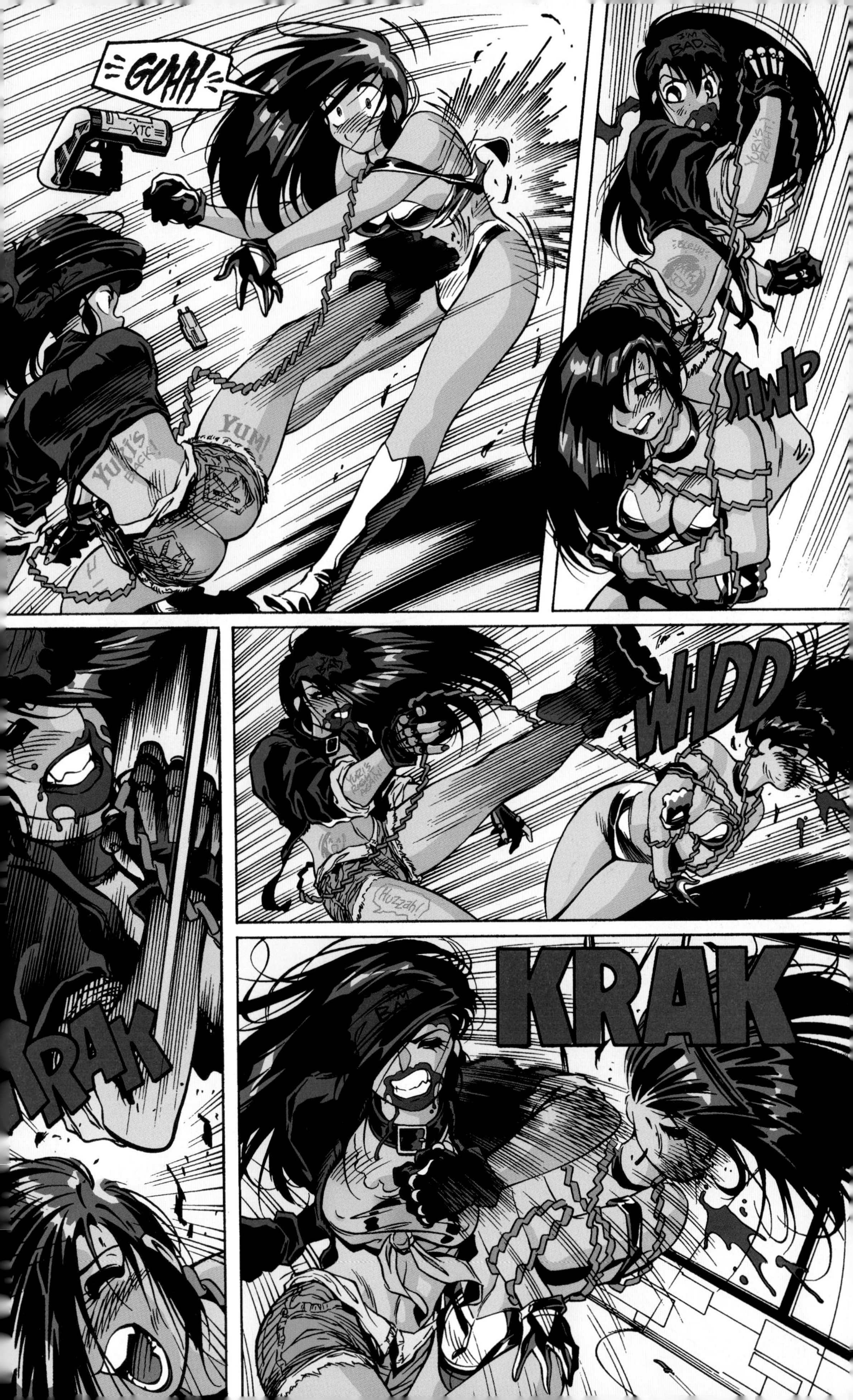
GUHH
XTC
YUM!
YURI'S BACK!
I'M BAD.
YURI'S RIGHT!
SHWIP
RAK
WHDD
YURI'S RIGHT AGAIN!
Huzzah!
KRAK

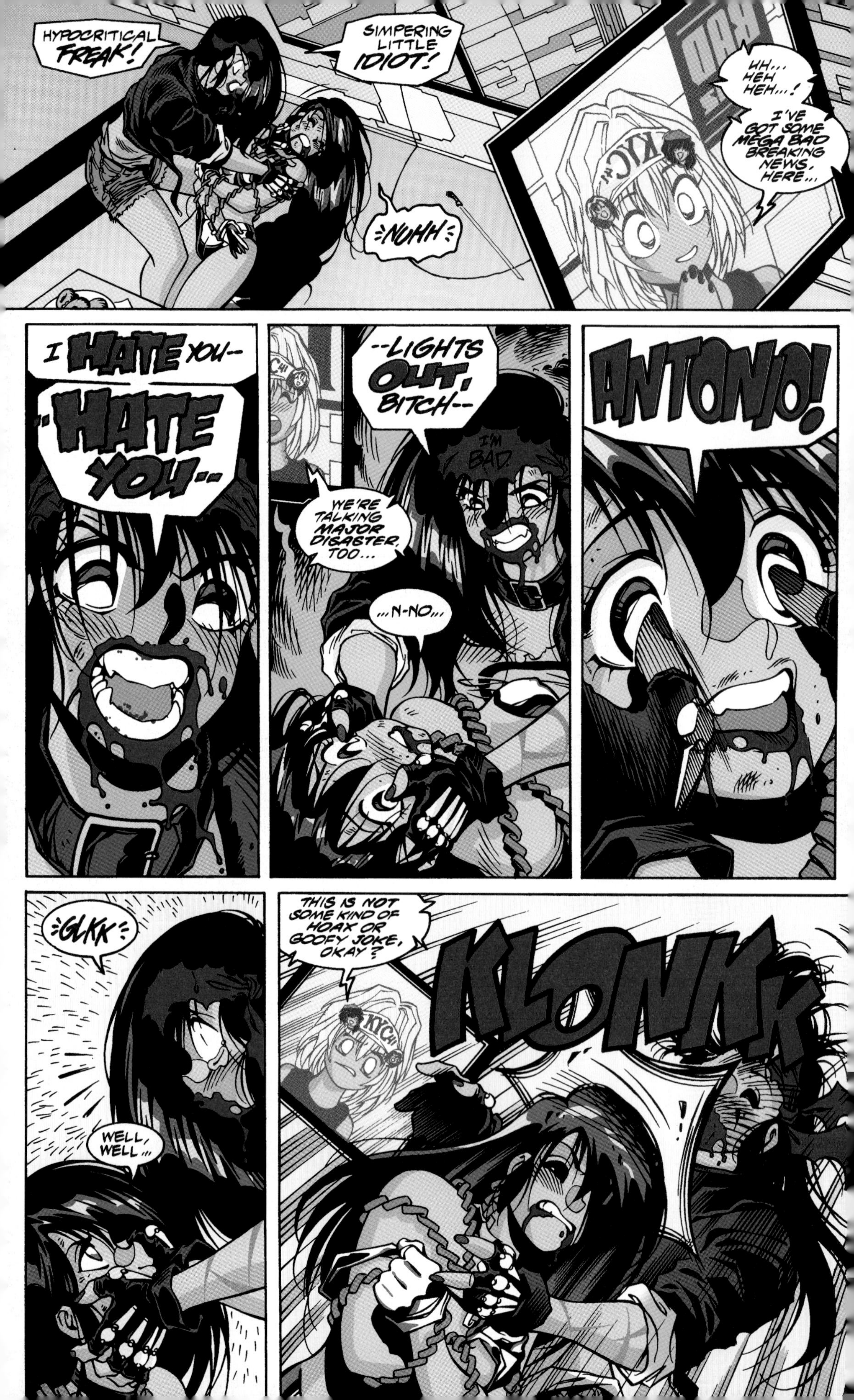
HYPOCRITICAL FREAK!
SIMPERING LITTLE IDIOT!
NUHH
UH... HEH HEH...!
I'VE GOT SOME MEGA BAD BREAKING NEWS, HERE...
I HATE YOU--
--HATE YOU--
--LIGHTS OUT, BITCH--
I'M BAD
WE'RE TALKING MAJOR DISASTER, TOO...
...N-NO...
ANTONIO!
GLKK
WELL, WELL...
THIS IS NOT SOME KIND OF HOAX OR GOOFY JOKE, OKAY?
KLONKK

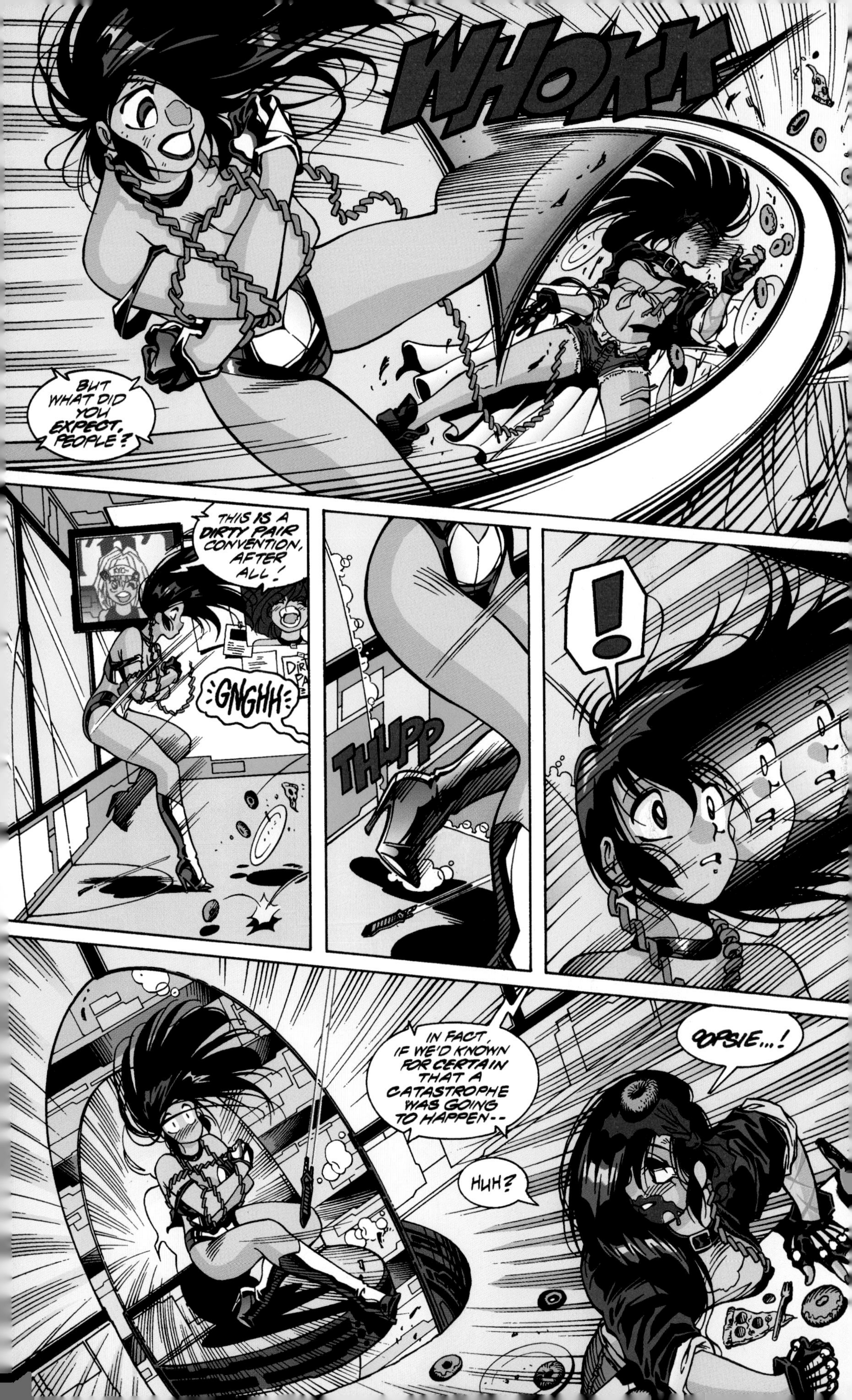
WHOKK
BUT WHAT DID YOU EXPECT, PEOPLE?
THIS IS A DIRTY PAIR CONVENTION, AFTER ALL!
GNGHH
THUPP
!
IN FACT, IF WE'D KNOWN FOR CERTAIN THAT A CATASTROPHE WAS GOING TO HAPPEN--
HUH?
OOPSIE...!

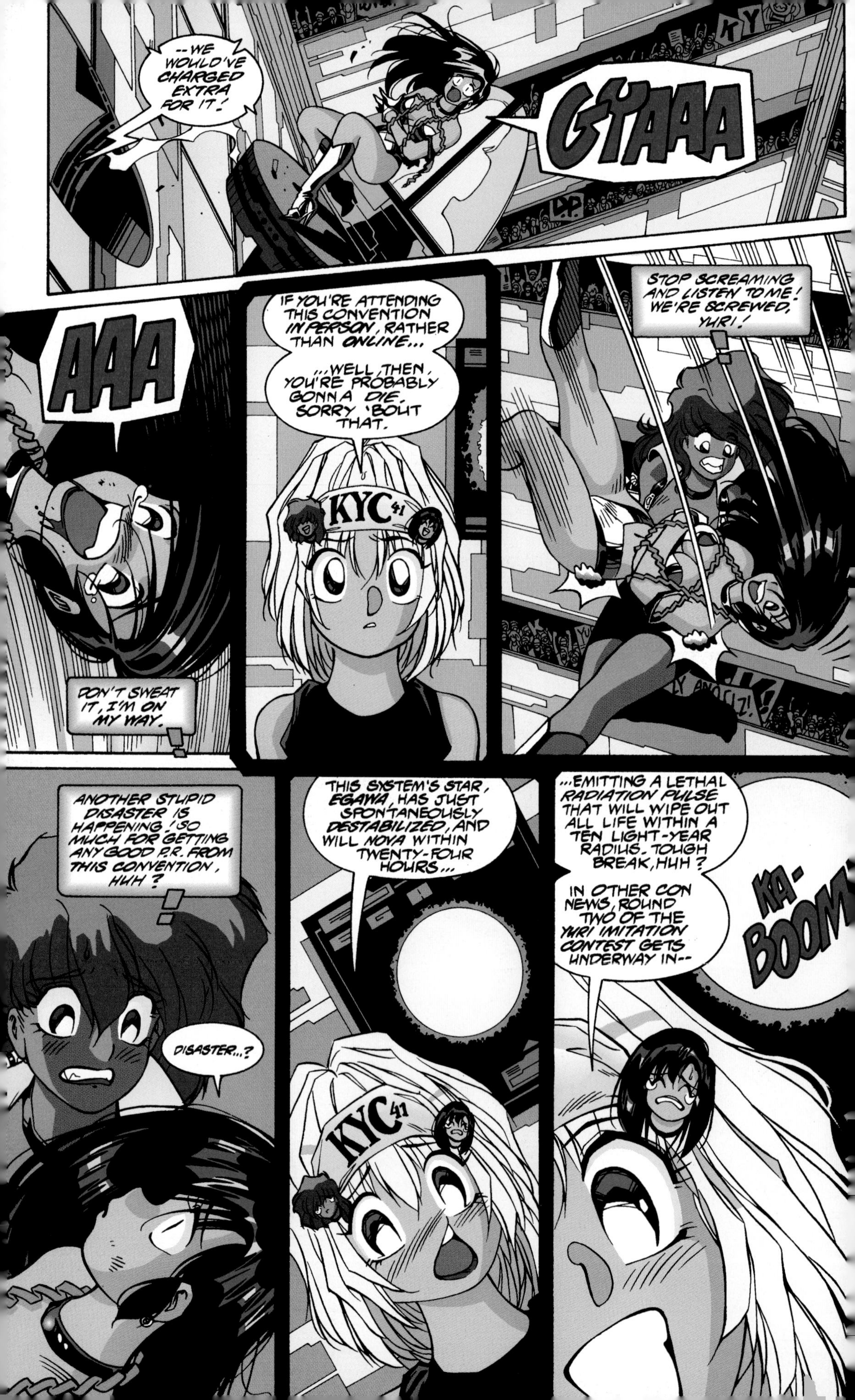
--WE WOULD'VE CHARGED EXTRA FOR IT!
GYAAA
AAA
DON'T SWEAT IT, I'M ON MY WAY.
IF YOU'RE ATTENDING THIS CONVENTION IN PERSON, RATHER THAN ONLINE...
...WELL, THEN, YOU'RE PROBABLY GONNA DIE. SORRY 'BOUT THAT.
KYC 41
STOP SCREAMING AND LISTEN TO ME! WE'RE SCREWED, YURI!
ANOTHER STUPID DISASTER IS HAPPENING! SO MUCH FOR GETTING ANY GOOD P.R. FROM THIS CONVENTION, HUH?
DISASTER...?
THIS SYSTEM'S STAR, EGAWA, HAS JUST SPONTANEOUSLY DESTABILIZED, AND WILL NOVA WITHIN TWENTY-FOUR HOURS...
KYC 41
...EMITTING A LETHAL RADIATION PULSE THAT WILL WIPE OUT ALL LIFE WITHIN A TEN LIGHT-YEAR RADIUS. TOUGH BREAK, HUH?
IN OTHER CON NEWS, ROUND TWO OF THE YURI IMITATION CONTEST GETS UNDERWAY IN--
KA-BOOM

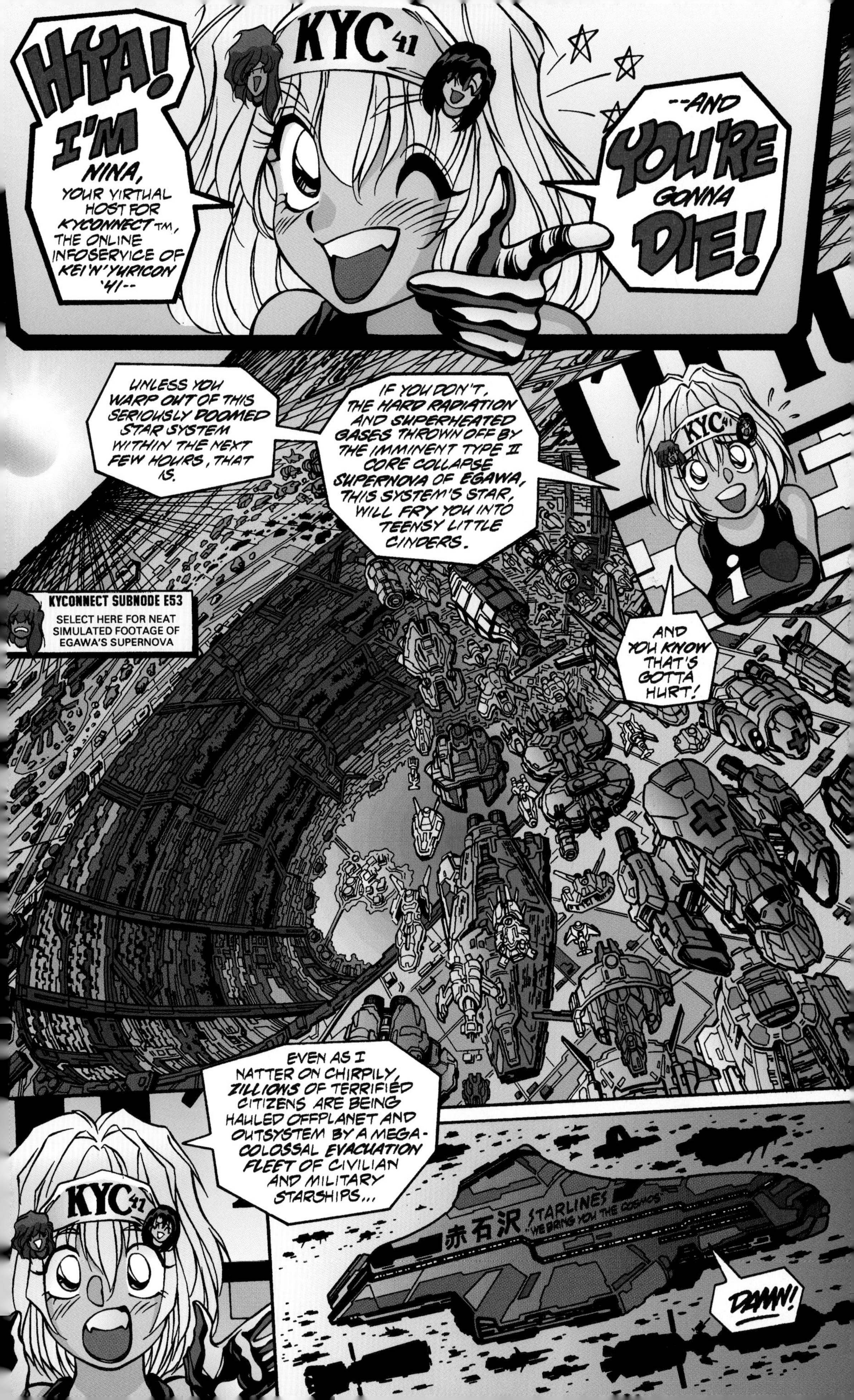
KYC 41
HIYA! I'M NINA, YOUR VIRTUAL HOST FOR KYCONNECT TM, THE ONLINE INFOSERVICE OF KEI'N'YURICON '41--
--AND YOU'RE GONNA DIE!
UNLESS YOU WARP OUT OF THIS SERIOUSLY DOOMED STAR SYSTEM WITHIN THE NEXT FEW HOURS, THAT IS.
IF YOU DON'T, THE HARD RADIATION AND SUPERHEATED GASES THROWN OFF BY THE IMMINENT TYPE II CORE COLLAPSE SUPERNOVA OF EGAWA, THIS SYSTEM'S STAR, WILL FRY YOU INTO TEENSY LITTLE CINDERS.
KYC 41
KYCONNECT SUBNODE E53
SELECT HERE FOR NEAT SIMULATED FOOTAGE OF EGAWA'S SUPERNOVA
AND YOU KNOW THAT'S GOTTA HURT!
EVEN AS I NATTER ON CHIRPILY, ZILLIONS OF TERRIFIED CITIZENS ARE BEING HAULED OFFPLANET AND OUTSYSTEM BY A MEGA-COLOSSAL EVACUATION FLEET OF CIVILIAN AND MILITARY STARSHIPS...
KYC 41
赤石沢 STARLINES "WE BRING YOU THE COSMOS"
DAMN!

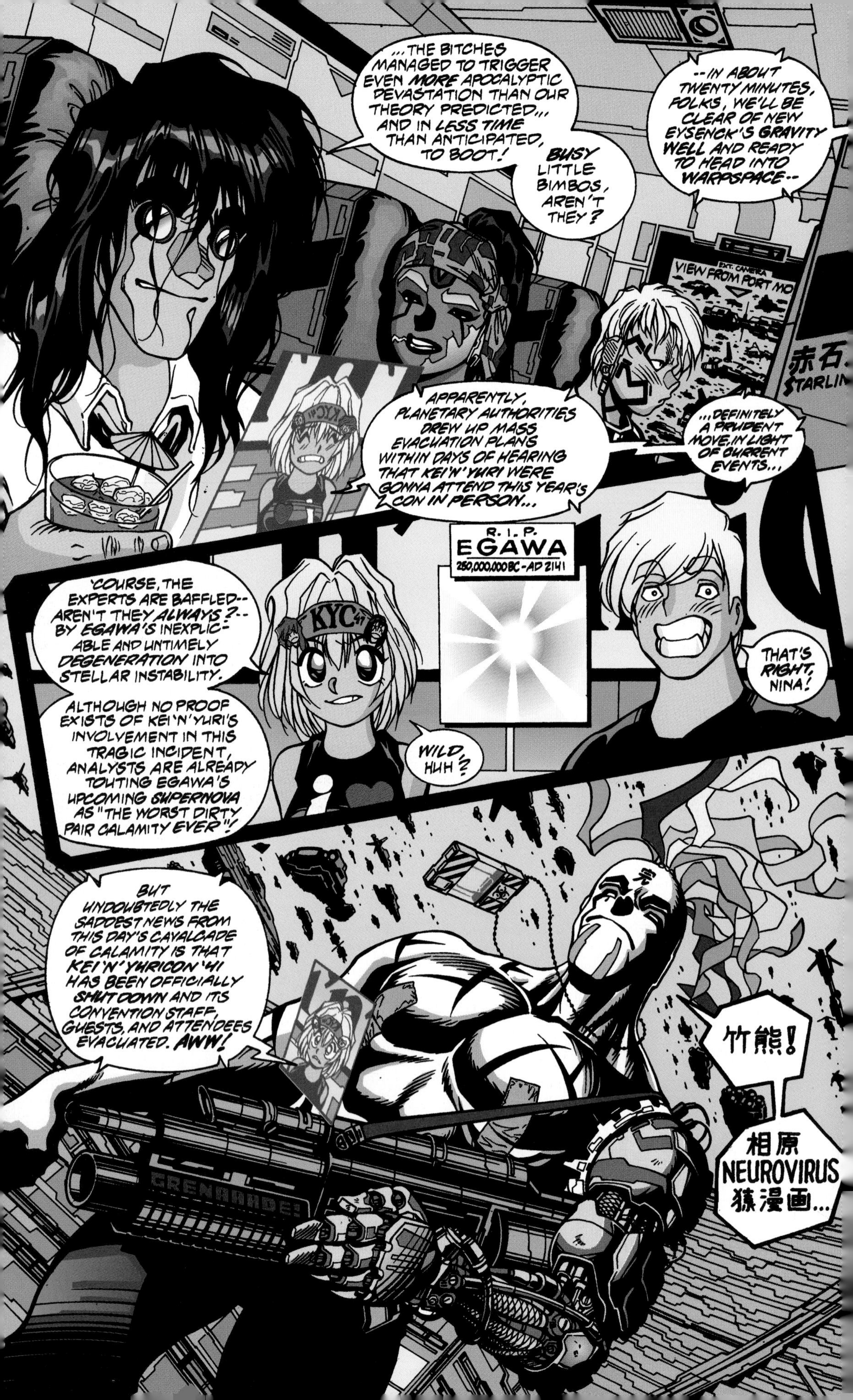
...THE BITCHES MANAGED TO TRIGGER EVEN MORE APOCALYPTIC DEVASTATION THAN OUR THEORY PREDICTED... AND IN LESS TIME THAN ANTICIPATED, TO BOOT!
BUSY LITTLE BIMBOS, AREN'T THEY?
--IN ABOUT TWENTY MINUTES, FOLKS, WE'LL BE CLEAR OF NEW EYSENCK'S GRAVITY WELL AND READY TO HEAD INTO WARPSPACE--
EXT. CAMERA
VIEW FROM PORT MO
赤石
STARLI
APPARENTLY, PLANETARY AUTHORITIES DREW UP MASS EVACUATION PLANS WITHIN DAYS OF HEARING THAT KEI'N'YURI WERE GONNA ATTEND THIS YEAR'S CON IN PERSON...
...DEFINITELY A PRUDENT MOVE, IN LIGHT OF CURRENT EVENTS...
R.I.P.
EGAWA
250,000,000 BC - AD 2141
'COURSE, THE EXPERTS ARE BAFFLED-- AREN'T THEY ALWAYS?-- BY EGAWA'S INEXPLICABLE AND UNTIMELY DEGENERATION INTO STELLAR INSTABILITY.
ALTHOUGH NO PROOF EXISTS OF KEI'N'YURI'S INVOLVEMENT IN THIS TRAGIC INCIDENT, ANALYSTS ARE ALREADY TOUTING EGAWA'S UPCOMING SUPERNOVA AS "THE WORST DIRTY PAIR CALAMITY EVER"!
KYC 41
WILD, HUH?
THAT'S RIGHT, NINA!
BUT UNDOUBTEDLY THE SADDEST NEWS FROM THIS DAY'S CAVALCADE OF CALAMITY IS THAT KEI'N'YURICON '41 HAS BEEN OFFICIALLY SHUT DOWN AND ITS CONVENTION STAFF, GUESTS, AND ATTENDEES EVACUATED. AWW!
竹熊!
相原
NEUROVIRUS
猿漫画...
GRENAAADE!

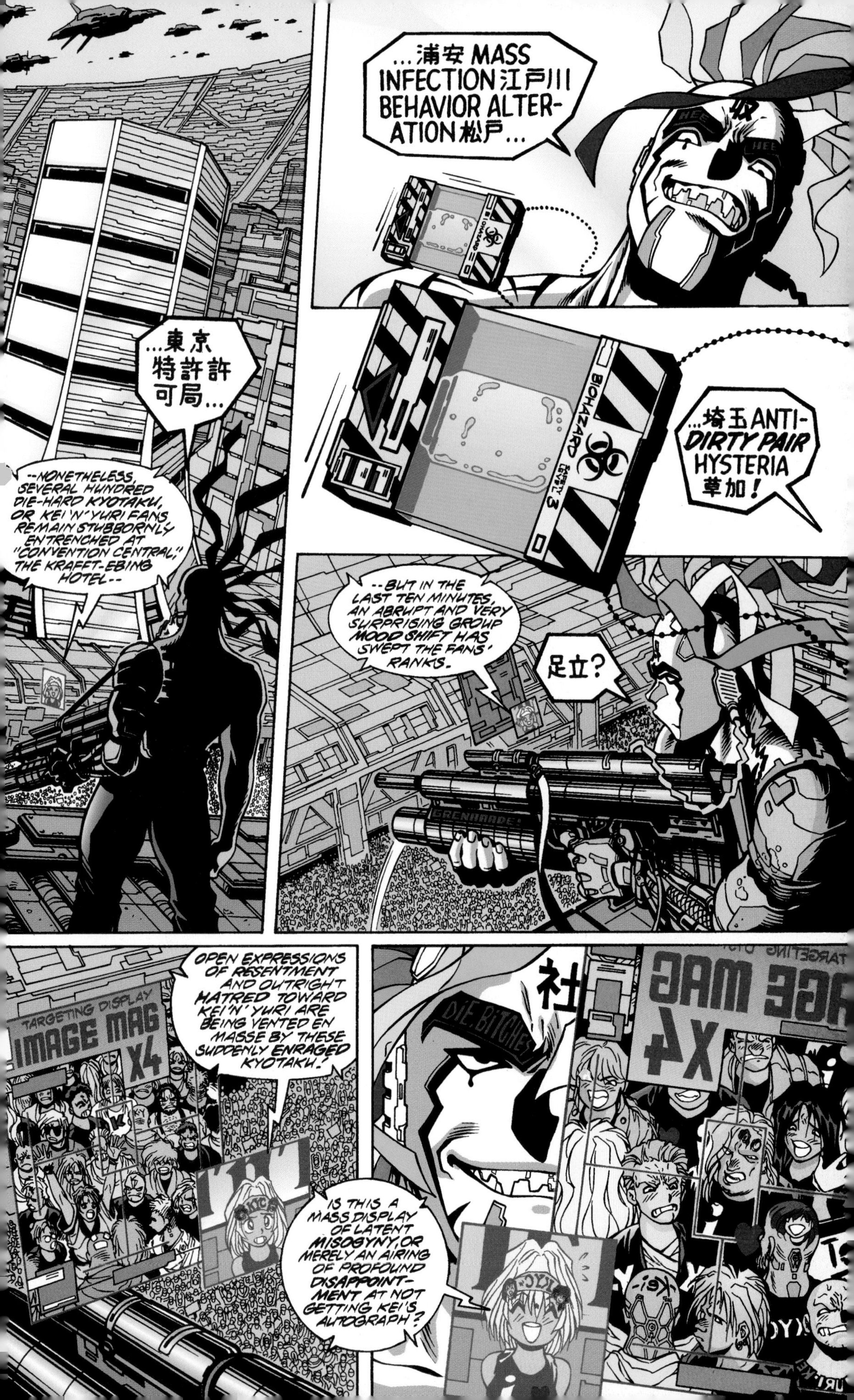
...東京特許許可局...
--NONETHELESS, SEVERAL HUNDRED DIE-HARD KYOTAKU, OR KEI 'N' YURI FANS REMAIN STUBBORNLY ENTRENCHED AT "CONVENTION CENTRAL," THE KRAFFT-EBING HOTEL--
...浦安 MASS INFECTION 江戸川 BEHAVIOR ALTER-ATION 松戸...
BIOHAZARD
SAFETY LEVEL 3
...埼玉 ANTI-DIRTY PAIR HYSTERIA 草加!
--BUT IN THE LAST TEN MINUTES, AN ABRUPT AND VERY SURPRISING GROUP MOOD SHIFT HAS SWEPT THE FANS' RANKS.
足立?
TARGETING DISPLAY
IMAGE MAG X4
OPEN EXPRESSIONS OF RESENTMENT AND OUTRIGHT HATRED TOWARD KEI 'N' YURI ARE BEING VENTED EN MASSE BY THESE SUDDENLY ENRAGED KYOTAKU!
DIE, BITCHES
IS THIS A MASS DISPLAY OF LATENT MISOGYNY, OR MERELY AN AIRING OF PROFOUND DISAPPOINT-MENT AT NOT GETTING KEI'S AUTOGRAPH?

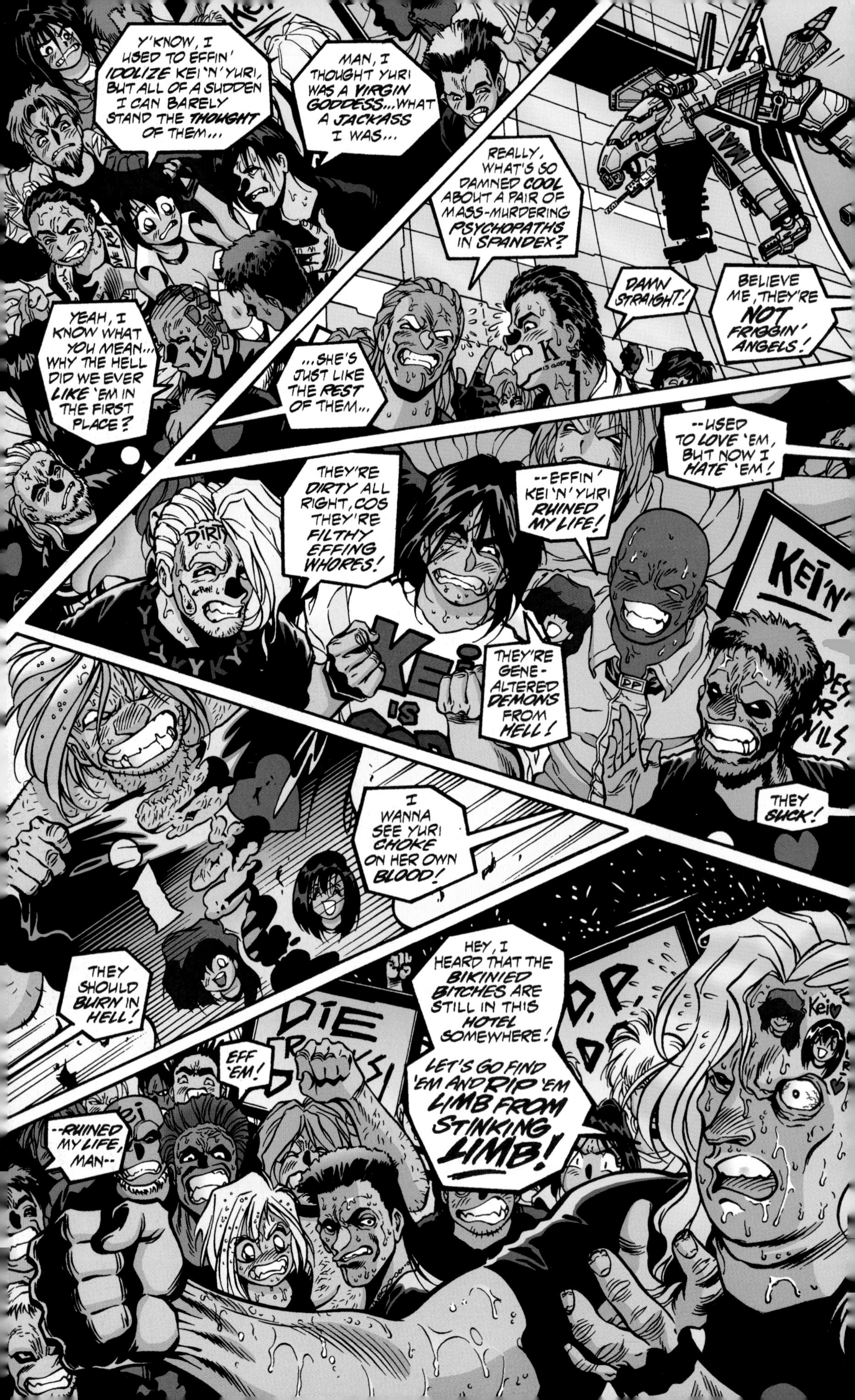
Y'KNOW, I USED TO EFFIN' IDOLIZE KEI 'N' YURI, BUT ALL OF A SUDDEN I CAN BARELY STAND THE THOUGHT OF THEM...
MAN, I THOUGHT YURI WAS A VIRGIN GODDESS... WHAT A JACKASS I WAS...
YEAH, I KNOW WHAT YOU MEAN... WHY THE HELL DID WE EVER LIKE 'EM IN THE FIRST PLACE?
REALLY, WHAT'S SO DAMNED COOL ABOUT A PAIR OF MASS-MURDERING PSYCHOPATHS IN SPANDEX?
...SHE'S JUST LIKE THE REST OF THEM...
DAMN STRAIGHT!
BELIEVE ME, THEY'RE NOT FRIGGIN' ANGELS!
MAI!
DIRTY
THEY'RE DIRTY ALL RIGHT, COS THEY'RE FILTHY EFFING WHORES!
--EFFIN' KEI 'N' YURI RUINED MY LIFE!
--USED TO LOVE 'EM, BUT NOW I HATE 'EM!
KEI 'N'
THEY'RE GENE-ALTERED DEMONS FROM HELL!
THEY SUCK!
I WANNA SEE YURI CHOKE ON HER OWN BLOOD!
THEY SHOULD BURN IN HELL!
DIE
HEY, I HEARD THAT THE BIKINIED BITCHES ARE STILL IN THIS HOTEL SOMEWHERE!
LET'S GO FIND 'EM AND RIP 'EM LIMB FROM STINKING LIMB!
EFF 'EM!
--RUINED MY LIFE, MAN--
Kei

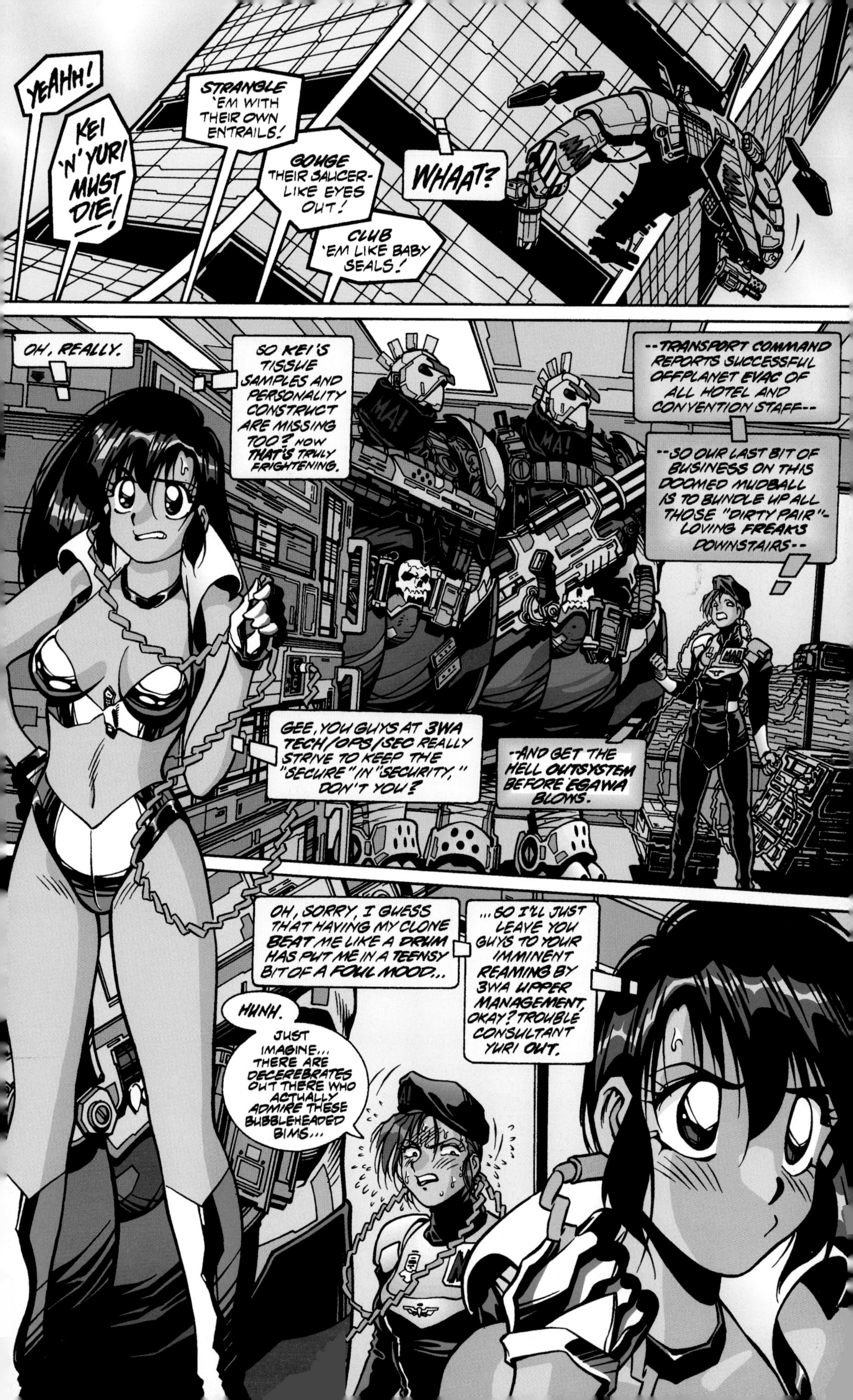
YEAHH!
KEI 'N' YURI MUST DIE!
STRANGLE 'EM WITH THEIR OWN ENTRAILS!
GOUGE THEIR SAUCER-LIKE EYES OUT!
CLUB 'EM LIKE BABY SEALS!
WHAAT?
OH, REALLY.
SO KEI'S TISSUE SAMPLES AND PERSONALITY CONSTRUCT ARE MISSING TOO? NOW THAT'S TRULY FRIGHTENING.
--TRANSPORT COMMAND REPORTS SUCCESSFUL OFFPLANET EVAC OF ALL HOTEL AND CONVENTION STAFF--
--SO OUR LAST BIT OF BUSINESS ON THIS DOOMED MUDBALL IS TO BUNDLE UP ALL THOSE "DIRTY PAIR"-LOVING FREAKS DOWNSTAIRS--
GEE, YOU GUYS AT 3WA TECH/OPS/SEC REALLY STRIVE TO KEEP THE "SECURE" IN "SECURITY," DON'T YOU?
--AND GET THE HELL OUTSYSTEM BEFORE EGAWA BLOWS.
OH, SORRY, I GUESS THAT HAVING MY CLONE BEAT ME LIKE A DRUM HAS PUT ME IN A TEENSY BIT OF A FOUL MOOD...
...SO I'LL JUST LEAVE YOU GUYS TO YOUR IMMINENT REAMING BY 3WA UPPER MANAGEMENT, OKAY? TROUBLE CONSULTANT YURI OUT.
HUNH.
JUST IMAGINE... THERE ARE DECEREBRATES OUT THERE WHO ACTUALLY ADMIRE THESE BUBBLEHEADED BIMS...

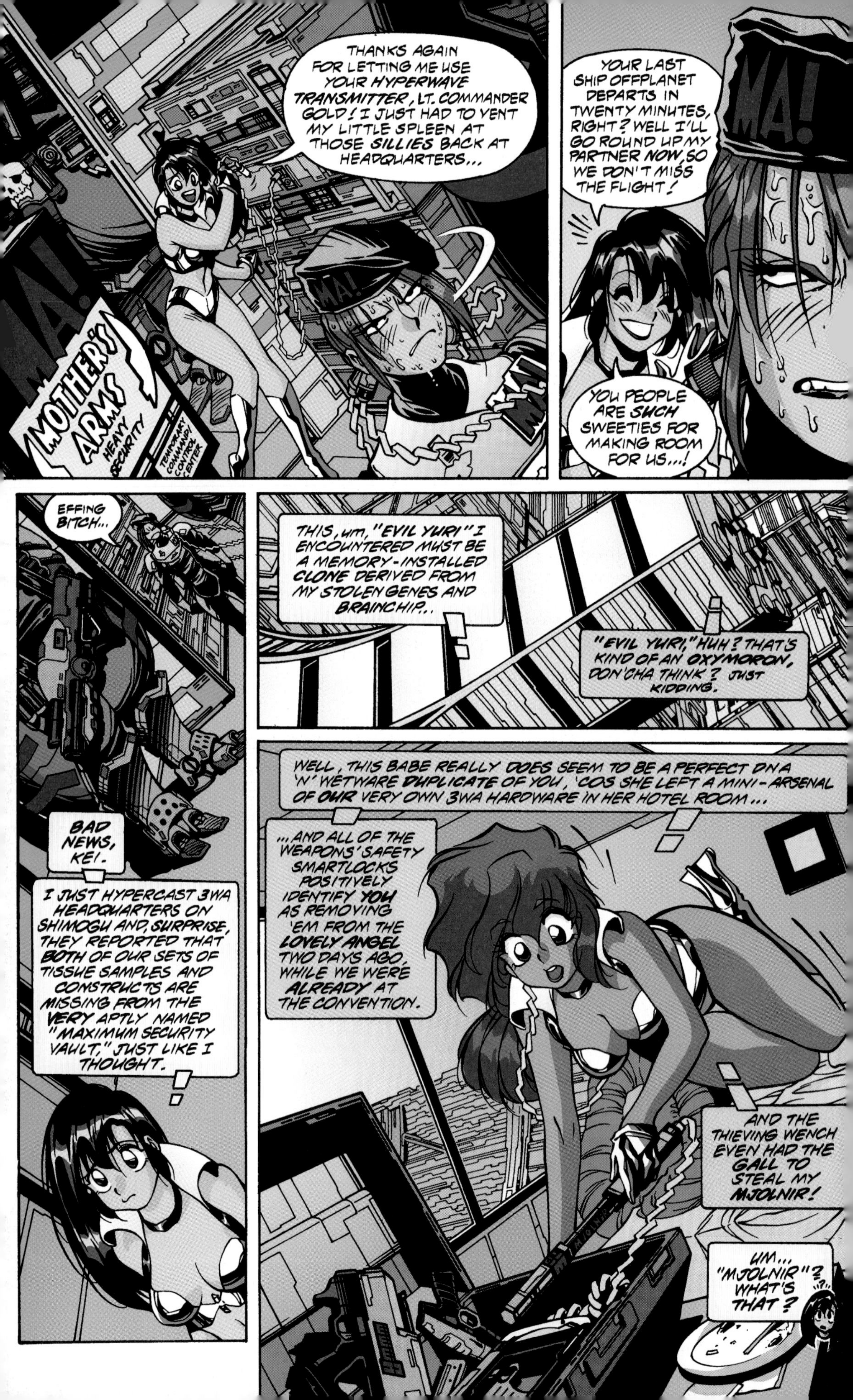
THANKS AGAIN FOR LETTING ME USE YOUR HYPERWAVE TRANSMITTER, LT. COMMANDER GOLD! I JUST HAD TO VENT MY LITTLE SPLEEN AT THOSE SILLIES BACK AT HEADQUARTERS...
MA!
MOTHER'S ARMS HEAVY SECURITY
TEMPORARY COMMAND/CONTROL CENTER
YOUR LAST SHIP OFFPLANET DEPARTS IN TWENTY MINUTES, RIGHT? WELL I'LL GO ROUND UP MY PARTNER NOW, SO WE DON'T MISS THE FLIGHT!
MA!
YOU PEOPLE ARE SUCH SWEETIES FOR MAKING ROOM FOR US...!
EFFING BITCH...
BAD NEWS, KEI.
I JUST HYPERCAST 3WA HEADQUARTERS ON SHIMOGU AND, SURPRISE, THEY REPORTED THAT BOTH OF OUR SETS OF TISSUE SAMPLES AND CONSTRUCTS ARE MISSING FROM THE VERY APTLY NAMED "MAXIMUM SECURITY VAULT," JUST LIKE I THOUGHT.
THIS, UM, "EVIL YURI" I ENCOUNTERED MUST BE A MEMORY-INSTALLED CLONE DERIVED FROM MY STOLEN GENES AND BRAINCHIP...
"EVIL YURI," HUH? THAT'S KIND OF AN OXYMORON, DON'CHA THINK? JUST KIDDING.
WELL, THIS BABE REALLY DOES SEEM TO BE A PERFECT DNA 'N' WETWARE DUPLICATE OF YOU, 'COS SHE LEFT A MINI-ARSENAL OF OUR VERY OWN 3WA HARDWARE IN HER HOTEL ROOM...
...AND ALL OF THE WEAPONS' SAFETY SMARTLOCKS POSITIVELY IDENTIFY YOU AS REMOVING 'EM FROM THE LOVELY ANGEL TWO DAYS AGO, WHILE WE WERE ALREADY AT THE CONVENTION.
AND THE THIEVING WENCH EVEN HAD THE GALL TO STEAL MY MJOLNIR!
UM... "MJOLNIR"? WHAT'S THAT?

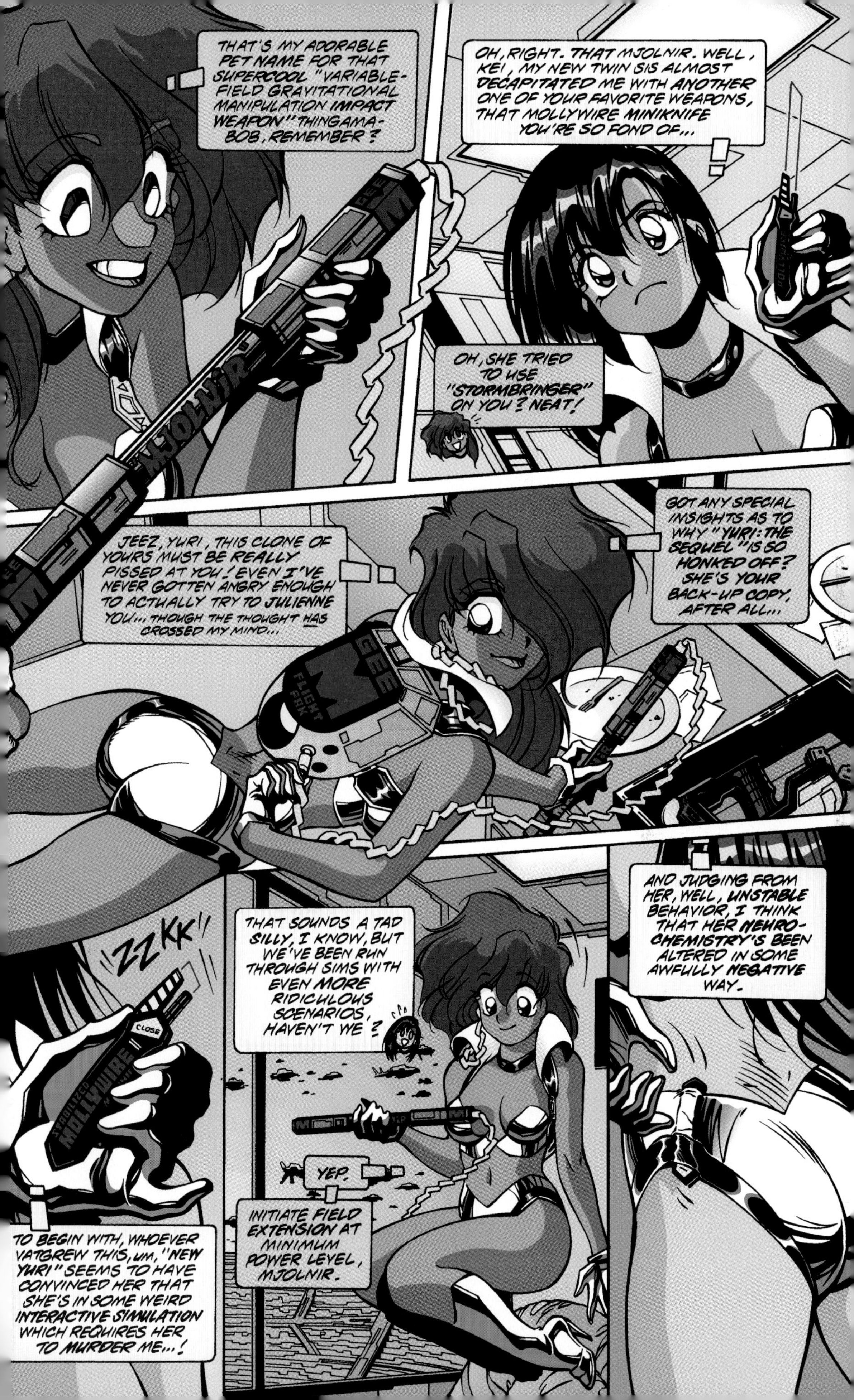
THAT'S MY ADORABLE PET NAME FOR THAT SUPERCOOL "VARIABLE-FIELD GRAVITATIONAL MANIPULATION IMPACT WEAPON" THINGAMA-BOB, REMEMBER?
GEE
MJOLNIR
OH, RIGHT. THAT MJOLNIR. WELL, KEI, MY NEW TWIN SIS ALMOST DECAPITATED ME WITH ANOTHER ONE OF YOUR FAVORITE WEAPONS, THAT MOLLYWIRE MINIKNIFE YOU'RE SO FOND OF...
OH, SHE TRIED TO USE "STORMBRINGER" ON YOU? NEAT!
JEEZ, YURI, THIS CLONE OF YOURS MUST BE REALLY PISSED AT YOU! EVEN I'VE NEVER GOTTEN ANGRY ENOUGH TO ACTUALLY TRY TO JULIENNE YOU... THOUGH THE THOUGHT HAS CROSSED MY MIND...
GEE
FLIGHT PAK
GOT ANY SPECIAL INSIGHTS AS TO WHY "YURI: THE SEQUEL" IS SO HONKED OFF? SHE'S YOUR BACK-UP COPY, AFTER ALL...
ZZKK
CLOSE
MOLLYWIRE
TO BEGIN WITH, WHOEVER VATGREW THIS, UM, "NEW YURI" SEEMS TO HAVE CONVINCED HER THAT SHE'S IN SOME WEIRD INTERACTIVE SIMULATION WHICH REQUIRES HER TO MURDER ME...!
THAT SOUNDS A TAD SILLY, I KNOW, BUT WE'VE BEEN RUN THROUGH SIMS WITH EVEN MORE RIDICULOUS SCENARIOS, HAVEN'T WE?
YEP.
INITIATE FIELD EXTENSION AT MINIMUM POWER LEVEL, MJOLNIR.
AND JUDGING FROM HER, WELL, UNSTABLE BEHAVIOR, I THINK THAT HER NEURO-CHEMISTRY'S BEEN ALTERED IN SOME AWFULLY NEGATIVE WAY.

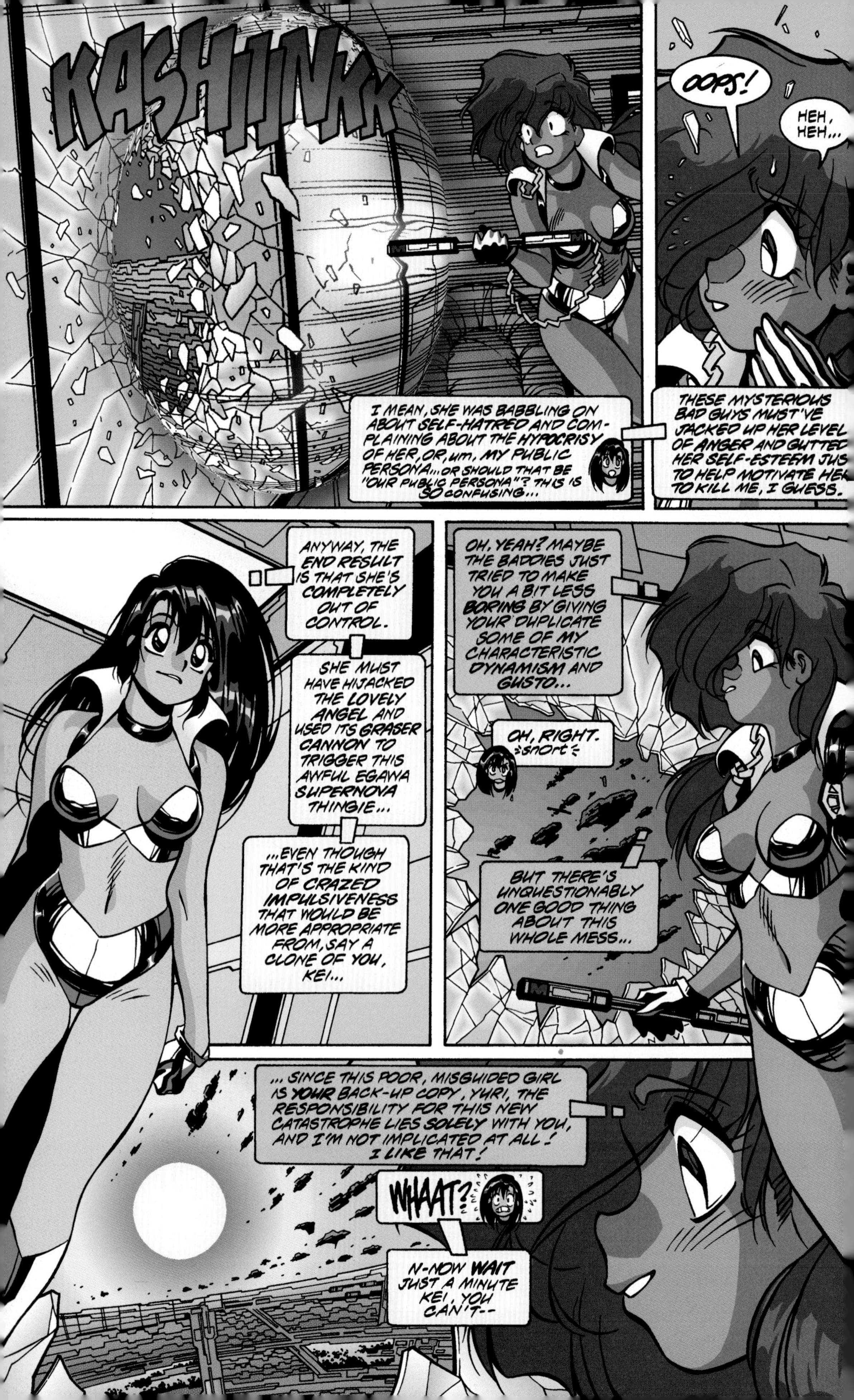
KASHIINKK
I MEAN, SHE WAS BABBLING ON ABOUT SELF-HATRED AND COMPLAINING ABOUT THE HYPOCRISY OF HER, OR, um, MY PUBLIC PERSONA... OR SHOULD THAT BE "OUR PUBLIC PERSONA"? THIS IS SO CONFUSING...
OOPS!
HEH, HEH...
THESE MYSTERIOUS BAD GUYS MUST'VE JACKED UP HER LEVEL OF ANGER AND GUTTED HER SELF-ESTEEM JUS TO HELP MOTIVATE HE TO KILL ME, I GUESS.
ANYWAY, THE END RESULT IS THAT SHE'S COMPLETELY OUT OF CONTROL.
SHE MUST HAVE HIJACKED THE LOVELY ANGEL AND USED ITS GRASER CANNON TO TRIGGER THIS AWFUL EGAWA SUPERNOVA THINGIE...
...EVEN THOUGH THAT'S THE KIND OF CRAZED IMPULSIVENESS THAT WOULD BE MORE APPROPRIATE FROM, SAY A CLONE OF YOU, KEI...
OH, YEAH? MAYBE THE BADDIES JUST TRIED TO MAKE YOU A BIT LESS BORING BY GIVING YOUR DUPLICATE SOME OF MY CHARACTERISTIC DYNAMISM AND GUSTO...
OH, RIGHT. snort
BUT THERE'S UNQUESTIONABLY ONE GOOD THING ABOUT THIS WHOLE MESS...
... SINCE THIS POOR, MISGUIDED GIRL IS YOUR BACK-UP COPY, YURI, THE RESPONSIBILITY FOR THIS NEW CATASTROPHE LIES SOLELY WITH YOU, AND I'M NOT IMPLICATED AT ALL! I LIKE THAT!
WHAAT?
N-NOW WAIT JUST A MINUTE KEI, YOU CAN'T--

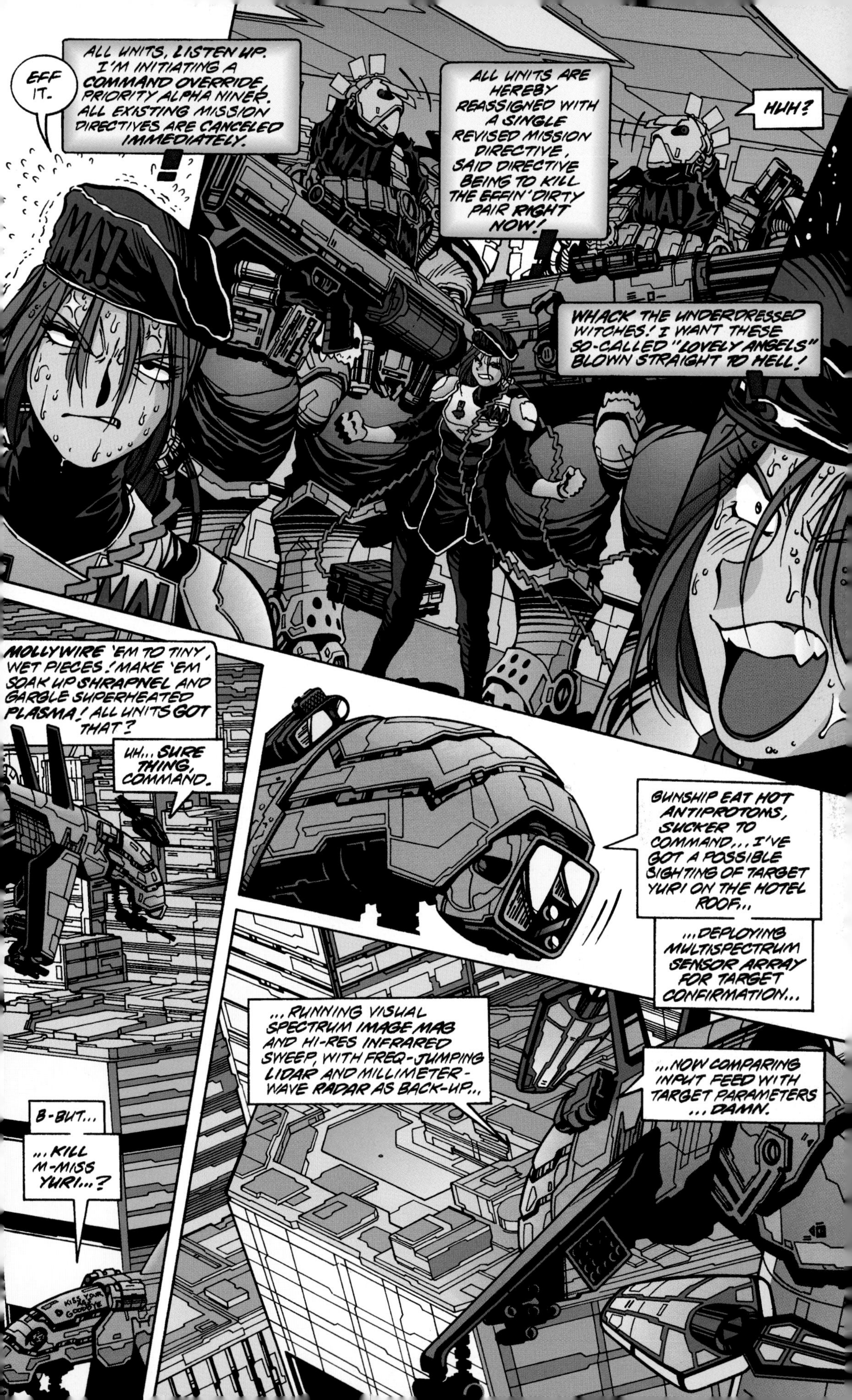
EFF IT.
ALL UNITS, LISTEN UP. I'M INITIATING A COMMAND OVERRIDE, PRIORITY ALPHA NINER. ALL EXISTING MISSION DIRECTIVES ARE CANCELED IMMEDIATELY.
!
ALL UNITS ARE HEREBY REASSIGNED WITH A SINGLE REVISED MISSION DIRECTIVE, SAID DIRECTIVE BEING TO KILL THE EFFIN' DIRTY PAIR RIGHT NOW!
HUH?
WHACK THE UNDERDRESSED WITCHES! I WANT THESE SO-CALLED "LOVELY ANGELS" BLOWN STRAIGHT TO HELL!
MOLLYWIRE 'EM TO TINY, WET PIECES! MAKE 'EM SOAK UP SHRAPNEL AND GARGLE SUPERHEATED PLASMA! ALL UNITS GOT THAT?
UH... SURE THING, COMMAND.
B-BUT...
...KILL M-MISS YURI...?
GUNSHIP EAT HOT ANTIPROTONS, SUCKER TO COMMAND... I'VE GOT A POSSIBLE SIGHTING OF TARGET YURI ON THE HOTEL ROOF...
...DEPLOYING MULTISPECTRUM SENSOR ARRAY FOR TARGET CONFIRMATION...
...RUNNING VISUAL SPECTRUM IMAGE MAG AND HI-RES INFRARED SWEEP, WITH FREQ-JUMPING LIDAR AND MILLIMETER-WAVE RADAR AS BACK-UP...
...NOW COMPARING INPUT FEED WITH TARGET PARAMETERS ... DAMN.

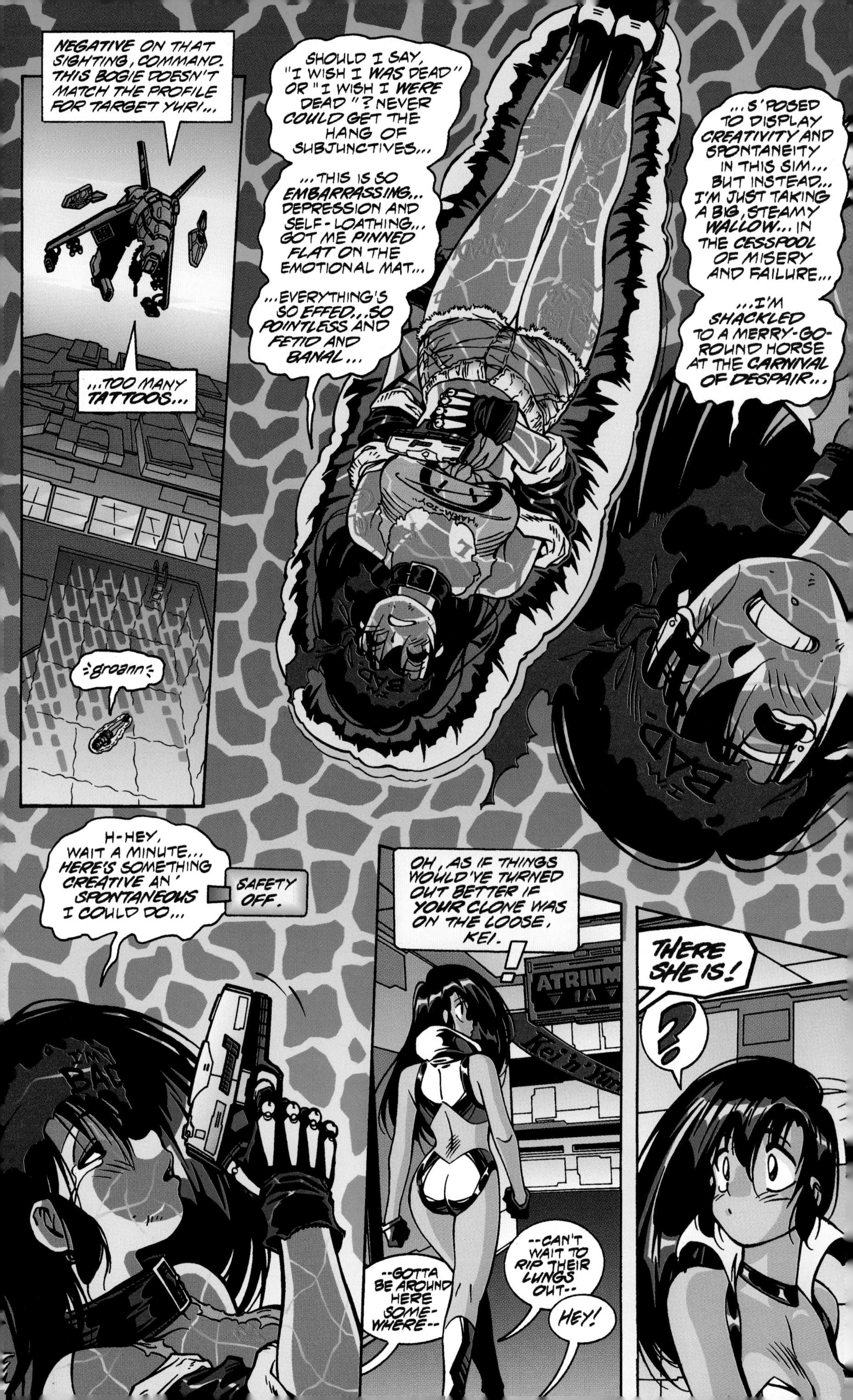
NEGATIVE ON THAT SIGHTING, COMMAND. THIS BOGIE DOESN'T MATCH THE PROFILE FOR TARGET YURI...
...TOO MANY TATTOOS...
groann
SHOULD I SAY, "I WISH I WAS DEAD" OR "I WISH I WERE DEAD"? NEVER COULD GET THE HANG OF SUBJUNCTIVES...
...THIS IS SO EMBARRASSING... DEPRESSION AND SELF-LOATHING... GOT ME PINNED FLAT ON THE EMOTIONAL MAT...
...EVERYTHING'S SO EFFED... SO POINTLESS AND FETID AND BANAL...
...S'POSED TO DISPLAY CREATIVITY AND SPONTANEITY IN THIS SIM... BUT INSTEAD... I'M JUST TAKING A BIG, STEAMY WALLOW... IN THE CESSPOOL OF MISERY AND FAILURE...
...I'M SHACKLED TO A MERRY-GO-ROUND HORSE AT THE CARNIVAL OF DESPAIR...
H-HEY, WAIT A MINUTE... HERE'S SOMETHING CREATIVE AN' SPONTANEOUS I COULD DO...
SAFETY OFF.
OH, AS IF THINGS WOULD'VE TURNED OUT BETTER IF YOUR CLONE WAS ON THE LOOSE, KEI.
!
ATRIUM
1A
--GOTTA BE AROUND HERE SOME-WHERE--
--CAN'T WAIT TO RIP THEIR LUNGS OUT--
HEY!
THERE SHE IS!
?

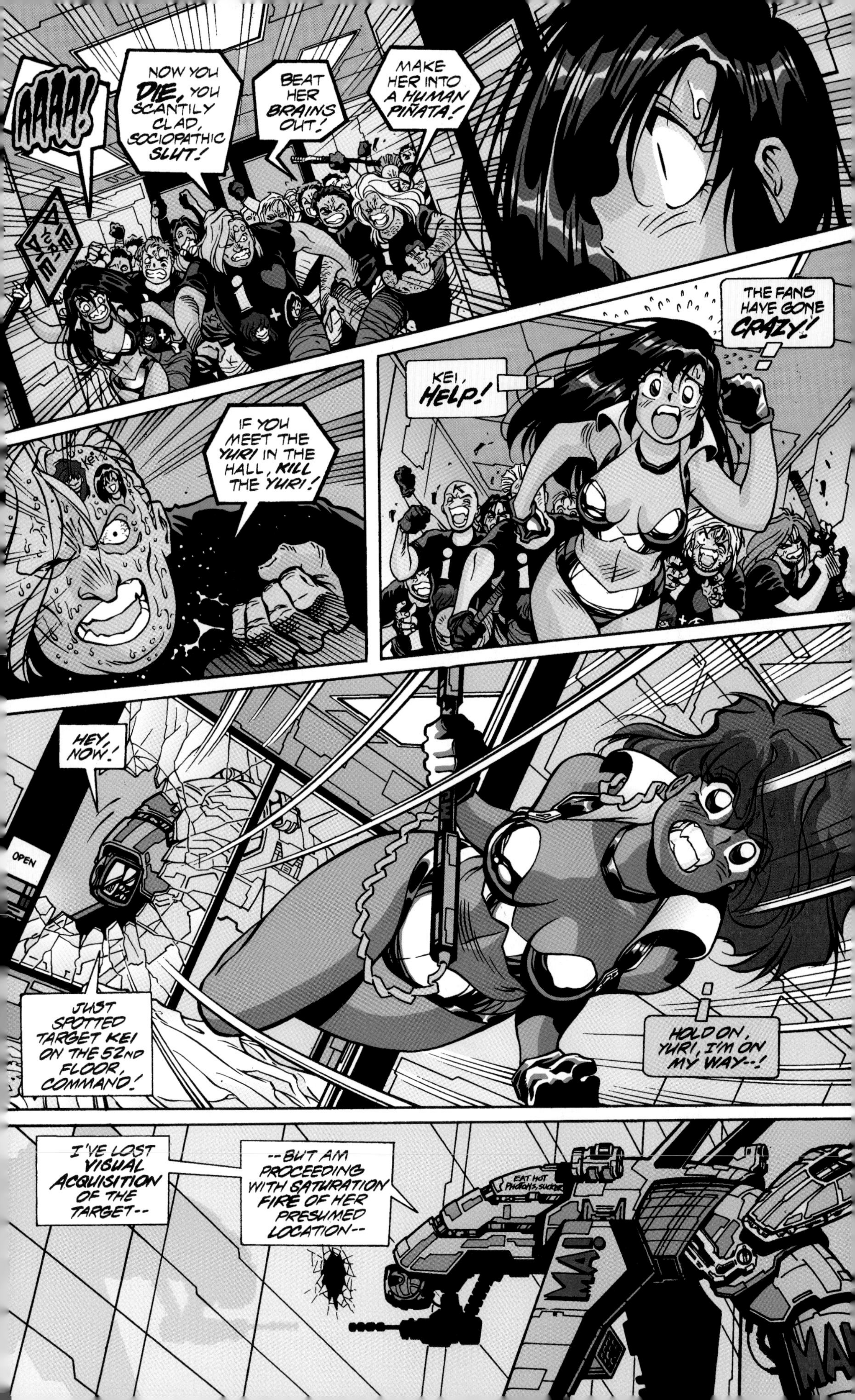
AAAA!
NOW YOU DIE, YOU SCANTILY CLAD, SOCIOPATHIC SLUT!
BEAT HER BRAINS OUT!
MAKE HER INTO A HUMAN PIÑATA!
IF YOU MEET THE YURI IN THE HALL, KILL THE YURI!
THE FANS HAVE GONE CRAZY!
KEI, HELP!
HEY, NOW!
OPEN
JUST SPOTTED TARGET KEI ON THE 52ND FLOOR, COMMAND!
HOLD ON, YURI, I'M ON MY WAY--!
I'VE LOST VISUAL ACQUISITION OF THE TARGET--
--BUT AM PROCEEDING WITH SATURATION FIRE OF HER PRESUMED LOCATION--
EAT HOT PHOTONS, SUCKER
MAI

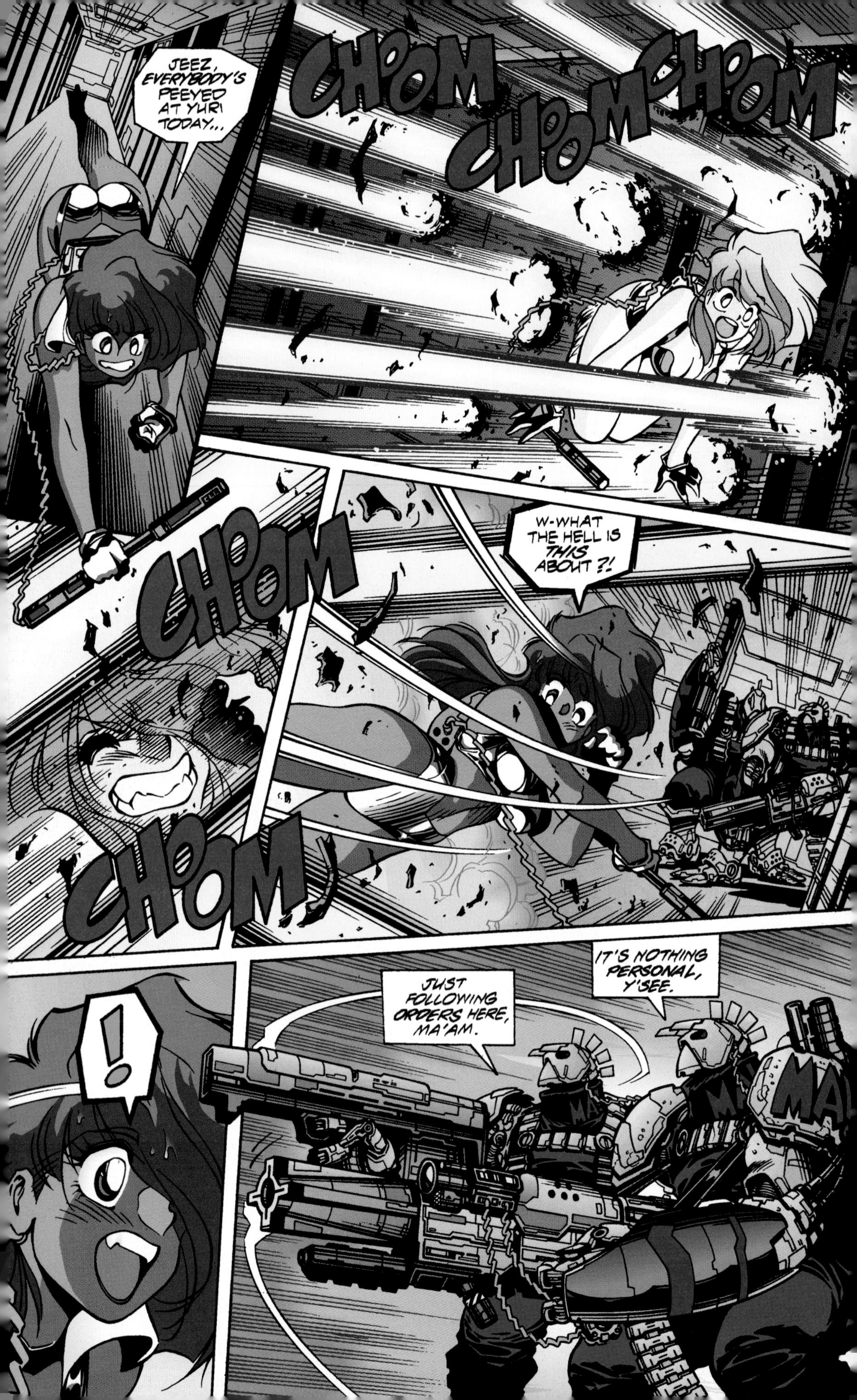
JEEZ, EVERYBODY'S PEEYED AT YURI TODAY...
CHOOM
CHOOM CHOOM
CHOOM
W-WHAT THE HELL IS THIS ABOUT ?!
CHOOM
!
JUST FOLLOWING ORDERS HERE, MA'AM.
IT'S NOTHING PERSONAL, Y'SEE.
MA
MA
MA

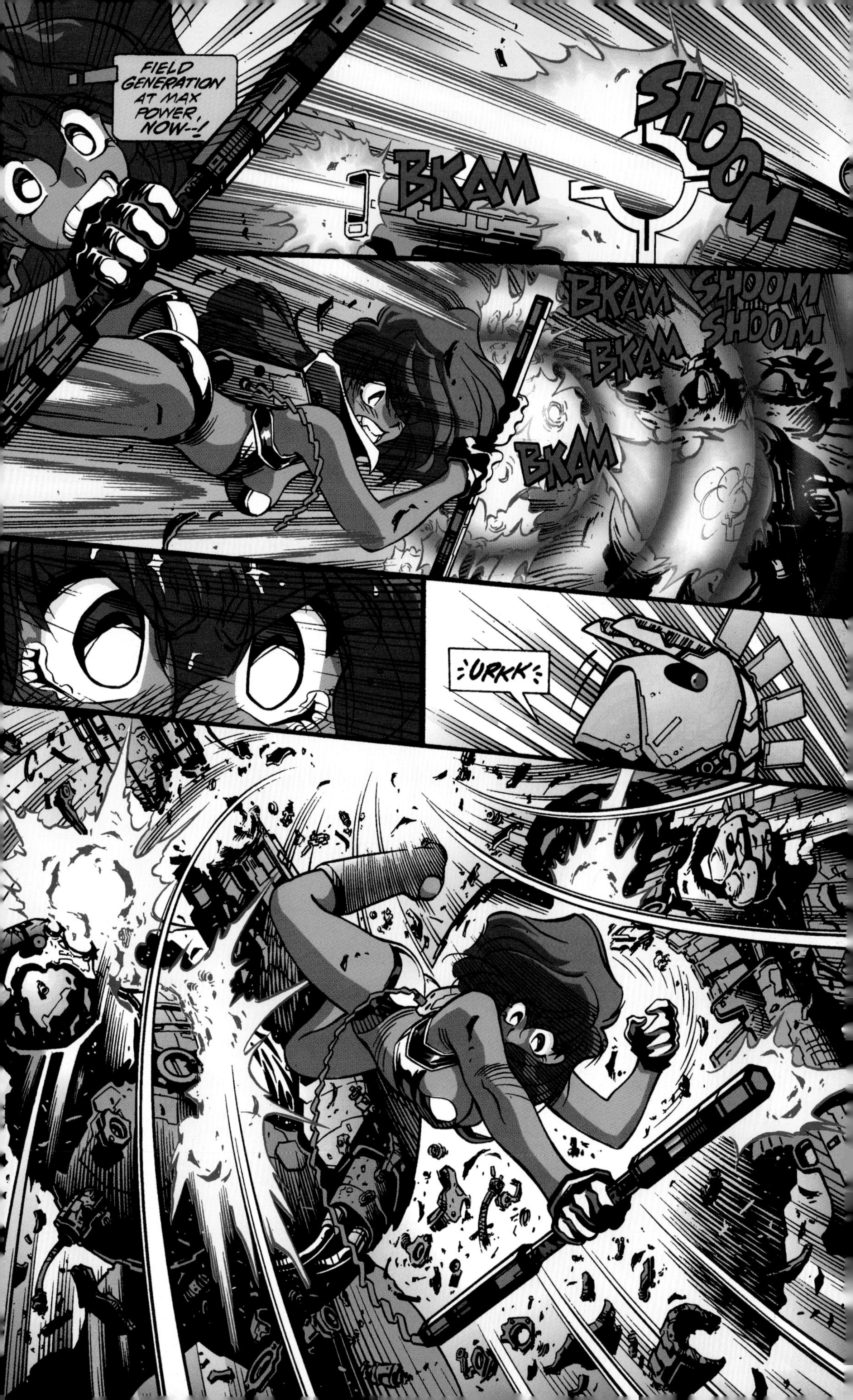
FIELD GENERATION AT MAX POWER, NOW--!
BKAM
SHOOM
BKAM
SHOOM
BKAM
SHOOM
BKAM
URKK

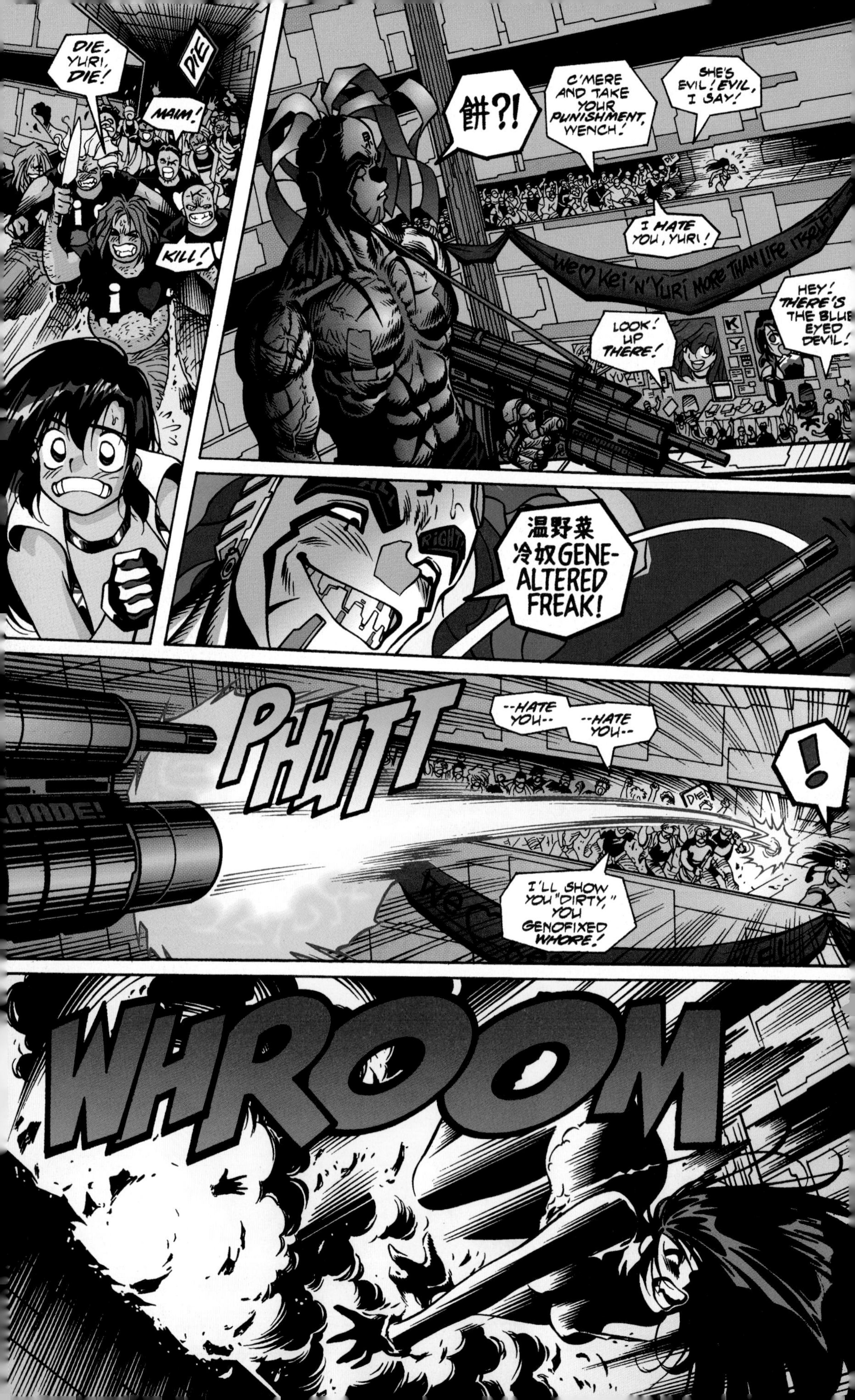
DIE, YURI, DIE!
DIE
MAIM!
KILL!
餅?!
C'MERE AND TAKE YOUR PUNISHMENT, WENCH!
SHE'S EVIL! EVIL, I SAY!
I HATE YOU, YURI!
We ♥ Kei 'N' Yuri MORE THAN LIFE ITSELF
LOOK! UP THERE!
HEY! THERE'S THE BLUE EYED DEVIL!
温野菜 冷奴 GENE-ALTERED FREAK!
PHUTT
--HATE YOU--
--HATE YOU--
!
I'LL SHOW YOU "DIRTY," YOU GENOFIXED WHORE!
WHROOM

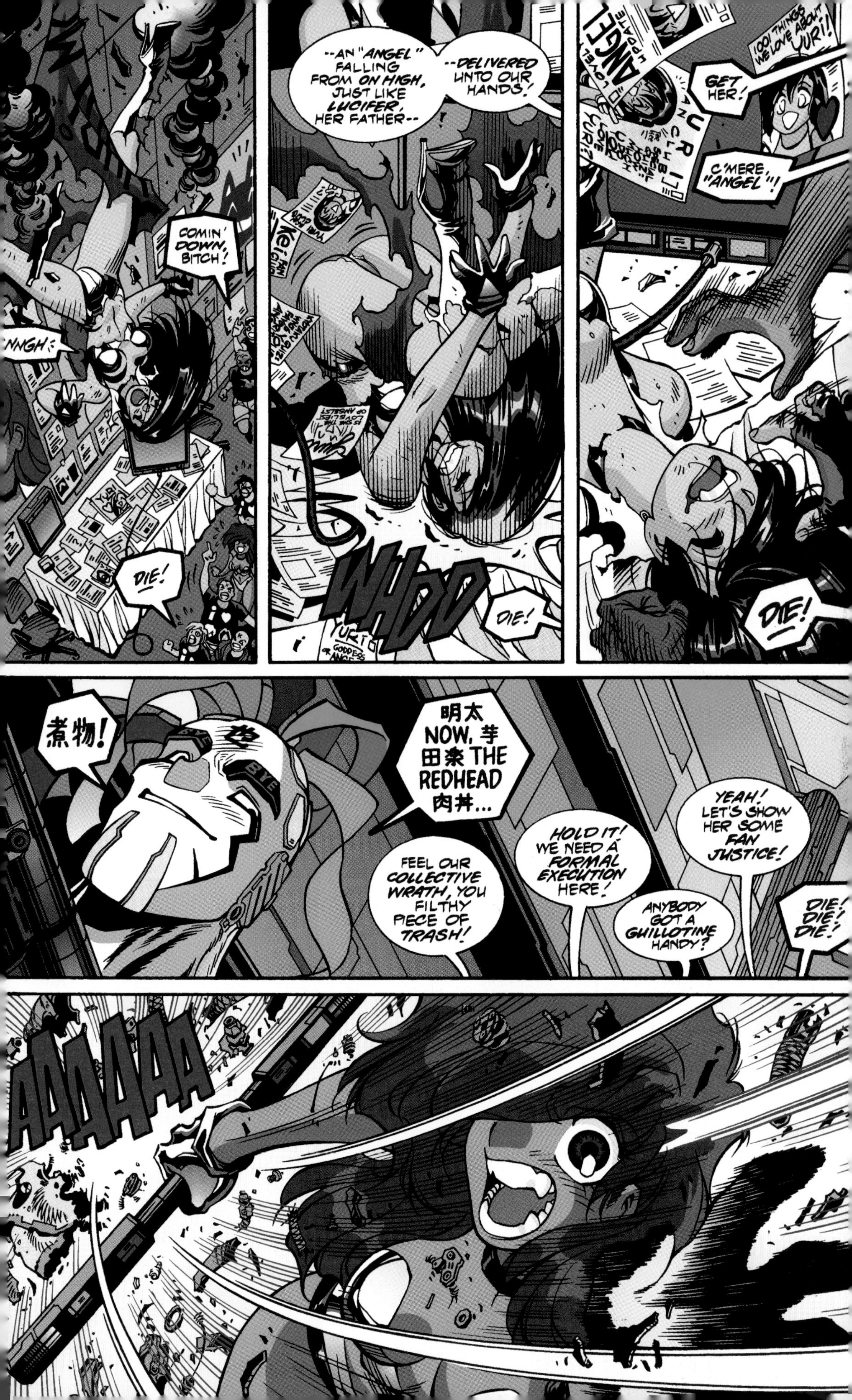
COMIN' DOWN, BITCH!
NNGH!
DIE!
--AN "ANGEL" FALLING FROM ON HIGH, JUST LIKE LUCIFER, HER FATHER--
--DELIVERED UNTO OUR HANDS!
WHDD
DIE!
1001 THINGS WE LOVE ABOUT YURI!
GET HER!
C'MERE, "ANGEL"!
DIE!
煮物!
明太 NOW, 芋田楽 THE REDHEAD 肉丼...
FEEL OUR COLLECTIVE WRATH, YOU FILTHY PIECE OF TRASH!
HOLD IT! WE NEED A FORMAL EXECUTION HERE!
YEAH! LET'S SHOW HER SOME FAN JUSTICE!
ANYBODY GOT A GUILLOTINE HANDY?
DIE! DIE! DIE!
AAAAAA

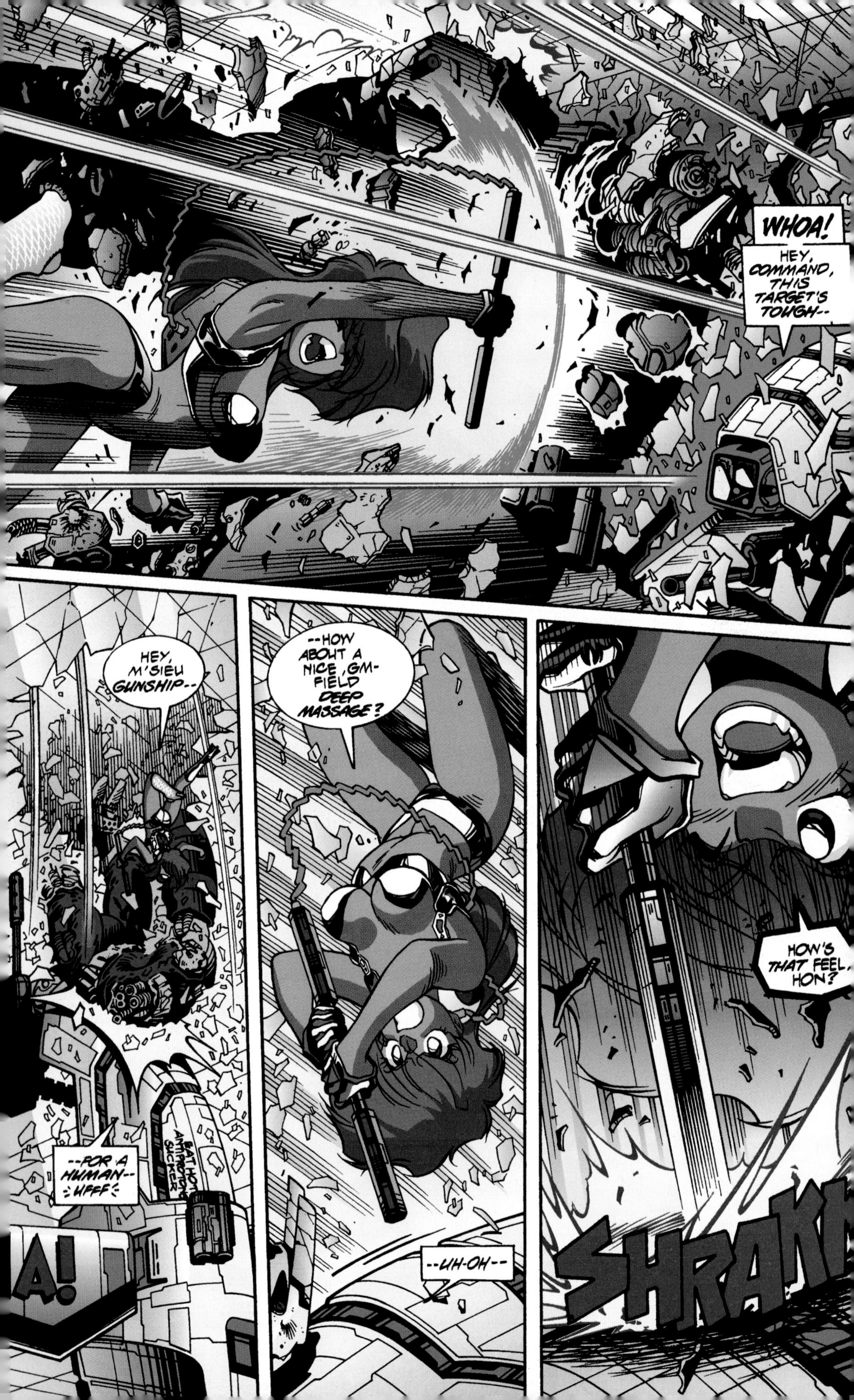
WHOA!
HEY, COMMAND, THIS TARGET'S TOUGH--
HEY, M'SIEU GUNSHIP--
EAT HOT ANTIPROTON SUCKER
--FOR A HUMAN-- :UFFF:
--HOW ABOUT A NICE, GM-FIELD DEEP MASSAGE?
--UH-OH--
HOW'S THAT FEEL, HON?

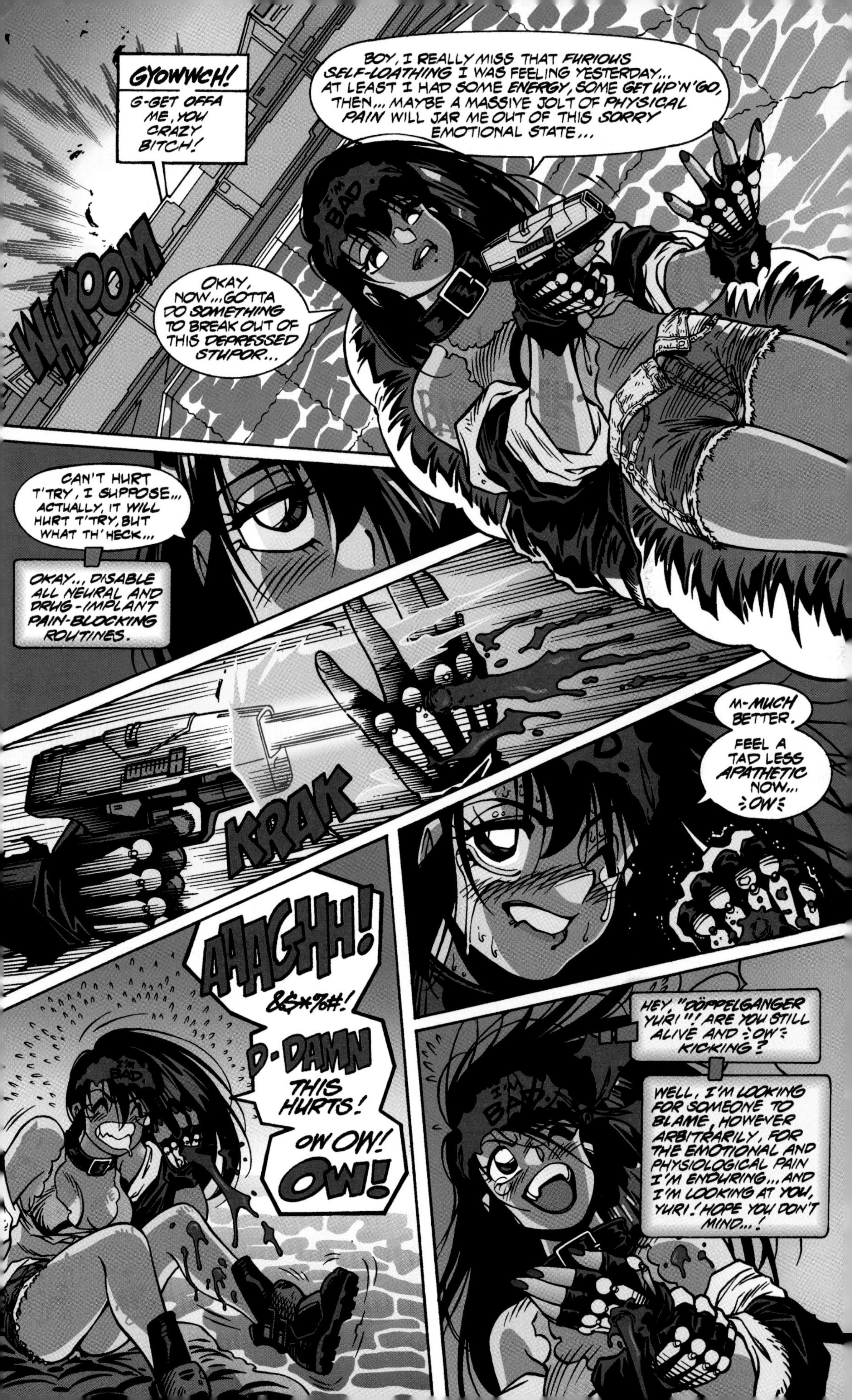
GYOWWCH!
G-GET OFFA ME, YOU CRAZY BITCH!
BOY, I REALLY MISS THAT FURIOUS SELF-LOATHING I WAS FEELING YESTERDAY... AT LEAST I HAD SOME ENERGY, SOME GET UP 'N' GO, THEN... MAYBE A MASSIVE JOLT OF PHYSICAL PAIN WILL JAR ME OUT OF THIS SORRY EMOTIONAL STATE...
WHKOOM
OKAY, NOW... GOTTA DO SOMETHING TO BREAK OUT OF THIS DEPRESSED STUPOR...
CAN'T HURT T'TRY, I SUPPOSE... ACTUALLY, IT WILL HURT T'TRY, BUT WHAT TH' HECK...
OKAY... DISABLE ALL NEURAL AND DRUG-IMPLANT PAIN-BLOCKING ROUTINES.
KRAK
M-MUCH BETTER.
FEEL A TAD LESS APATHETIC NOW... OW
AAAGHH!
&$*%#!
D-DAMN THIS HURTS!
OW OW! OW!
HEY, "DÖPPELGANGER YURI"! ARE YOU STILL ALIVE AND OW KICKING?
WELL, I'M LOOKING FOR SOMEONE TO BLAME, HOWEVER ARBITRARILY, FOR THE EMOTIONAL AND PHYSIOLOGICAL PAIN I'M ENDURING... AND I'M LOOKING AT YOU, YURI! HOPE YOU DON'T MIND...!

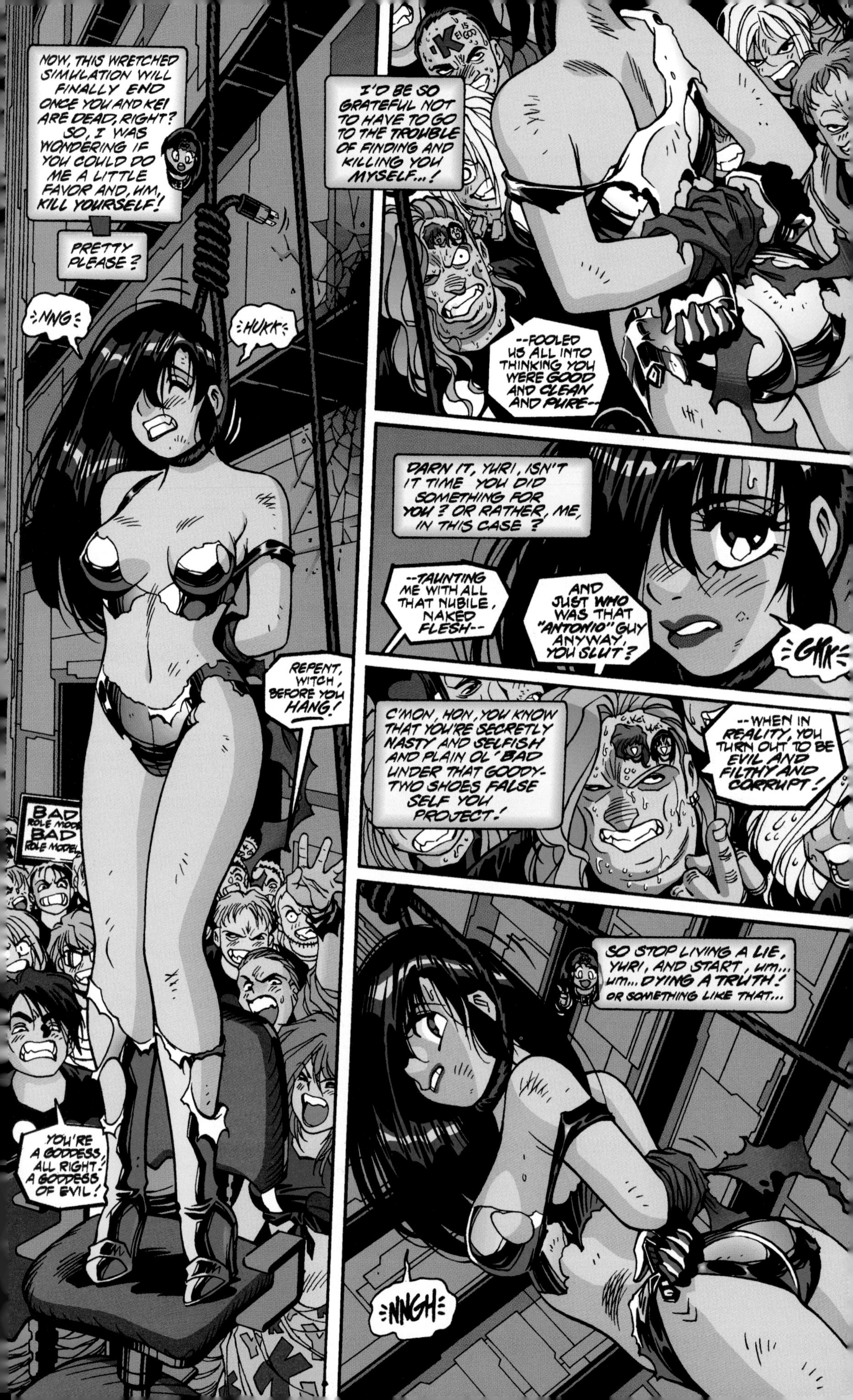
NOW, THIS WRETCHED SIMULATION WILL FINALLY END ONCE YOU AND KEI ARE DEAD, RIGHT? SO, I WAS WONDERING IF YOU COULD DO ME A LITTLE FAVOR AND, UM, KILL YOURSELF!
PRETTY PLEASE?
NNG
HUKK
REPENT, WITCH, BEFORE YOU HANG!
BAD ROLE MODEL
BAD ROLE MODEL
YOU'RE A GODDESS, ALL RIGHT! A GODDESS OF EVIL!
I'D BE SO GRATEFUL NOT TO HAVE TO GO TO THE TROUBLE OF FINDING AND KILLING YOU MYSELF...!
--FOOLED US ALL INTO THINKING YOU WERE GOOD AND CLEAN AND PURE--
DARN IT, YURI, ISN'T IT TIME YOU DID SOMETHING FOR YOU? OR RATHER, ME, IN THIS CASE?
--TAUNTING ME WITH ALL THAT NUBILE, NAKED FLESH--
AND JUST WHO WAS THAT "ANTONIO" GUY ANYWAY, YOU SLUT?
GAK
C'MON, HON, YOU KNOW THAT YOU'RE SECRETLY NASTY AND SELFISH AND PLAIN OL' BAD UNDER THAT GOODY-TWO SHOES FALSE SELF YOU PROJECT!
--WHEN IN REALITY, YOU TURN OUT TO BE EVIL AND FILTHY AND CORRUPT!
SO STOP LIVING A LIE, YURI, AND START, UM... UM... DYING A TRUTH! OR SOMETHING LIKE THAT...
NNGH

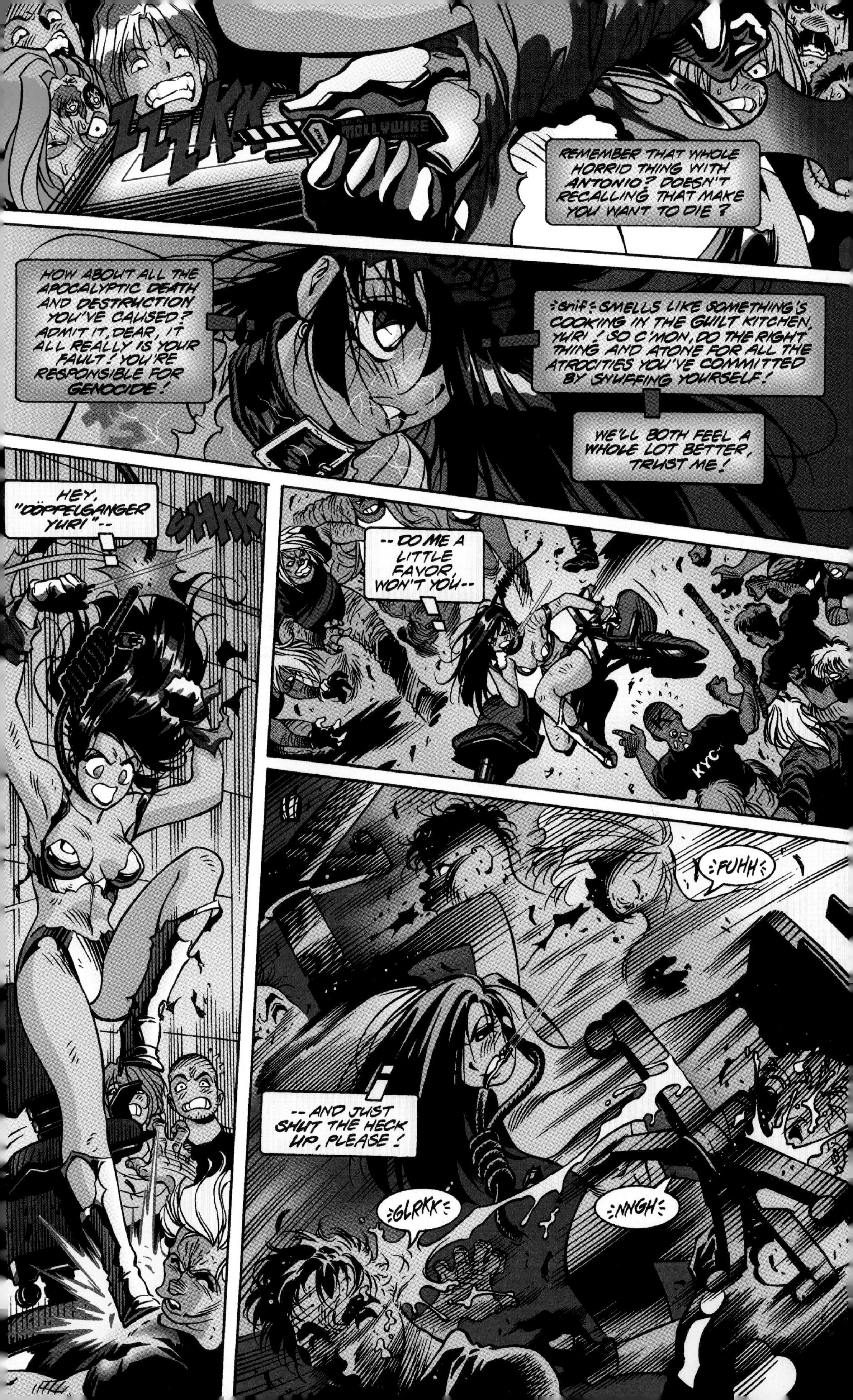
ZZZKK
MOLLYWIRE
REMEMBER THAT WHOLE HORRID THING WITH ANTONIO? DOESN'T RECALLING THAT MAKE YOU WANT TO DIE?
HOW ABOUT ALL THE APOCALYPTIC DEATH AND DESTRUCTION YOU'VE CAUSED? ADMIT IT, DEAR, IT ALL REALLY IS YOUR FAULT! YOU'RE RESPONSIBLE FOR GENOCIDE!
:SNIF: SMELLS LIKE SOMETHING'S COOKING IN THE GUILT KITCHEN, YURI! SO C'MON, DO THE RIGHT THING AND ATONE FOR ALL THE ATROCITIES YOU'VE COMMITTED BY SNUFFING YOURSELF!
WE'LL BOTH FEEL A WHOLE LOT BETTER, TRUST ME!
HEY, "DÖPPELGANGER YURI"--
SHKK
--DO ME A LITTLE FAVOR, WON'T YOU--
KYC
FUHH
--AND JUST SHUT THE HECK UP, PLEASE!
GLRKK
NNGH

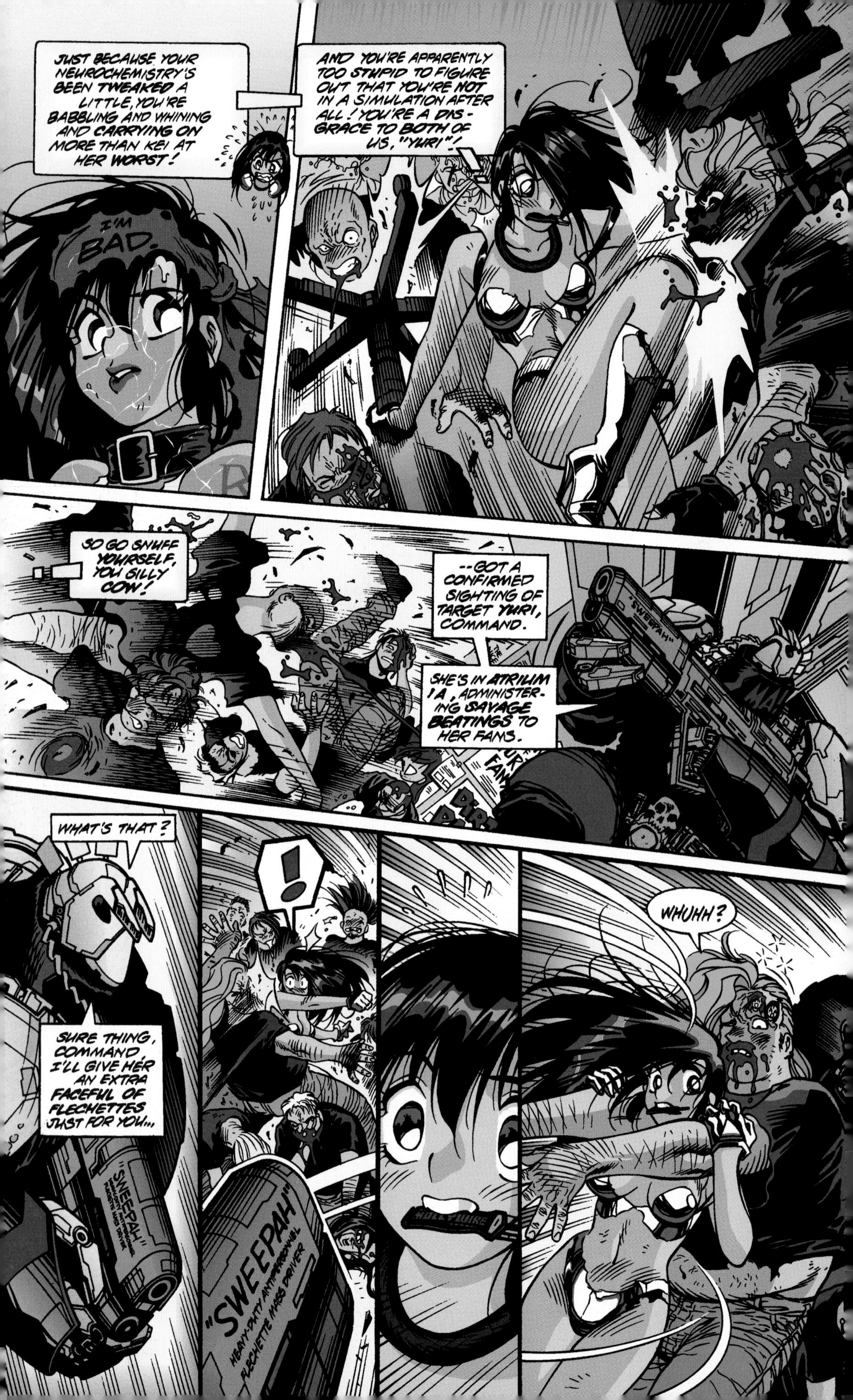
JUST BECAUSE YOUR NEUROCHEMISTRY'S BEEN TWEAKED A LITTLE, YOU'RE BABBLING AND WHINING AND CARRYING ON MORE THAN KEI AT HER WORST!
I'M BAD.
AND YOU'RE APPARENTLY TOO STUPID TO FIGURE OUT THAT YOU'RE NOT IN A SIMULATION AFTER ALL! YOU'RE A DIS-GRACE TO BOTH OF US, "YURI"!
SO GO SNUFF YOURSELF, YOU SILLY COW!
--GOT A CONFIRMED SIGHTING OF TARGET YURI, COMMAND.
SHE'S IN ATRIUM 1A, ADMINISTER-ING SAVAGE BEATINGS TO HER FANS.
"SWEEPAH"
WHAT'S THAT?
SURE THING, COMMAND. I'LL GIVE HER AN EXTRA FACEFUL OF FLECHETTES JUST FOR YOU...
"SWEEPAH"
!
"SWEEPAH"
HEAVY-DUTY ANTIPERSONNEL FLECHETTE MASS DRIVER
WHUHH?

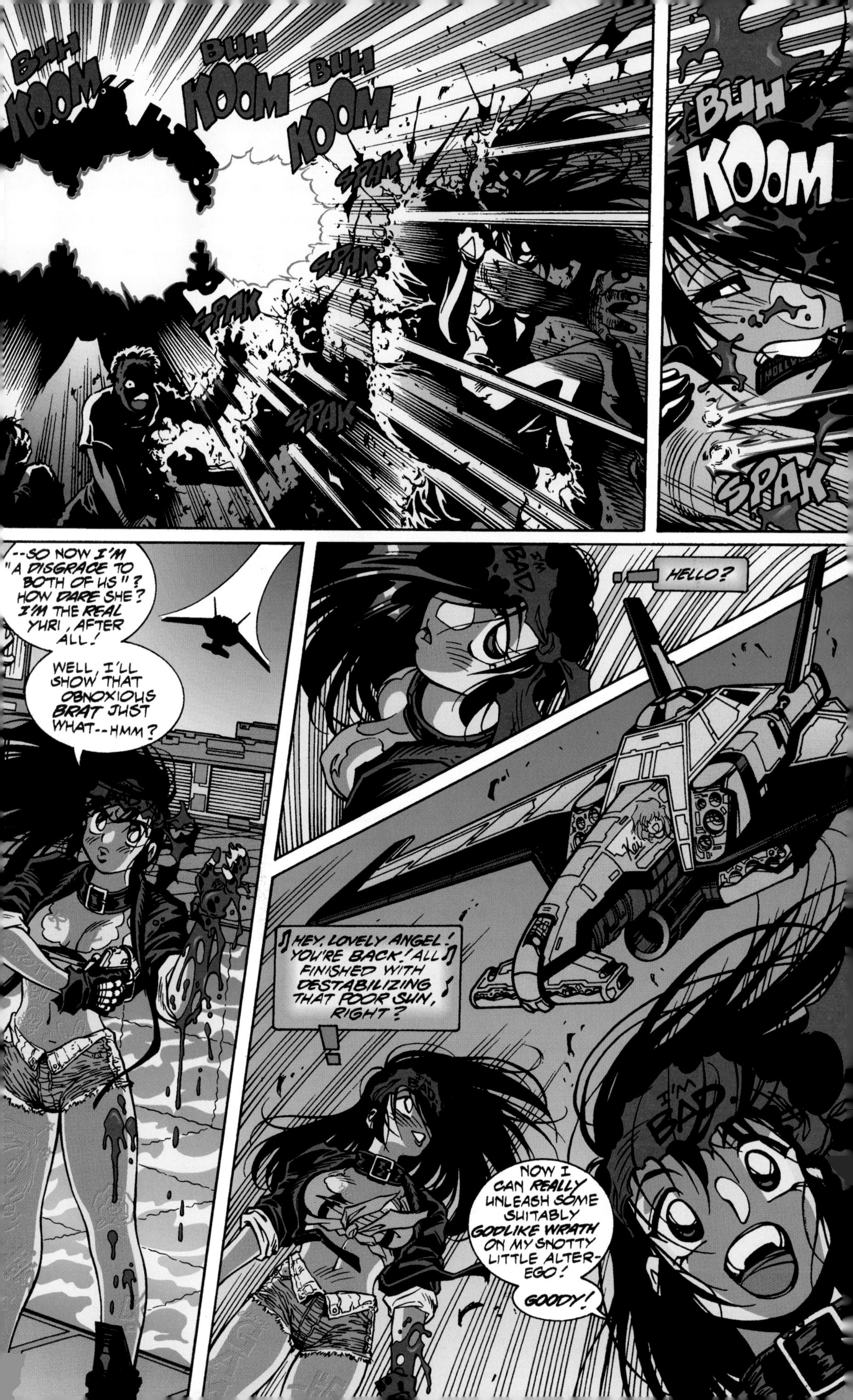
BUH KOOM
BUH KOOM
BUH KOOM
SPAK
SPAK
SPAK
SPAK
BUH KOOM
SPAK
--SO NOW I'M "A DISGRACE TO BOTH OF US"? HOW DARE SHE? I'M THE REAL YURI, AFTER ALL!
WELL, I'LL SHOW THAT OBNOXIOUS BRAT JUST WHAT--HMM?
I'M BAD
HELLO?
HEY, LOVELY ANGEL! YOU'RE BACK! ALL FINISHED WITH DESTABILIZING THAT POOR SUN, RIGHT?
!
I'M BAD
NOW I CAN REALLY UNLEASH SOME SUITABLY GODLIKE WRATH ON MY SNOTTY LITTLE ALTER-EGO!
GOODY!

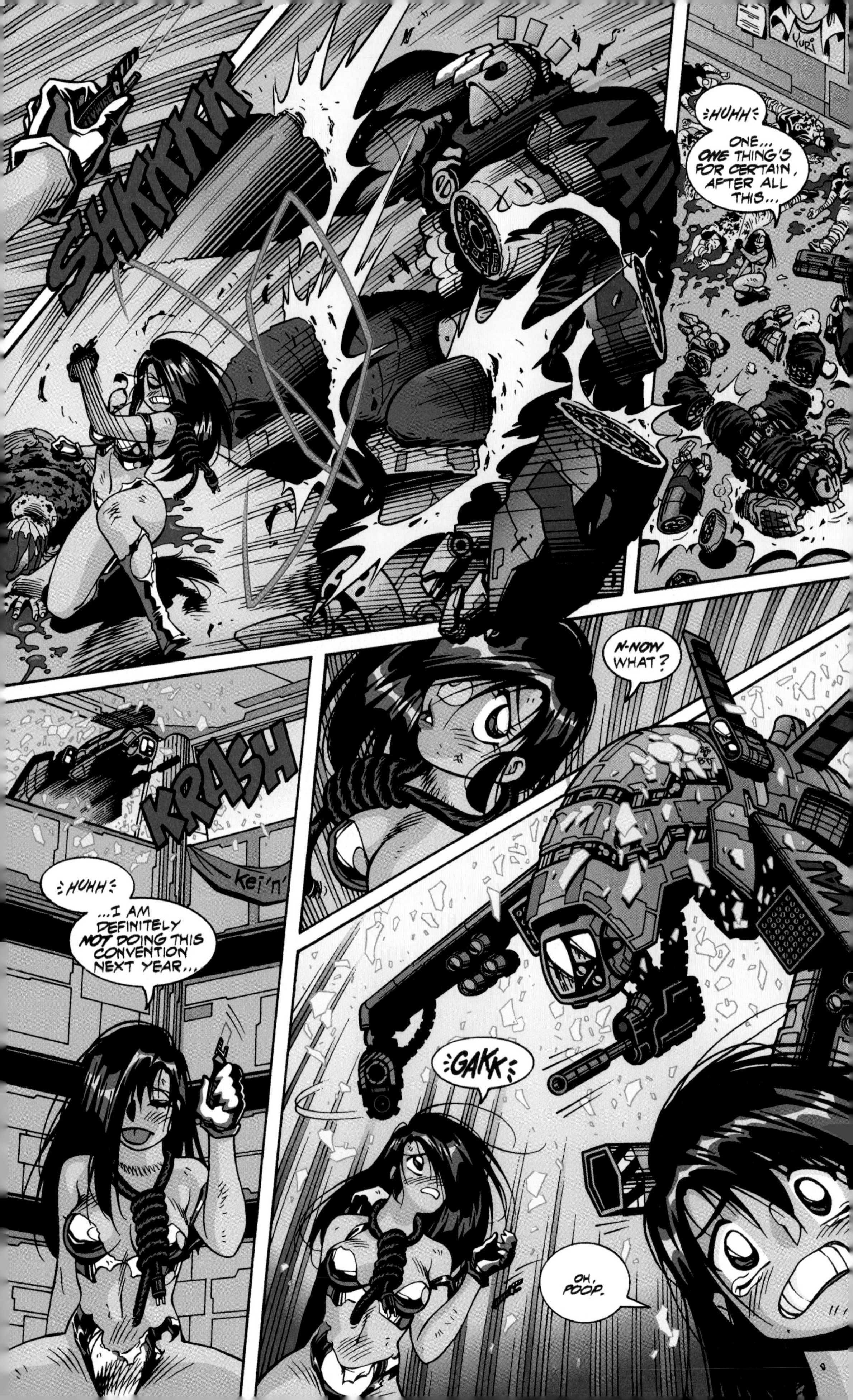
SHKKKK
MA!
YURI
HUHH
ONE... ONE THING'S FOR CERTAIN, AFTER ALL THIS...
KRASH
kei 'n'
HUHH
...I AM DEFINITELY NOT DOING THIS CONVENTION NEXT YEAR...
N-NOW WHAT?
GAKK
OH, POOP.

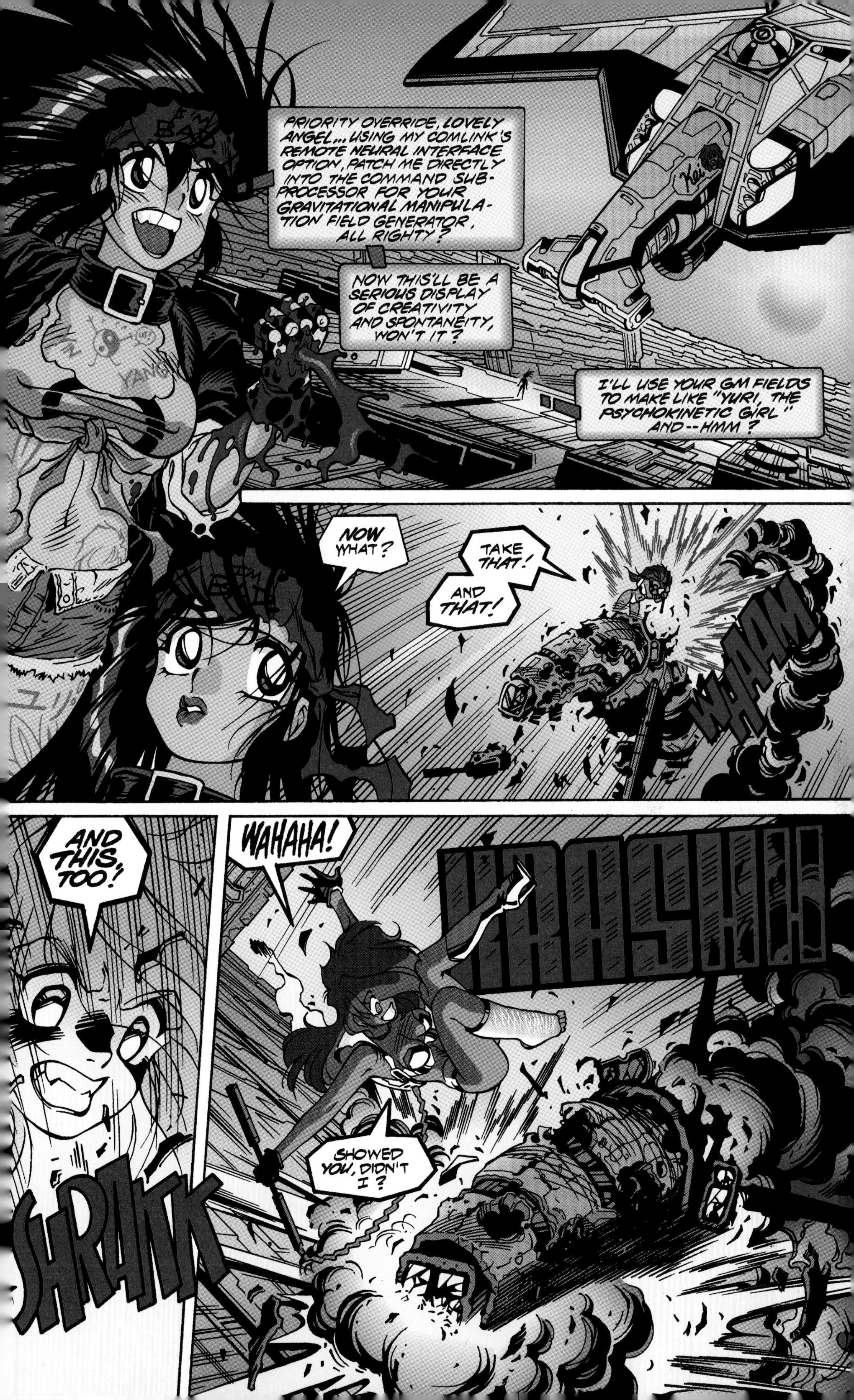
PRIORITY OVERRIDE, LOVELY ANGEL... USING MY COMLINK'S REMOTE NEURAL INTERFACE OPTION, PATCH ME DIRECTLY INTO THE COMMAND SUB-PROCESSOR FOR YOUR GRAVITATIONAL MANIPULATION FIELD GENERATOR, ALL RIGHTY?
NOW THIS'LL BE A SERIOUS DISPLAY OF CREATIVITY AND SPONTANEITY, WON'T IT?
I'LL USE YOUR GM FIELDS TO MAKE LIKE "YURI, THE PSYCHOKINETIC GIRL" AND--HMM?
NOW WHAT?
TAKE THAT!
AND THAT!
WHAM
AND THIS, TOO!
WAHAHA!
KRASH
SHOWED YOU, DIDN'T I?

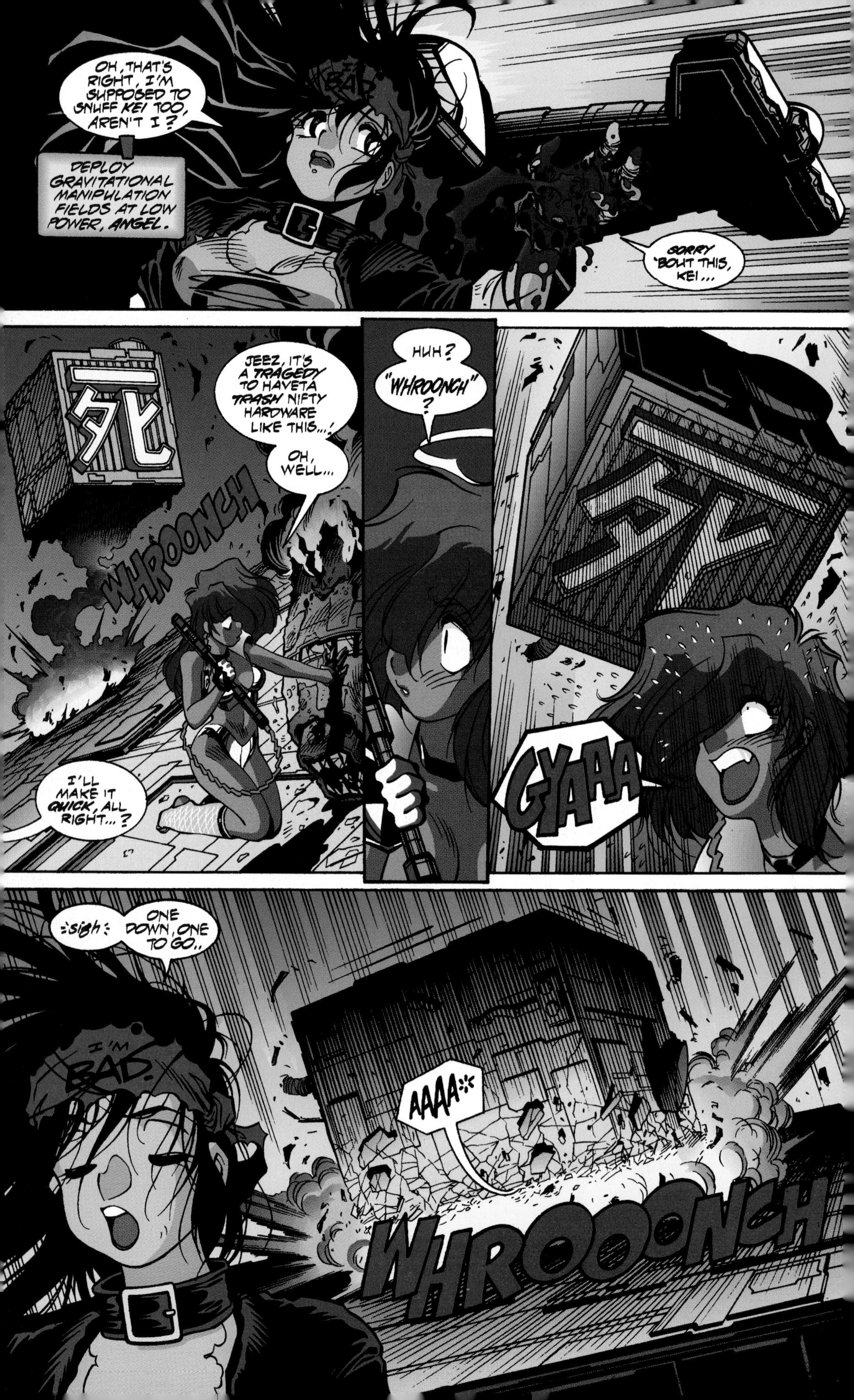
OH, THAT'S RIGHT, I'M SUPPOSED TO SNUFF KEI TOO, AREN'T I?
DEPLOY GRAVITATIONAL MANIPULATION FIELDS AT LOW POWER, ANGEL.
I'M BAD.
SORRY 'BOUT THIS, KEI...
死
WHROONCH
JEEZ, IT'S A TRAGEDY TO HAVETA TRASH NIFTY HARDWARE LIKE THIS...!
OH, WELL...
I'LL MAKE IT QUICK, ALL RIGHT...?
HUH? "WHROONCH"?
GYAAA
:sigh: ONE DOWN, ONE TO GO..
I'M BAD.
AAAA
WHROOONCH

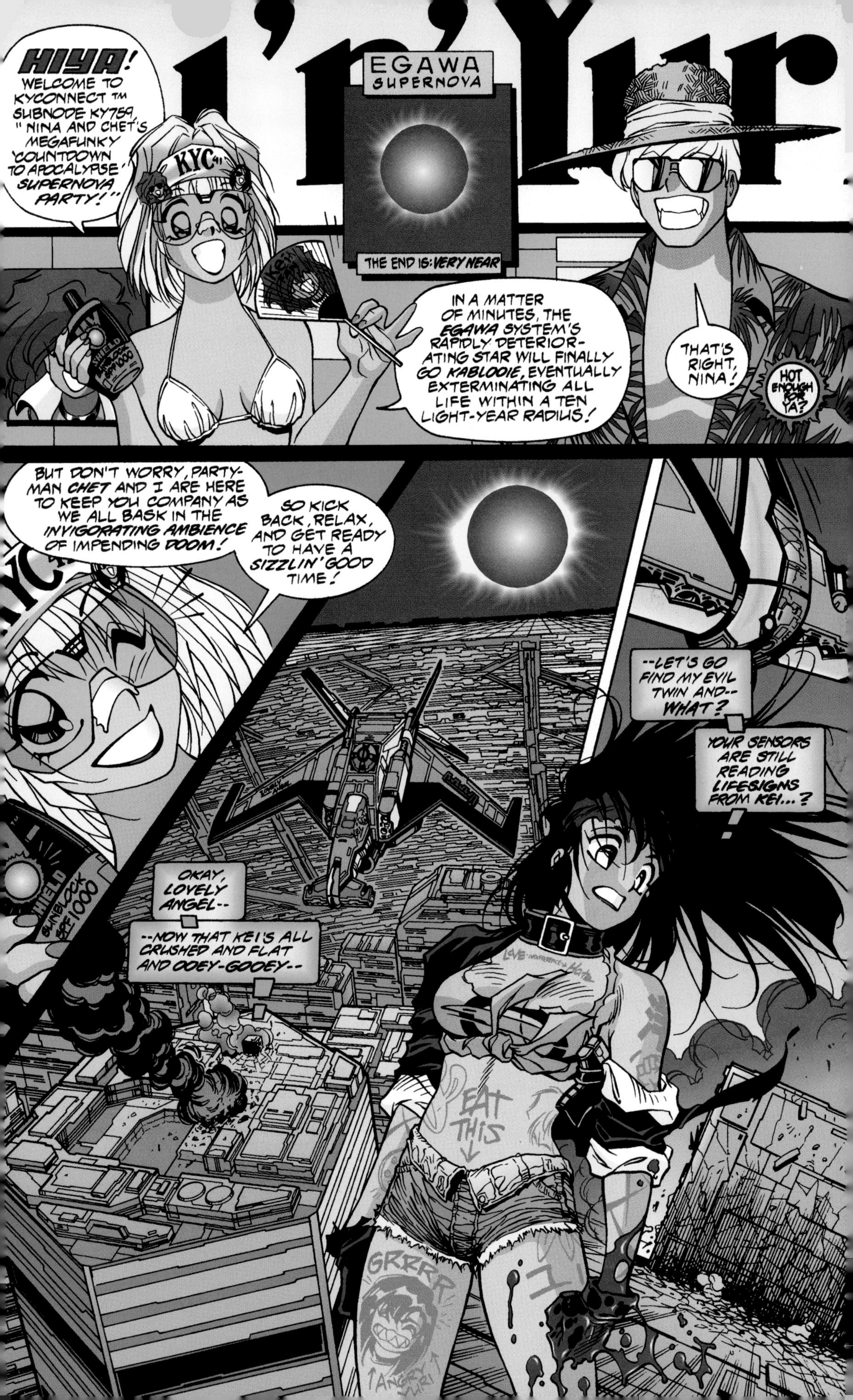

HIYA! WELCOME TO KYCONNECT ™ SUBNODE KY759, "NINA AND CHET'S MEGAFUNKY 'COUNTDOWN TO APOCALYPSE' SUPERNOVA PARTY!"
EGAWA SUPERNOVA
THE END IS: VERY NEAR
KYC
IN A MATTER OF MINUTES, THE EGAWA SYSTEM'S RAPIDLY DETERIORATING STAR WILL FINALLY GO KABLOOIE, EVENTUALLY EXTERMINATING ALL LIFE WITHIN A TEN LIGHT-YEAR RADIUS!
THAT'S RIGHT, NINA!
HOT ENOUGH FOR YA?
BUT DON'T WORRY, PARTY-MAN CHET AND I ARE HERE TO KEEP YOU COMPANY AS WE ALL BASK IN THE INVIGORATING AMBIENCE OF IMPENDING DOOM!
SO KICK BACK, RELAX, AND GET READY TO HAVE A SIZZLIN' GOOD TIME!
SUNBLOCK SPF 1000
OKAY, LOVELY ANGEL--
--NOW THAT KEI'S ALL CRUSHED AND FLAT AND OOEY-GOOEY--
--LET'S GO FIND MY EVIL TWIN AND-- WHAT?
YOUR SENSORS ARE STILL READING LIFESIGNS FROM KEI...?
EAT THIS
GRRRR

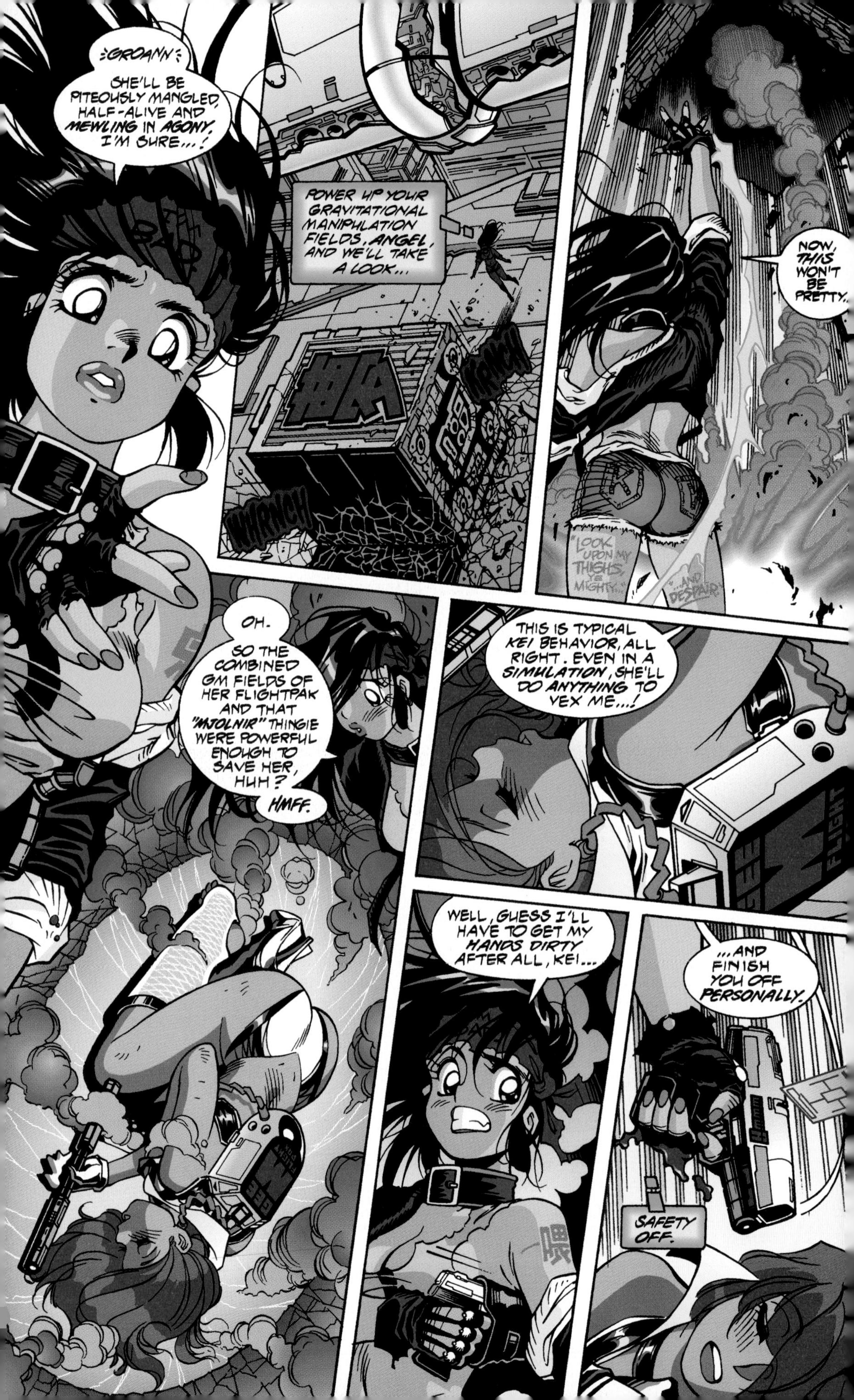
:GROANN:
SHE'LL BE PITEOUSLY MANGLED, HALF-ALIVE AND MEWLING IN AGONY, I'M SURE...!
POWER UP YOUR GRAVITATIONAL MANIPULATION FIELDS, ANGEL, AND WE'LL TAKE A LOOK...
WHRNCH
NOW, THIS WON'T BE PRETTY.
"LOOK UPON MY THIGHS, YE MIGHTY..."
"...AND DESPAIR"
OH.
SO THE COMBINED GM FIELDS OF HER FLIGHTPAK AND THAT "MJOLNIR" THINGIE WERE POWERFUL ENOUGH TO SAVE HER, HUH?
HMFF.
THIS IS TYPICAL KEI BEHAVIOR, ALL RIGHT. EVEN IN A SIMULATION, SHE'LL DO ANYTHING TO VEX ME...!
WELL, GUESS I'LL HAVE TO GET MY HANDS DIRTY AFTER ALL, KEI...
...AND FINISH YOU OFF PERSONALLY.
SAFETY OFF.

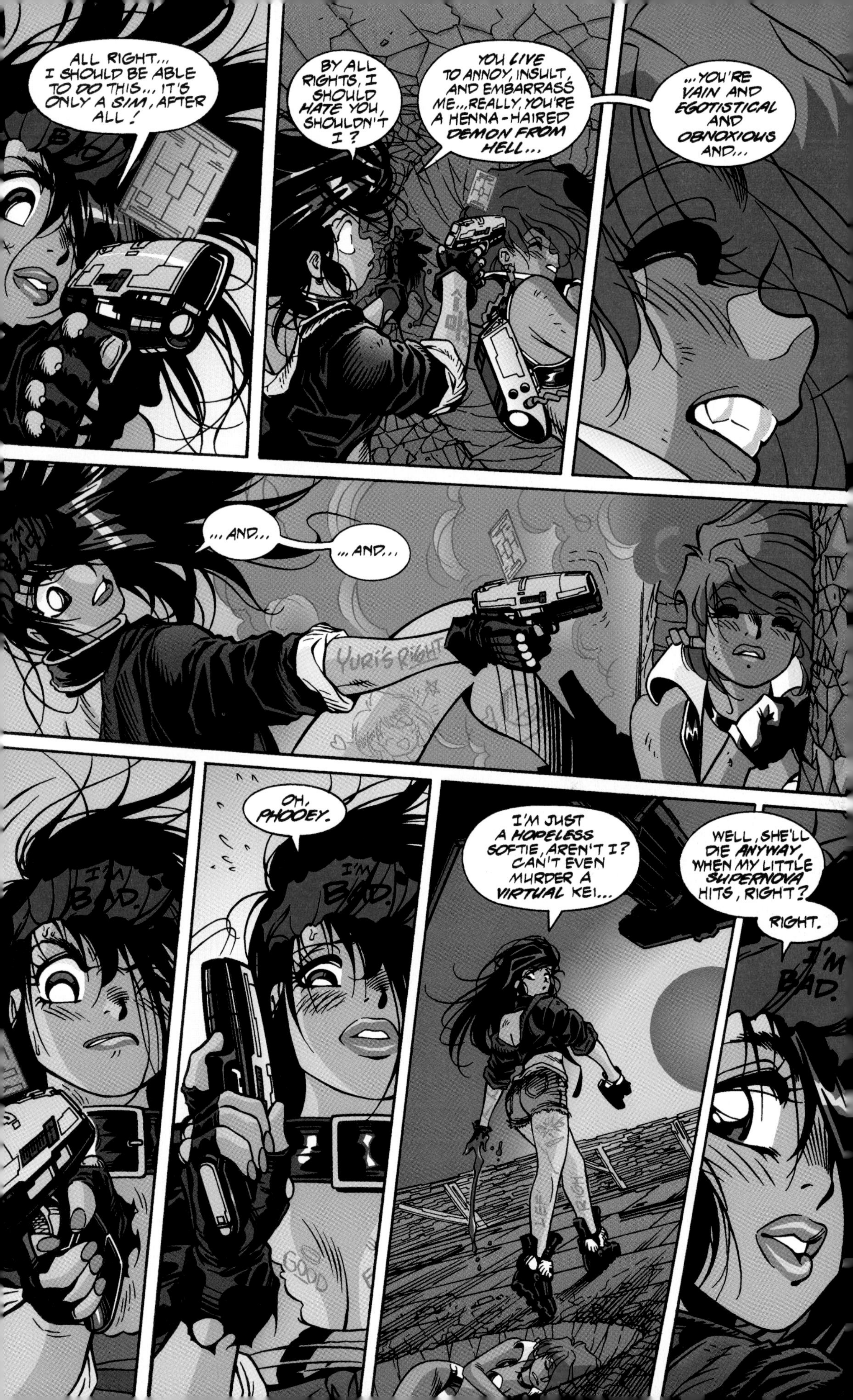
ALL RIGHT... I SHOULD BE ABLE TO DO THIS... IT'S ONLY A SIM, AFTER ALL!
BY ALL RIGHTS, I SHOULD HATE YOU, SHOULDN'T I?
YOU LIVE TO ANNOY, INSULT, AND EMBARRASS ME... REALLY, YOU'RE A HENNA-HAIRED DEMON FROM HELL...
...YOU'RE VAIN AND EGOTISTICAL AND OBNOXIOUS AND...
...AND...
...AND...
YURI'S RIGHT
I'M BAD.
OH, PHOOEY.
I'M BAD.
GOOD
I'M JUST A HOPELESS SOFTIE, AREN'T I? CAN'T EVEN MURDER A VIRTUAL KEI...
WELL, SHE'LL DIE ANYWAY, WHEN MY LITTLE SUPERNOVA HITS, RIGHT?
RIGHT.
I'M BAD.

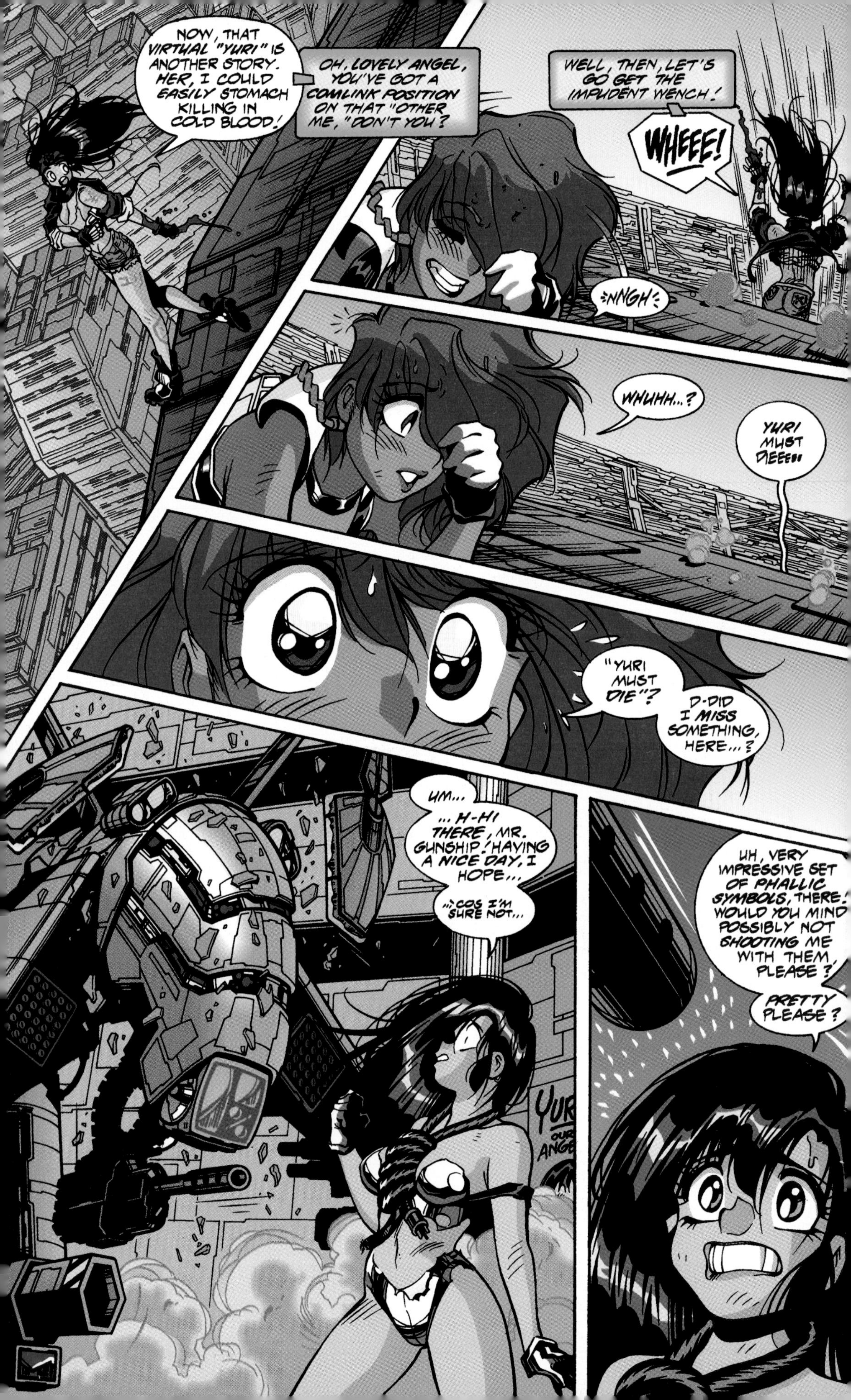
NOW, THAT VIRTUAL "YURI" IS ANOTHER STORY. HER, I COULD EASILY STOMACH KILLING IN COLD BLOOD!
OH, LOVELY ANGEL, YOU'VE GOT A COMLINK POSITION ON THAT "OTHER ME," DON'T YOU?
WELL, THEN, LET'S GO GET THE IMPUDENT WENCH!
WHEEE!
NNGH
WHUHH...?
YURI MUST DIEEE!!!
"YURI MUST DIE"?
D-DID I MISS SOMETHING, HERE...?
UM...
...H-HI THERE, MR. GUNSHIP! HAVING A NICE DAY, I HOPE...
...COS I'M SURE NOT...
UH, VERY IMPRESSIVE SET OF PHALLIC SYMBOLS, THERE! WOULD YOU MIND POSSIBLY NOT SHOOTING ME WITH THEM, PLEASE?
PRETTY PLEASE?

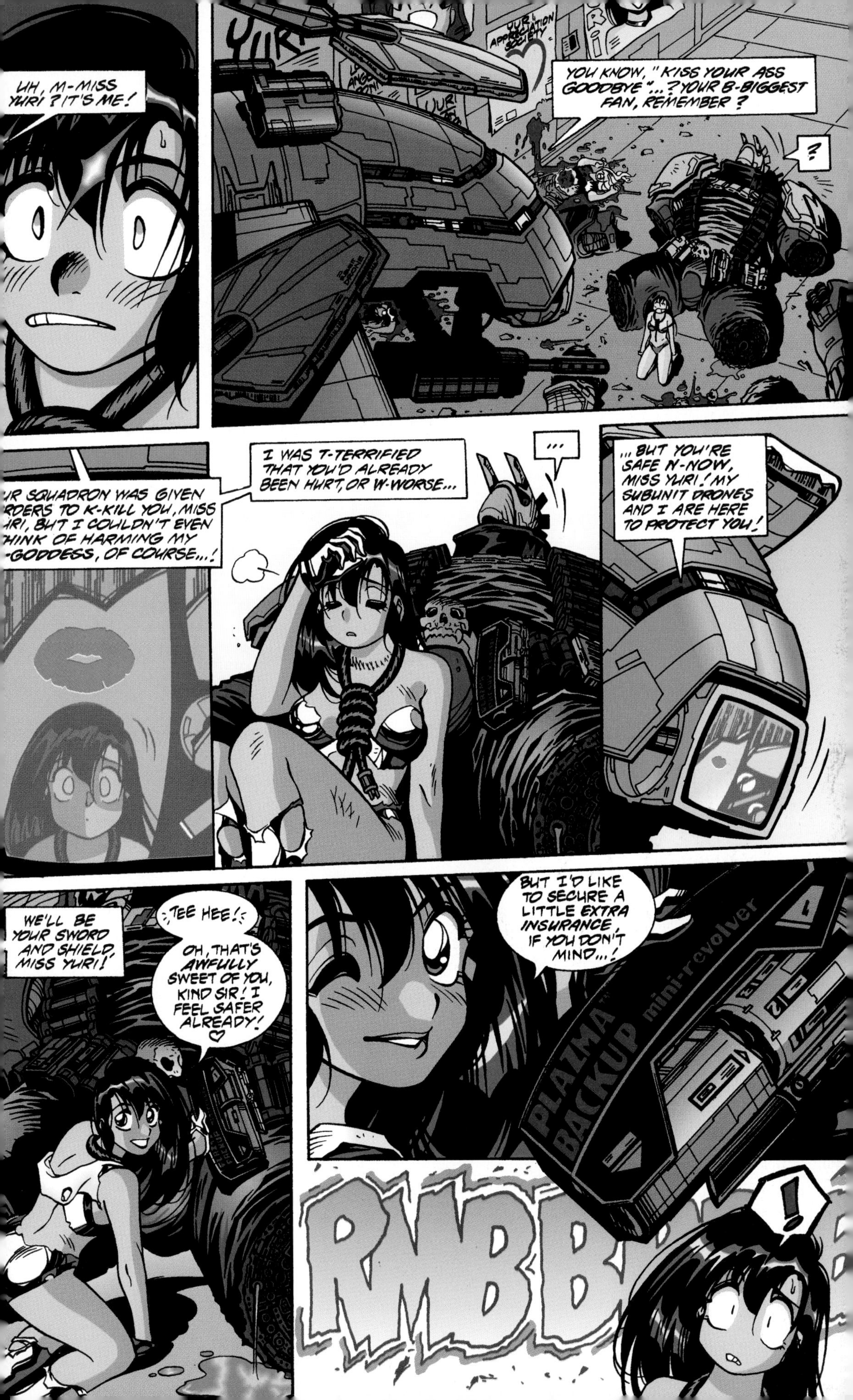
UH, M-MISS YURI ? IT'S ME!
YURI
YURI APPRECIATION SOCIETY
YOU KNOW, "KISS YOUR ASS GOODBYE"...? YOUR B-BIGGEST FAN, REMEMBER ?
?
UR SQUADRON WAS GIVEN RDERS TO K-KILL YOU, MISS URI, BUT I COULDN'T EVEN HINK OF HARMING MY -GODDESS, OF COURSE...!
I WAS T-TERRIFIED THAT YOU'D ALREADY BEEN HURT, OR W-WORSE...
...
... BUT YOU'RE SAFE N-NOW, MISS YURI! MY SUBUNIT DRONES AND I ARE HERE TO PROTECT YOU!
WE'LL BE YOUR SWORD AND SHIELD, MISS YURI!
TEE HEE!
OH, THAT'S AWFULLY SWEET OF YOU, KIND SIR! I FEEL SAFER ALREADY!
BUT I'D LIKE TO SECURE A LITTLE EXTRA INSURANCE, IF YOU DON'T MIND...!
PLAZMA BACKUP mini-revolver
RMBB
!

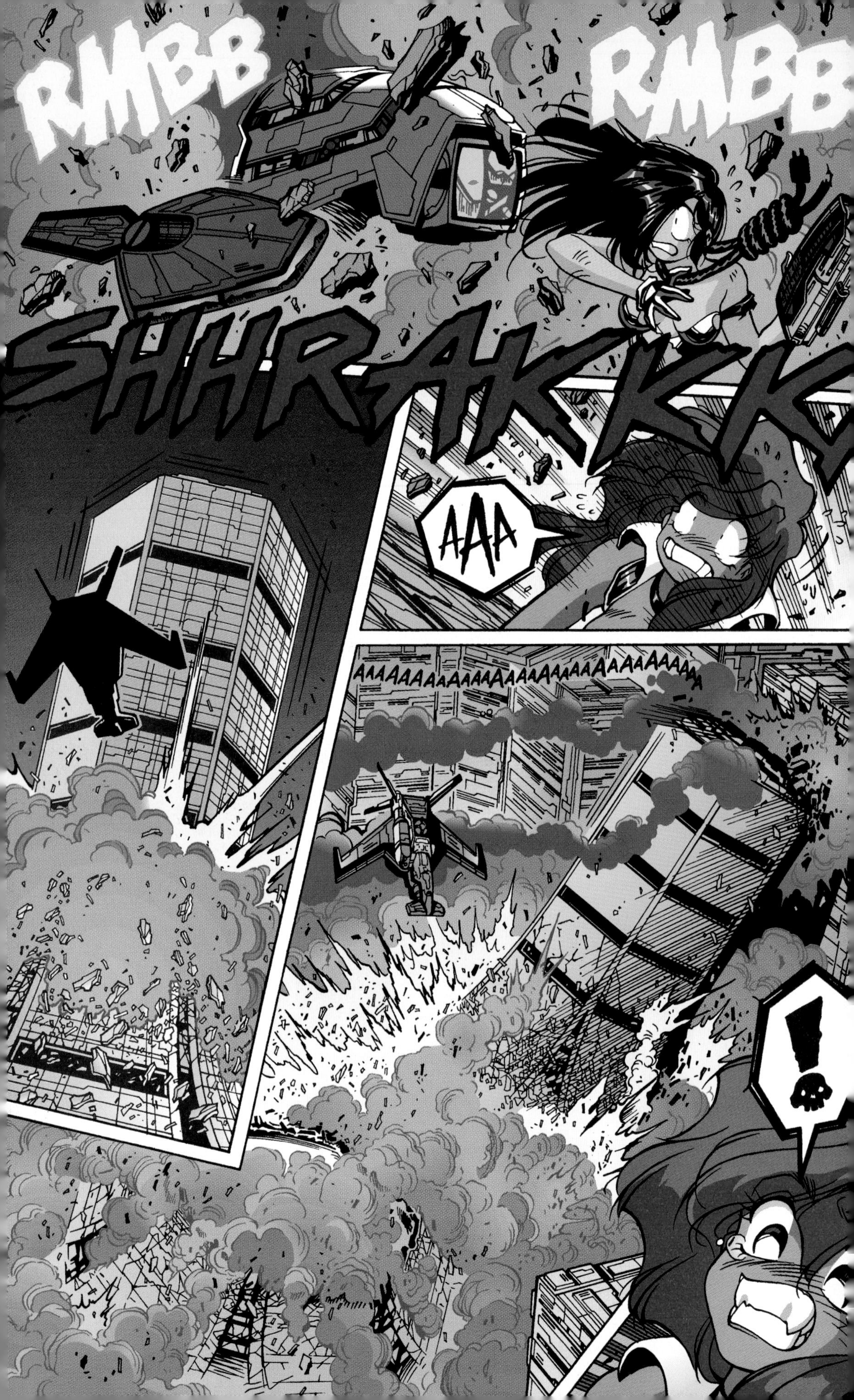
RMBB
RMBB
SHHRAKKK
AAA
AAAAAAAaAAAAAAAAAaaaAAAAaAAAAAA
!

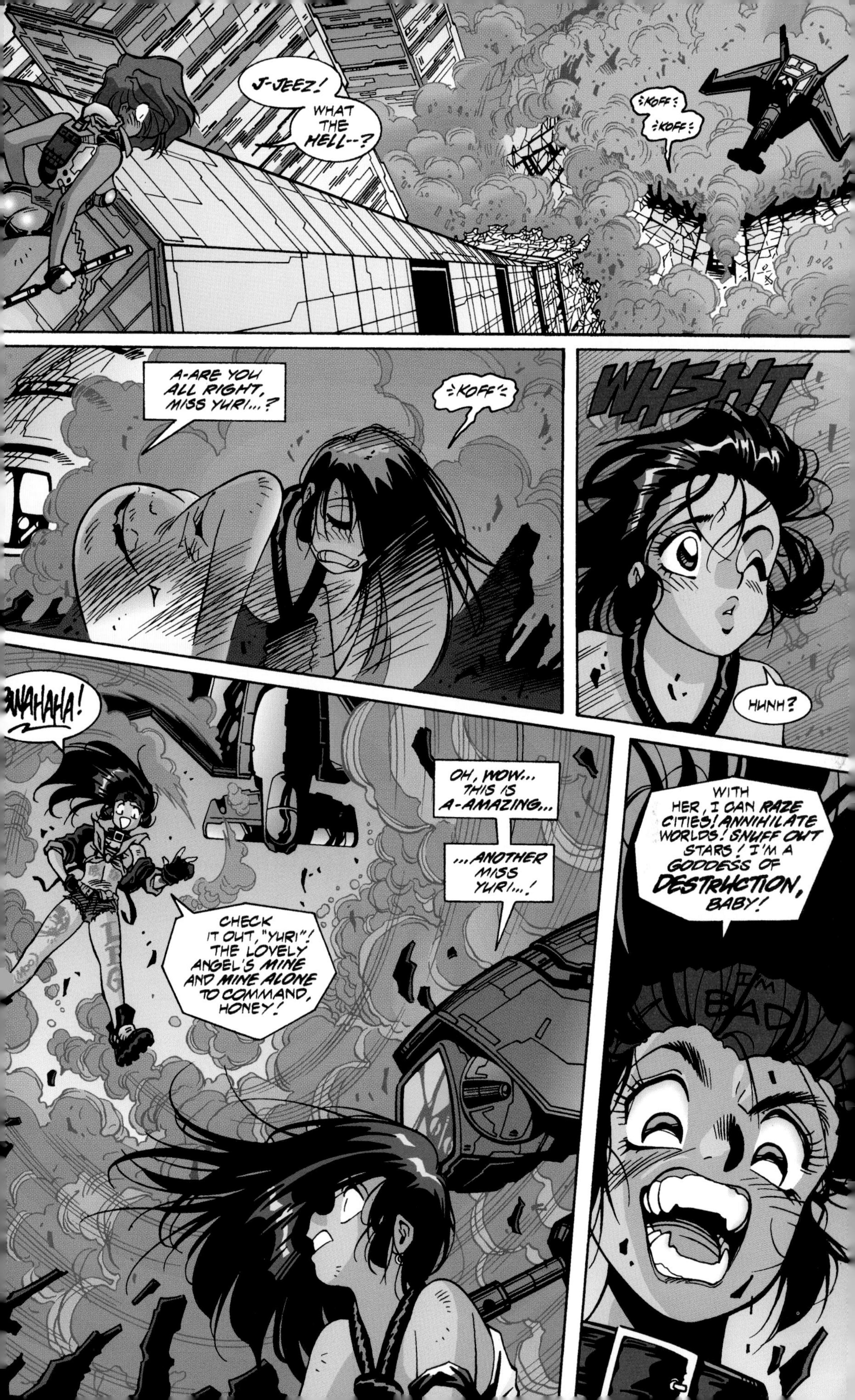
J-JEEZ!
WHAT THE HELL--?
KOFF
KOFF
A-ARE YOU ALL RIGHT, MISS YURI...?
KOFF
WHSHT
HUNH?
WAHAHA!
CHECK IT OUT, "YURI"! THE LOVELY ANGEL'S MINE AND MINE ALONE TO COMMAND, HONEY!
OH, WOW... THIS IS A-AMAZING...
...ANOTHER MISS YURI...!
WITH HER, I CAN RAZE CITIES! ANNIHILATE WORLDS! SNUFF OUT STARS! I'M A GODDESS OF DESTRUCTION, BABY!
I'M BAD

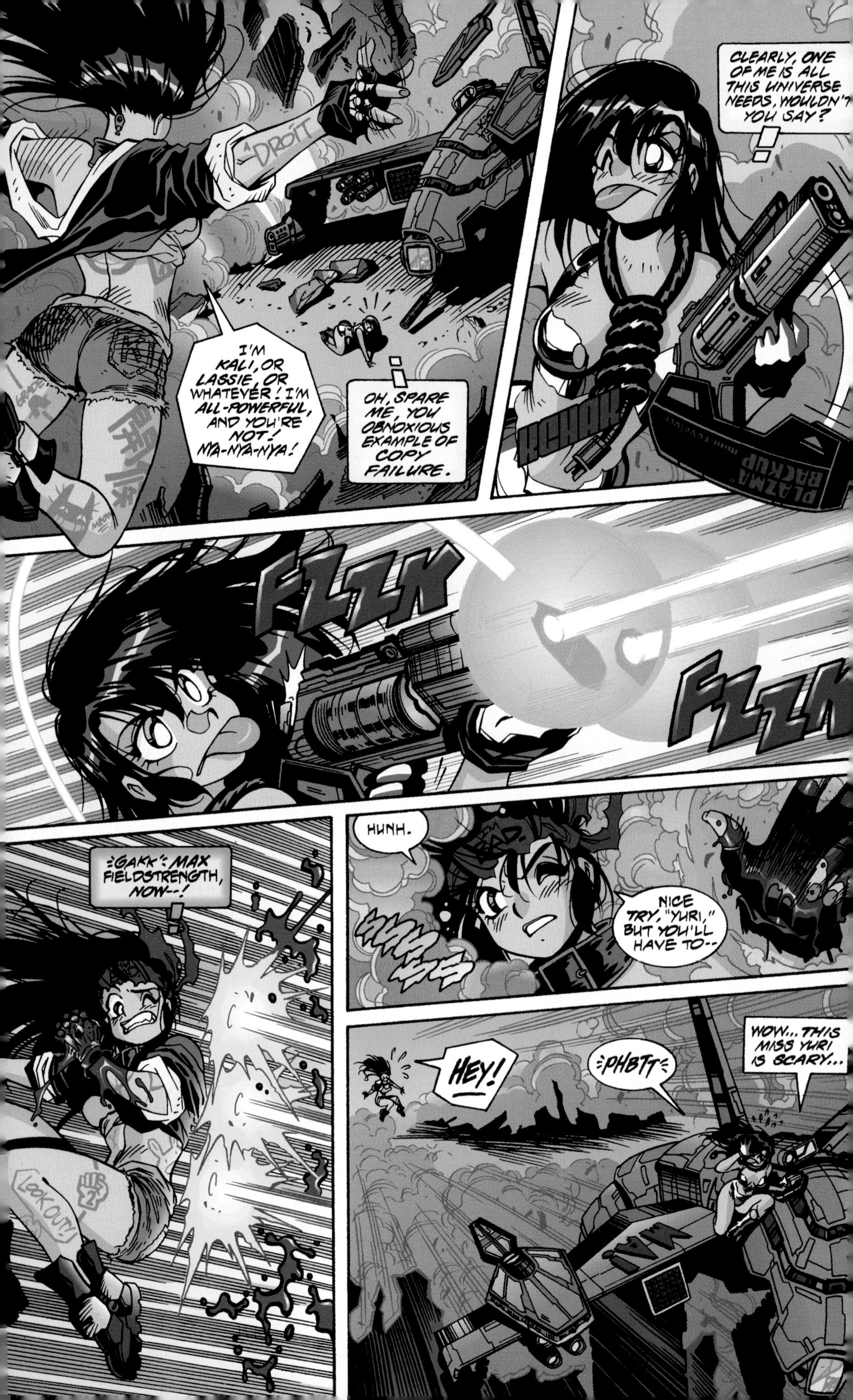
DROIT
I'M KALI, OR LASSIE, OR WHATEVER! I'M ALL-POWERFUL, AND YOU'RE NOT! NYA-NYA-NYA!
OH, SPARE ME, YOU OBNOXIOUS EXAMPLE OF COPY FAILURE.
CLEARLY, ONE OF ME IS ALL THIS UNIVERSE NEEDS, WOULDN'T YOU SAY?
!
KCHAK
PLAZMA BACKUP
FZZK
FZZK
:GAKK: MAX FIELDSTRENGTH, NOW--!
LOOK OUT!
HUNH.
NICE TRY, "YURI," BUT YOU'LL HAVE TO--
HEY!
PHBTT
WOW... THIS MISS YURI IS SCARY...

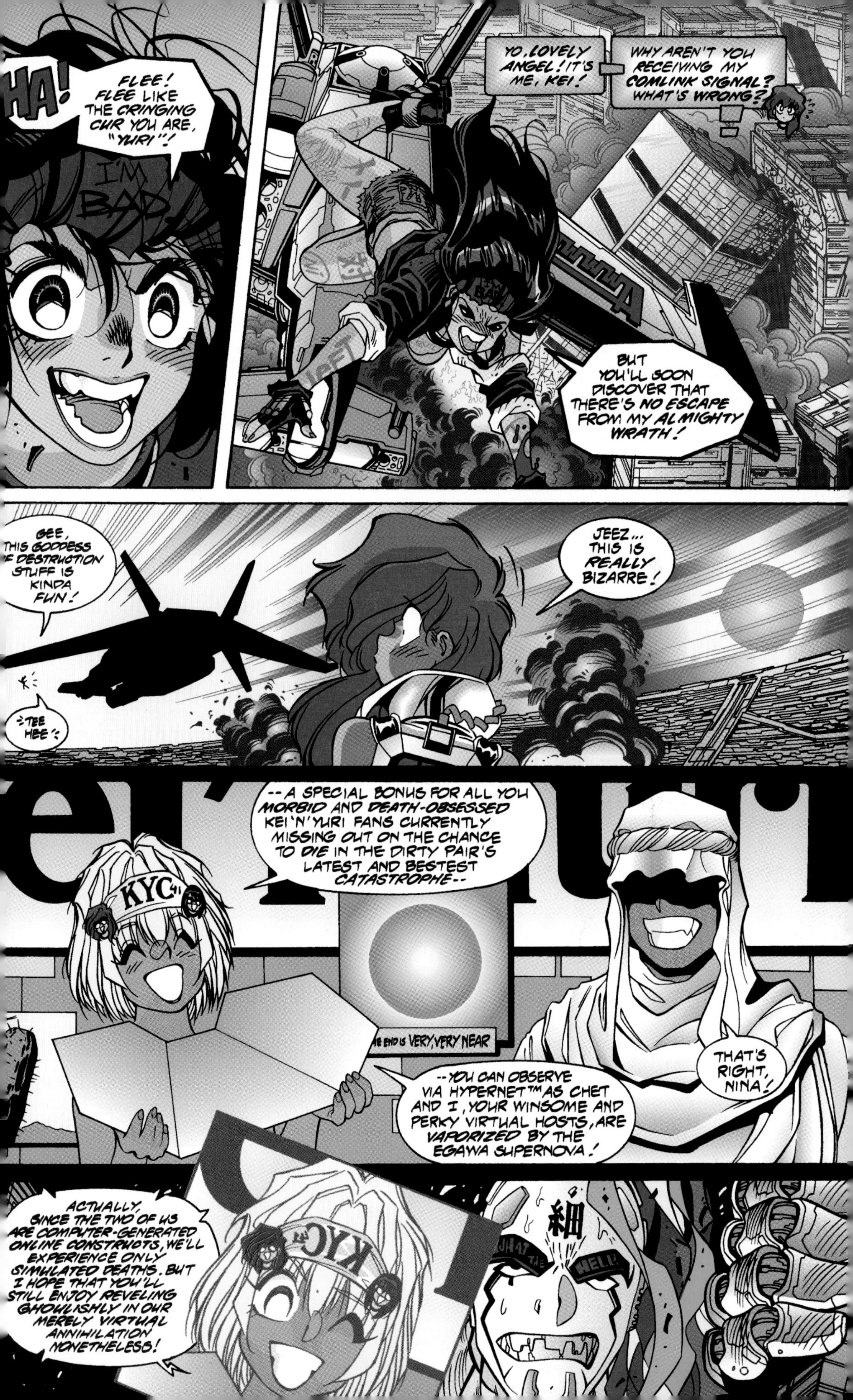
HA!
FLEE! FLEE LIKE THE CRINGING CUR YOU ARE, "YURI"!
I'M BAD
YO, LOVELY ANGEL! IT'S ME, KEI!
WHY AREN'T YOU RECEIVING MY COMLINK SIGNAL? WHAT'S WRONG?
BUT YOU'LL SOON DISCOVER THAT THERE'S NO ESCAPE FROM MY ALMIGHTY WRATH!
GEE, THIS GODDESS OF DESTRUCTION STUFF IS KINDA FUN!
TEE HEE
JEEZ... THIS IS REALLY BIZARRE!
-- A SPECIAL BONUS FOR ALL YOU MORBID AND DEATH-OBSESSED KEI'N'YURI FANS CURRENTLY MISSING OUT ON THE CHANCE TO DIE IN THE DIRTY PAIR'S LATEST AND BESTEST CATASTROPHE--
KYC
THE END IS VERY, VERY NEAR
--YOU CAN OBSERVE VIA HYPERNET™ AS CHET AND I, YOUR WINSOME AND PERKY VIRTUAL HOSTS, ARE VAPORIZED BY THE EGAWA SUPERNOVA!
THAT'S RIGHT, NINA!
ACTUALLY, SINCE THE TWO OF US ARE COMPUTER-GENERATED ONLINE CONSTRUCTS, WE'LL EXPERIENCE ONLY SIMULATED DEATHS. BUT I HOPE THAT YOU'LL STILL ENJOY REVELING GHOULISHLY IN OUR MERELY VIRTUAL ANNIHILATION NONETHELESS!
細
WHAT THE HELL

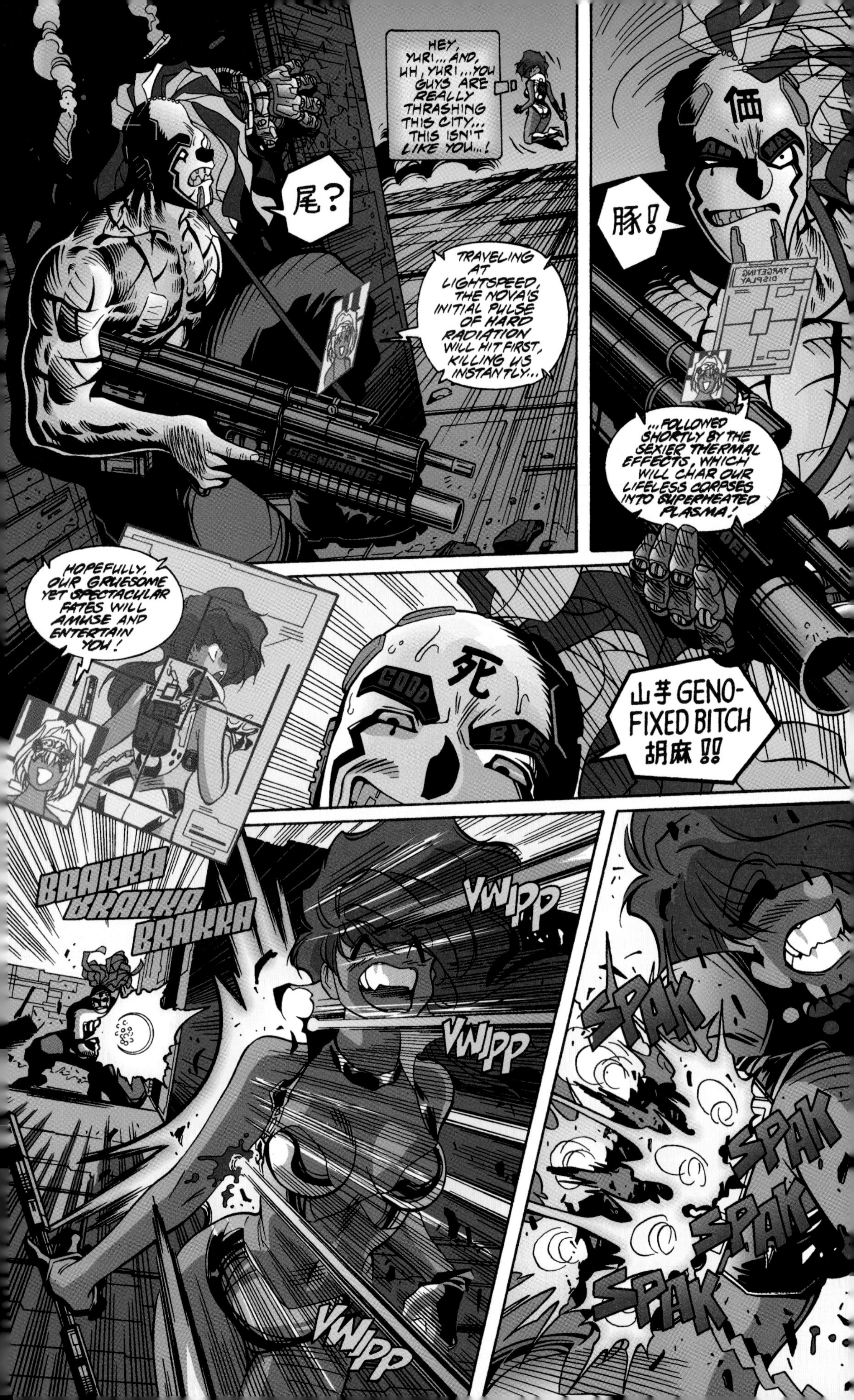
尾？
HEY, YURI... AND, UH, YURI... YOU GUYS ARE REALLY THRASHING THIS CITY... THIS ISN'T LIKE YOU...!
TRAVELING AT LIGHTSPEED, THE NOVA'S INITIAL PULSE OF HARD RADIATION WILL HIT FIRST, KILLING US INSTANTLY...
価
豚！
TARGETING DISPLAY
...FOLLOWED SHORTLY BY THE SEXIER THERMAL EFFECTS, WHICH WILL CHAR OUR LIFELESS CORPSES INTO SUPERHEATED PLASMA!
HOPEFULLY, OUR GRUESOME YET SPECTACULAR FATES WILL AMUSE AND ENTERTAIN YOU!
死
GOOD BYE
山芋 GENO-FIXED BITCH 胡麻!!
BRAKKA BRAKKA BRAKKA
VWIPP
VWIPP
VWIPP
SPAK
SPAK
SPAK
SPAK

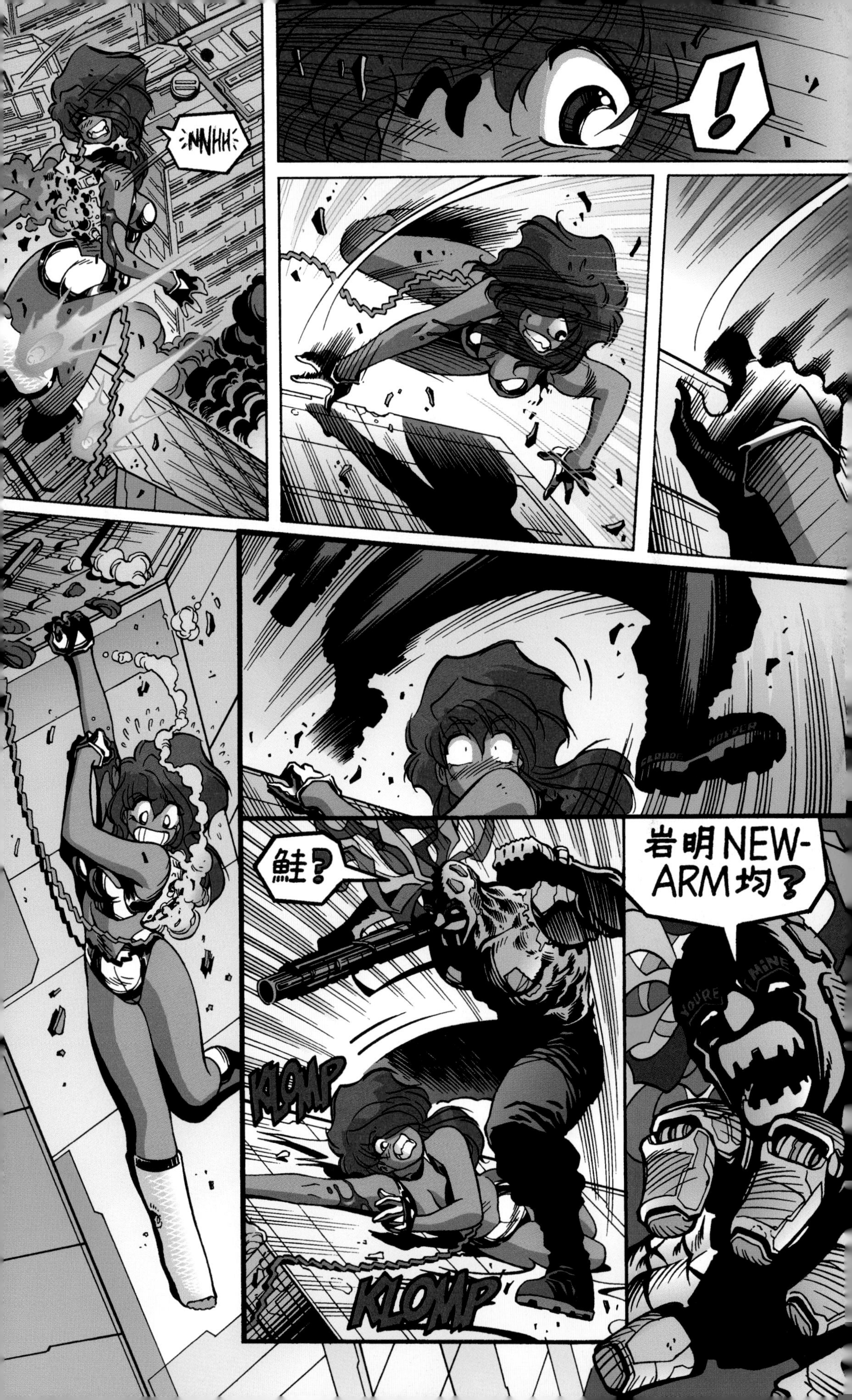
NNHH
!
鮭?
KLOMP
KLOMP
岩明NEW-ARM均?
YOU'RE MINE

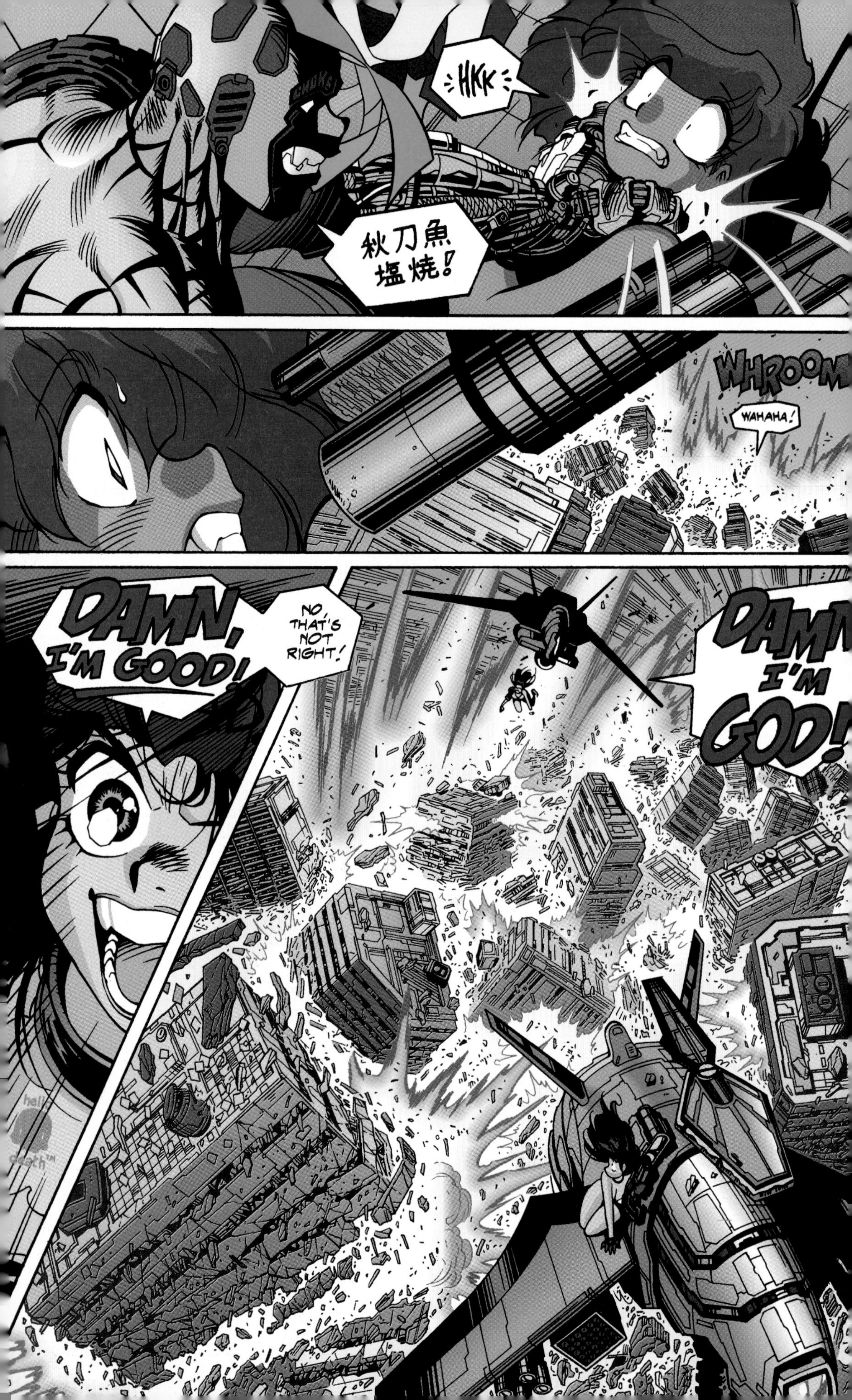
HKK
秋刀魚
塩焼!
WHROOM
WAHAHA!
DAMN, I'M GOOD!
NO THAT'S NOT RIGHT!
DAMN, I'M GOD!

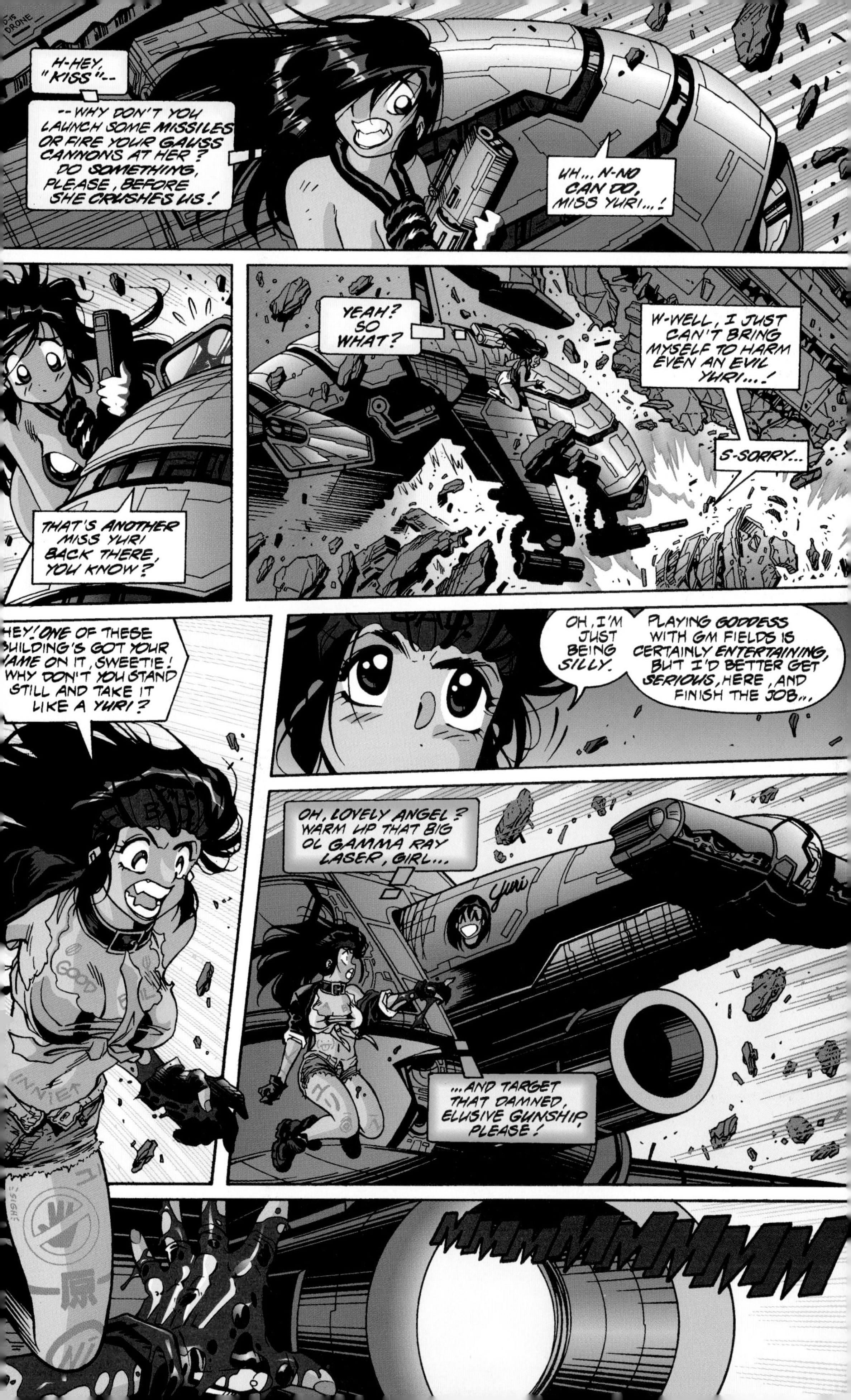

H-HEY, "KISS"--
--WHY DON'T YOU LAUNCH SOME MISSILES OR FIRE YOUR GAUSS CANNONS AT HER? DO SOMETHING, PLEASE, BEFORE SHE CRUSHES US!
UH... N-NO CAN DO, MISS YURI...!
THAT'S ANOTHER MISS YURI BACK THERE, YOU KNOW?
YEAH? SO WHAT?
W-WELL, I JUST CAN'T BRING MYSELF TO HARM EVEN AN EVIL YURI...!
S-SORRY...
HEY! ONE OF THESE BUILDING'S GOT YOUR NAME ON IT, SWEETIE! WHY DON'T YOU STAND STILL AND TAKE IT LIKE A YURI?
OH, I'M JUST BEING SILLY.
PLAYING GODDESS WITH GM FIELDS IS CERTAINLY ENTERTAINING, BUT I'D BETTER GET SERIOUS, HERE, AND FINISH THE JOB...
OH, LOVELY ANGEL? WARM UP THAT BIG OL GAMMA RAY LASER, GIRL...
Yuri
...AND TARGET THAT DAMNED, ELUSIVE GUNSHIP, PLEASE!
MMMMMMMMMMM

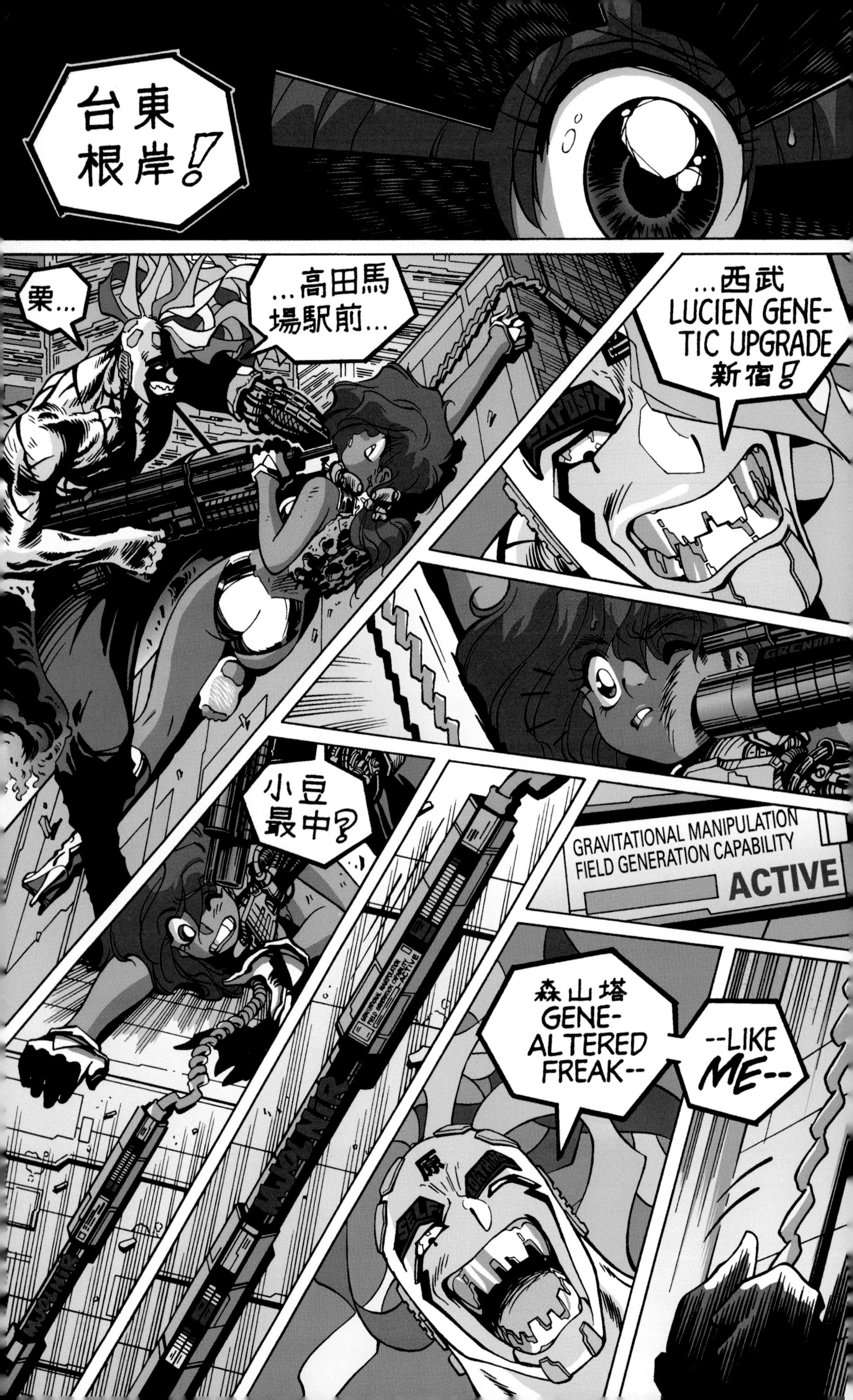
台東
根岸!
栗...
...高田馬
場駅前...
...西武
LUCIEN GENE-
TIC UPGRADE
新宿!
小豆
最中?
GRAVITATIONAL MANIPULATION
FIELD GENERATION CAPABILITY
ACTIVE
森山塔
GENE-
ALTERED
FREAK--
--LIKE
ME--

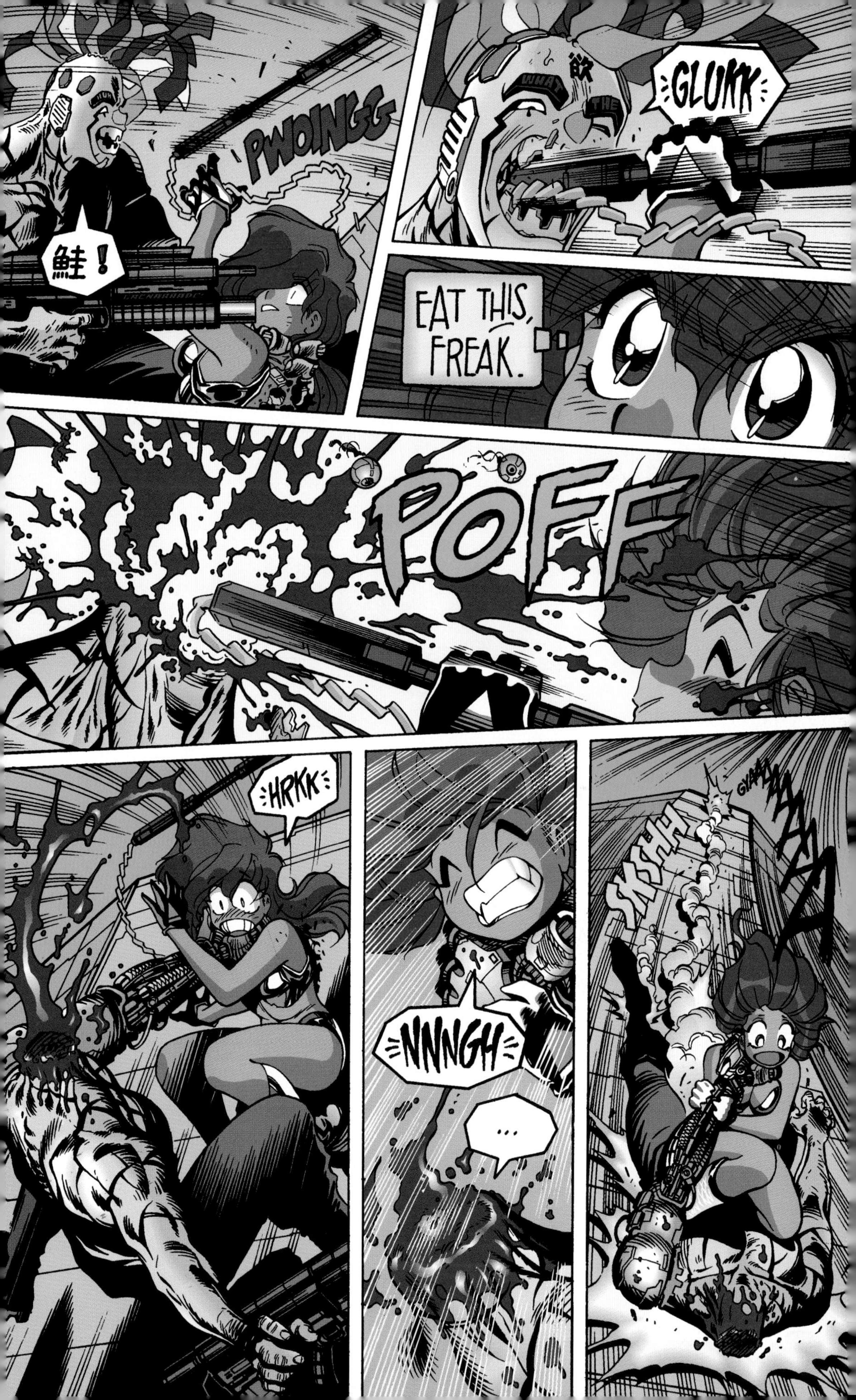
PWOINGG
鮭！
WHAT THE
GLUKK
EAT THIS, FREAK.
POFF
HRKK
NNNGH
...
SKSHH
GYAAA

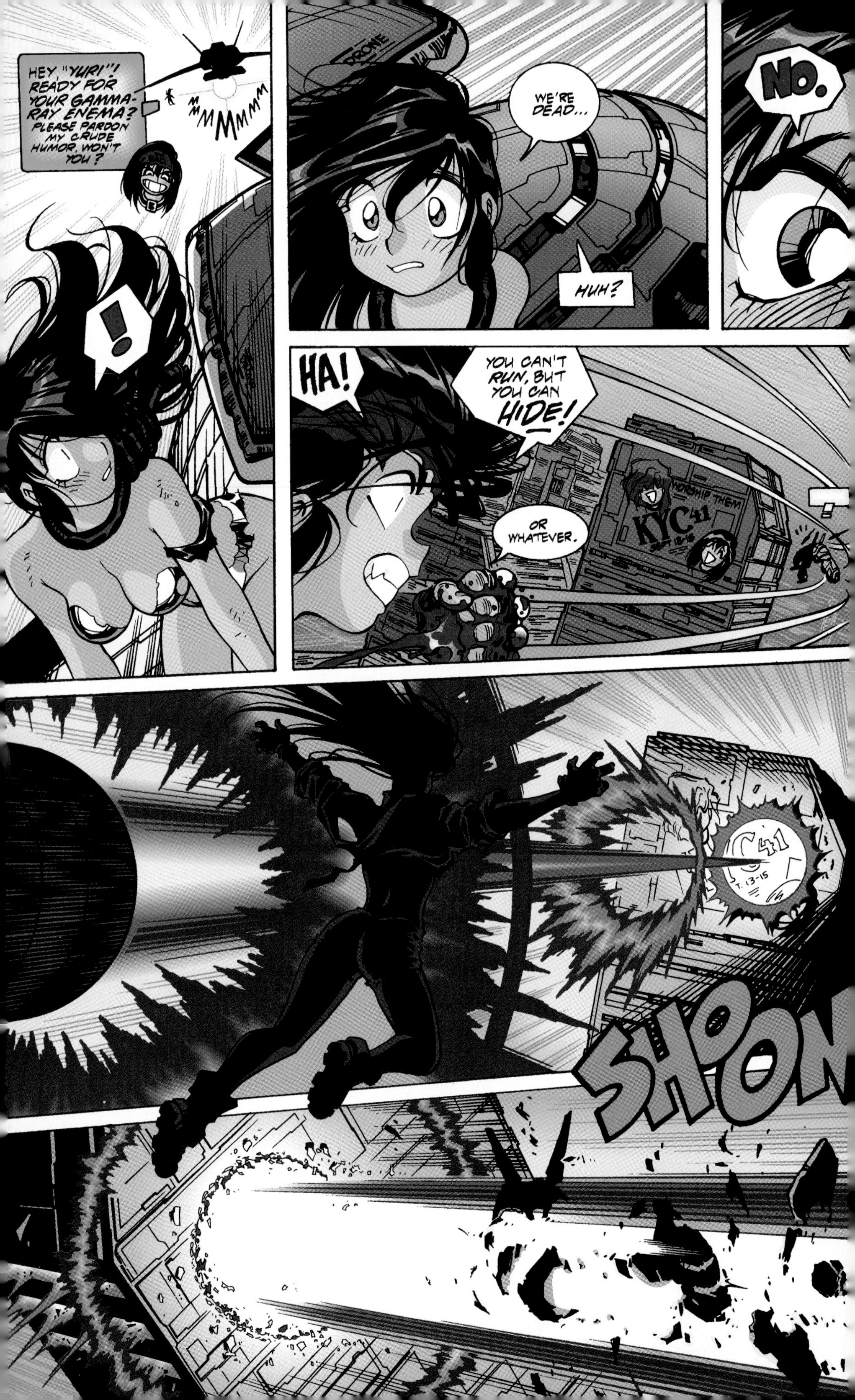

HEY, "YURI"! READY FOR YOUR GAMMA-RAY ENEMA? PLEASE PARDON MY CRUDE HUMOR, WON'T YOU?
MMMMMMMM
!
DRONE
WE'RE DEAD...
HUH?
NO.
HA!
YOU CAN'T RUN, BUT YOU CAN HIDE!
WORSHIP THEM
KYC 41
OR WHATEVER.
C 41
SHOOM

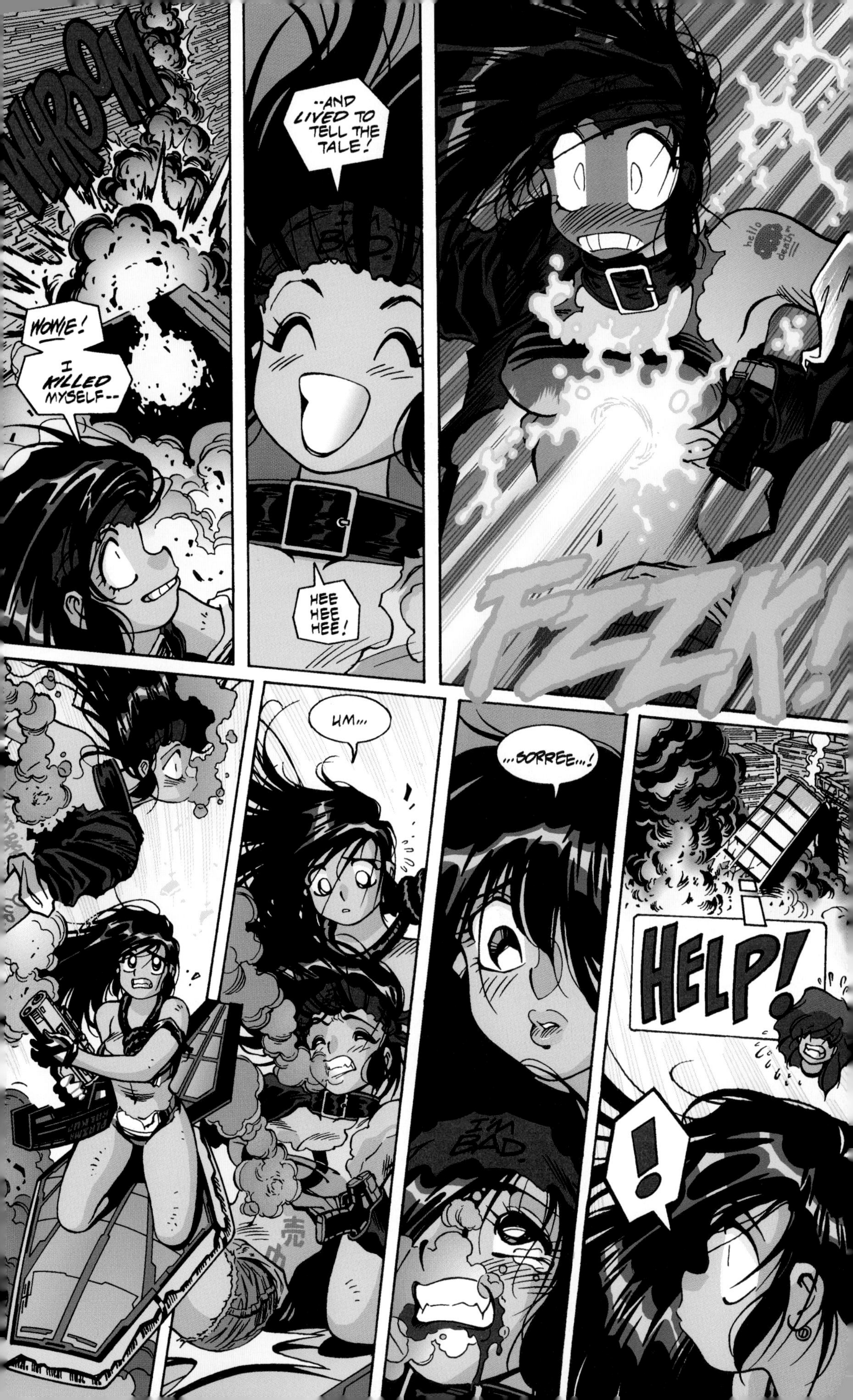
WHROOM!
WOWIE!
I KILLED MYSELF--
--AND LIVED TO TELL THE TALE!
I'M BAD
HEE HEE HEE!
hello death
FZZK!
UM...
...SORREE...!
I'M BAD
HELP!
!

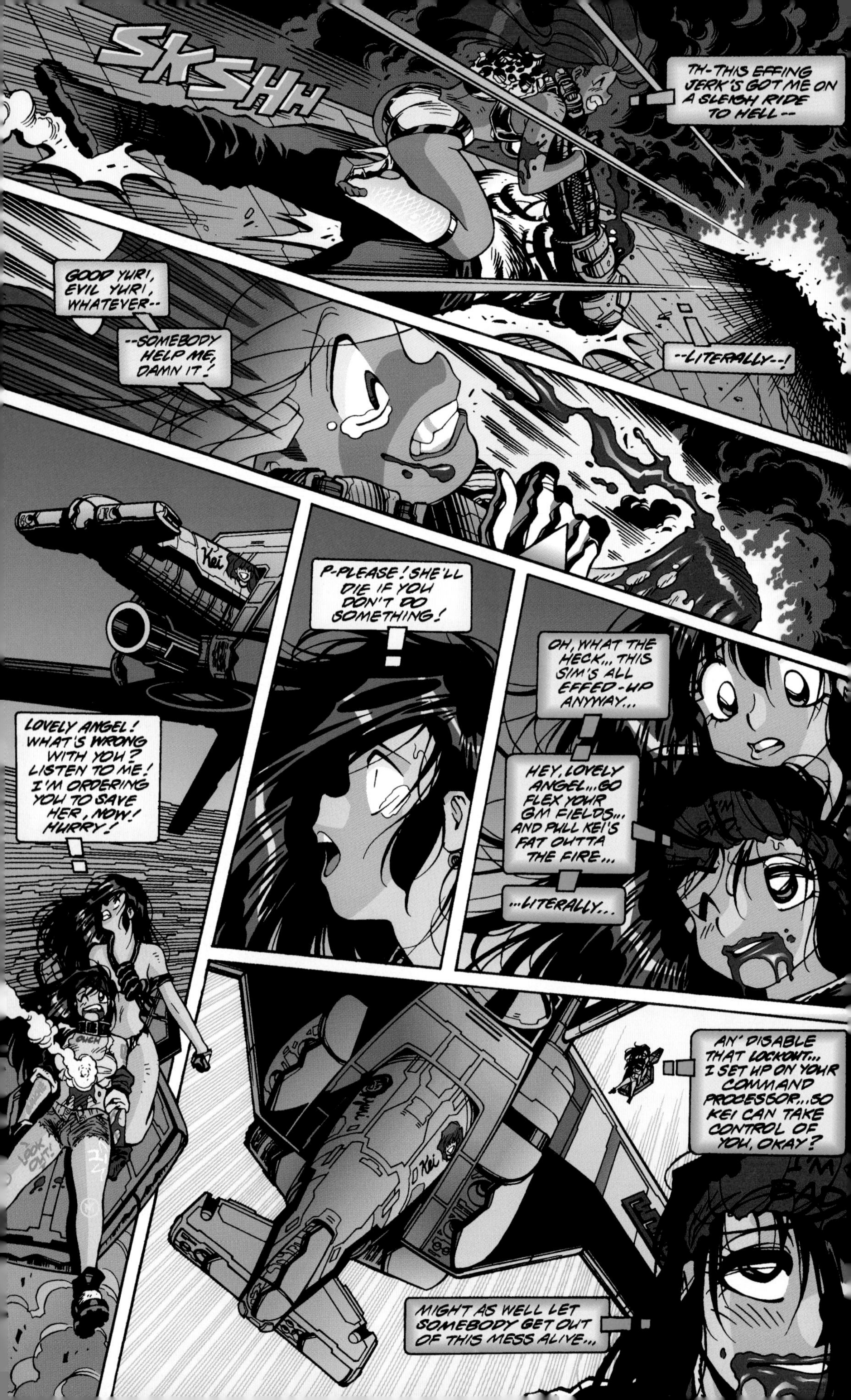
SKSHH
TH-THIS EFFING JERK'S GOT ME ON A SLEIGH RIDE TO HELL--
GOOD YURI, EVIL YURI, WHATEVER--
--SOMEBODY HELP ME, DAMN IT!
--LITERALLY--!
LOVELY ANGEL! WHAT'S WRONG WITH YOU? LISTEN TO ME! I'M ORDERING YOU TO SAVE HER, NOW! HURRY!
P-PLEASE! SHE'LL DIE IF YOU DON'T DO SOMETHING!
OH, WHAT THE HECK... THIS SIM'S ALL EFFED-UP ANYWAY...
HEY, LOVELY ANGEL... GO FLEX YOUR GM FIELDS... AND PULL KEI'S FAT OUTTA THE FIRE...
...LITERALLY...
AN' DISABLE THAT LOCKOUT... I SET UP ON YOUR COMMAND PROCESSOR... SO KEI CAN TAKE CONTROL OF YOU, OKAY?
MIGHT AS WELL LET SOMEBODY GET OUT OF THIS MESS ALIVE...

NOOO!

SHRAKK

OWAAAA!

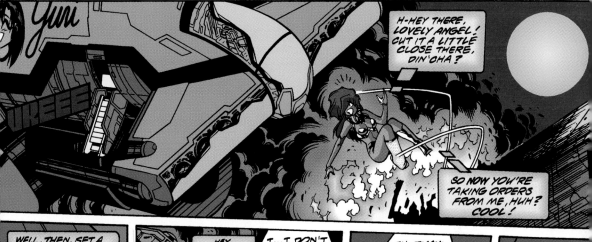

H-HEY THERE, LOVELY ANGEL! CUT IT A LITTLE CLOSE THERE, DIN'OHA?

SO NOW YOU'RE TAKING ORDERS FROM ME, HUH? COOL!

WELL, THEN, SET A SUPERFAST COURSE OUT OF THIS HELLHOLE'S GRAVITY WELL AND PREP YOUR WARP DRIVE FOR EMERGENCY WARP-SPACE INSERTION BEFORE THE DAMN SUN EXPLODES, ALL RIGHT?

HEY, WHERE'D THE YURI TWINS GO?

I...I DON'T BELIEVE IT...

...YOU SAVED HER, AFTER ALL!

TH-THANK YOU...
..."YURI".

YOU'RE WELCOME, "YURI".

SAFETY OFF.

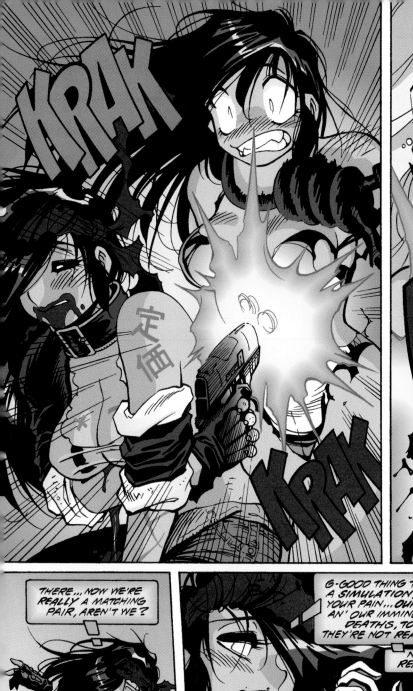

KRAK

KRAK

KRAK

THERE... NOW WE'RE REALLY A MATCHING PAIR, AREN'T WE?

:GUCHKK:

G-GOOD THING THIS IS A SIMULATION, HUH? YOUR PAIN... OUR PAIN... AN' OUR IMMINENT DEATHS, TOO... THEY'RE NOT REAL, SEE...?

NOT REAL...

:HKK:

WHAT? THEY'RE DYING?

NO!

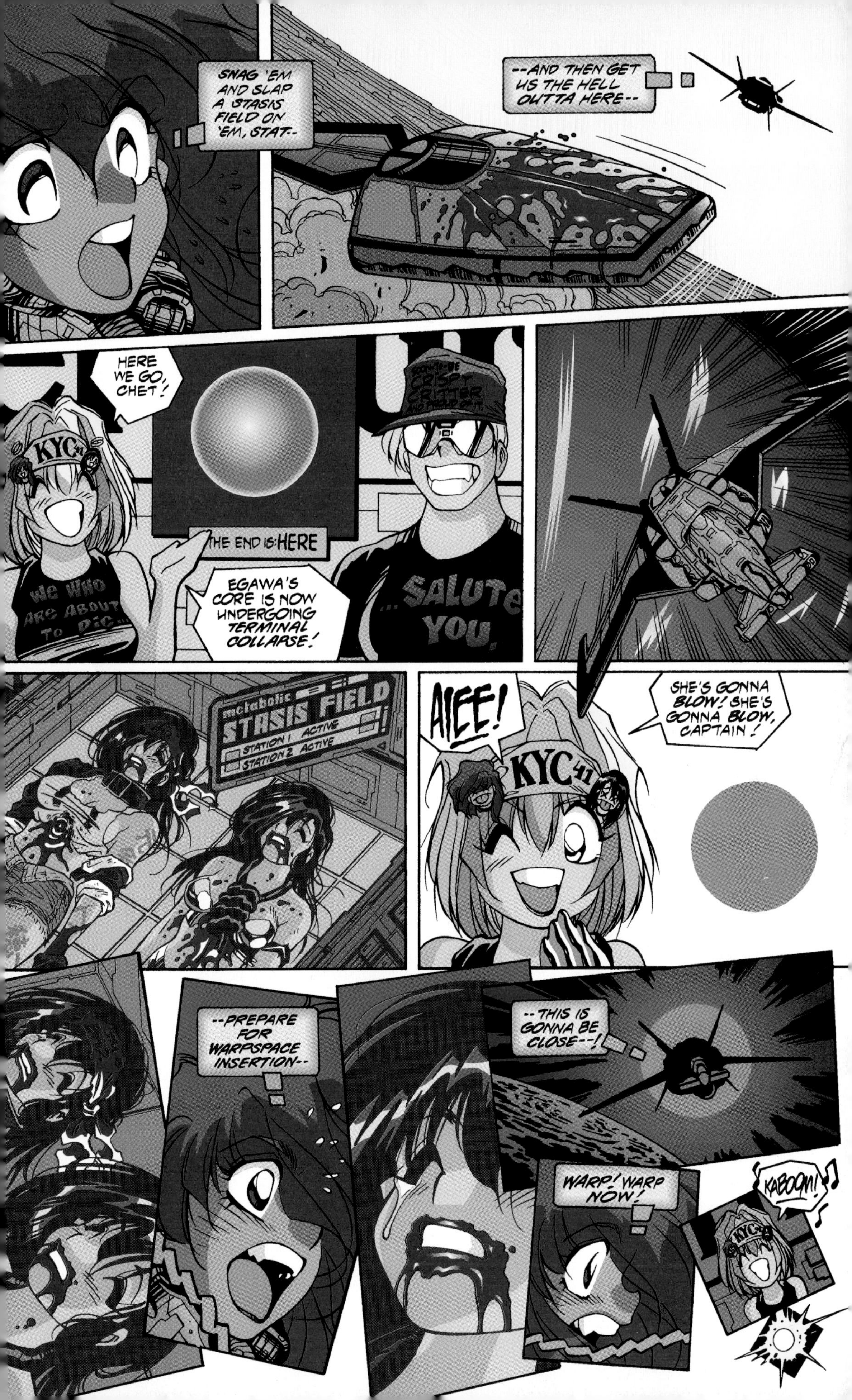
SNAG 'EM AND SLAP A STASIS FIELD ON 'EM, STAT-
--AND THEN GET US THE HELL OUTTA HERE--
HERE WE GO, CHET!
KYC 41
SOON-TO-BE CRISPY CRITTER AND PROUD OF IT
THE END IS: HERE
We WHO ARE ABOUT TO DIE...
EGAWA'S CORE IS NOW UNDERGOING TERMINAL COLLAPSE!
...SALUTE YOU.
metabolic STASIS FIELD
STATION 1 ACTIVE
STATION 2 ACTIVE
AIEE!
KYC 41
SHE'S GONNA BLOW! SHE'S GONNA BLOW, CAPTAIN!
--PREPARE FOR WARPSPACE INSERTION--
--THIS IS GONNA BE CLOSE--!
WARP! WARP NOW!
KABOOM!

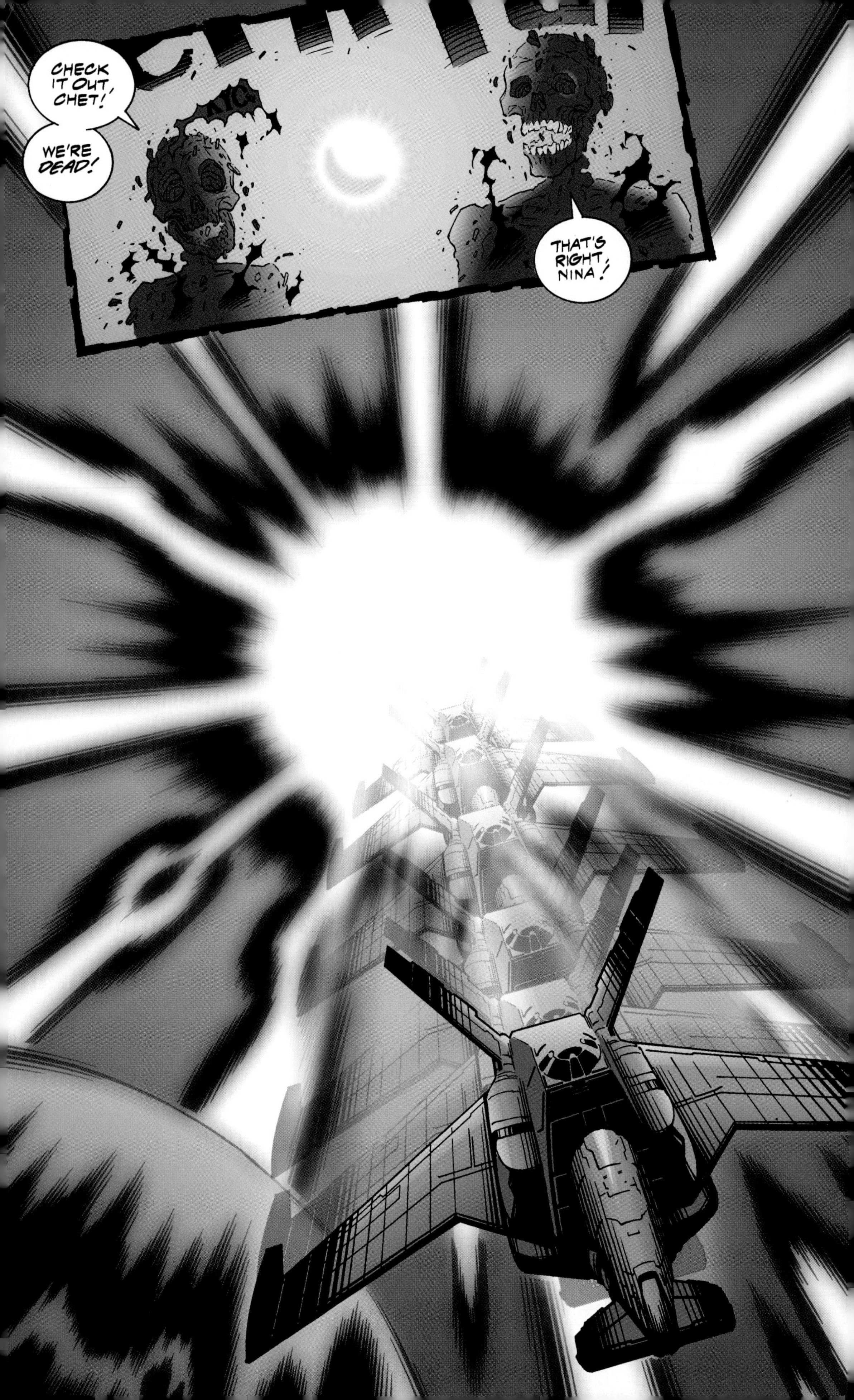
CHECK IT OUT, CHET!
WE'RE DEAD!
THAT'S RIGHT, NINA!

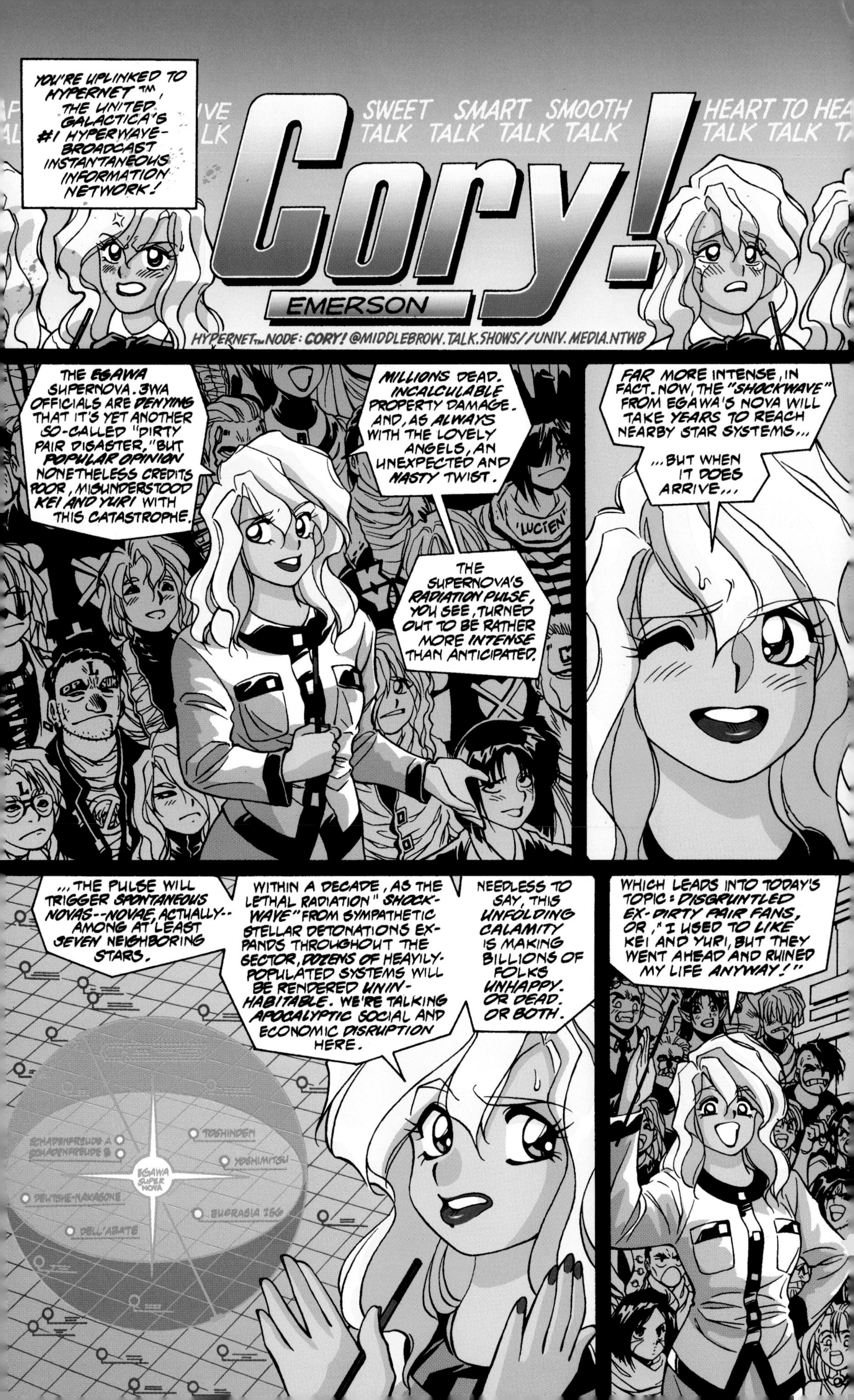
YOU'RE UPLINKED TO HYPERNET™, THE UNITED GALACTICA'S #1 HYPERWAVE-BROADCAST INSTANTANEOUS INFORMATION NETWORK!
SWEET TALK
SMART TALK
SMOOTH TALK
TALK
Cory!
EMERSON
HYPERNET™ NODE: CORY! @MIDDLEBROW.TALK.SHOWS//UNIV.MEDIA.NTWB
THE EGAWA SUPERNOVA. 3WA OFFICIALS ARE DENYING THAT IT'S YET ANOTHER SO-CALLED "DIRTY PAIR DISASTER," BUT POPULAR OPINION NONETHELESS CREDITS POOR, MISUNDERSTOOD KEI AND YURI WITH THIS CATASTROPHE.
MILLIONS DEAD. INCALCULABLE PROPERTY DAMAGE. AND, AS ALWAYS WITH THE LOVELY ANGELS, AN UNEXPECTED AND NASTY TWIST.
"LUCIEN"
THE SUPERNOVA'S RADIATION PULSE, YOU SEE, TURNED OUT TO BE RATHER MORE INTENSE THAN ANTICIPATED.
FAR MORE INTENSE, IN FACT. NOW, THE "SHOCKWAVE" FROM EGAWA'S NOVA WILL TAKE YEARS TO REACH NEARBY STAR SYSTEMS...
...BUT WHEN IT DOES ARRIVE...
...THE PULSE WILL TRIGGER SPONTANEOUS NOVAS--NOVAE, ACTUALLY--AMONG AT LEAST SEVEN NEIGHBORING STARS.
TOSHINDEN
YOSHIMITSU
EGAWA SUPER NOVA
DELL'ABATE
WITHIN A DECADE, AS THE LETHAL RADIATION "SHOCK-WAVE" FROM SYMPATHETIC STELLAR DETONATIONS EX-PANDS THROUGHOUT THE SECTOR, DOZENS OF HEAVILY-POPULATED SYSTEMS WILL BE RENDERED UNIN-HABITABLE. WE'RE TALKING APOCALYPTIC SOCIAL AND ECONOMIC DISRUPTION HERE.
NEEDLESS TO SAY, THIS UNFOLDING CALAMITY IS MAKING BILLIONS OF FOLKS UNHAPPY. OR DEAD. OR BOTH.
WHICH LEADS INTO TODAY'S TOPIC: DISGRUNTLED EX-DIRTY PAIR FANS, OR, "I USED TO LIKE KEI AND YURI, BUT THEY WENT AHEAD AND RUINED MY LIFE ANYWAY!"

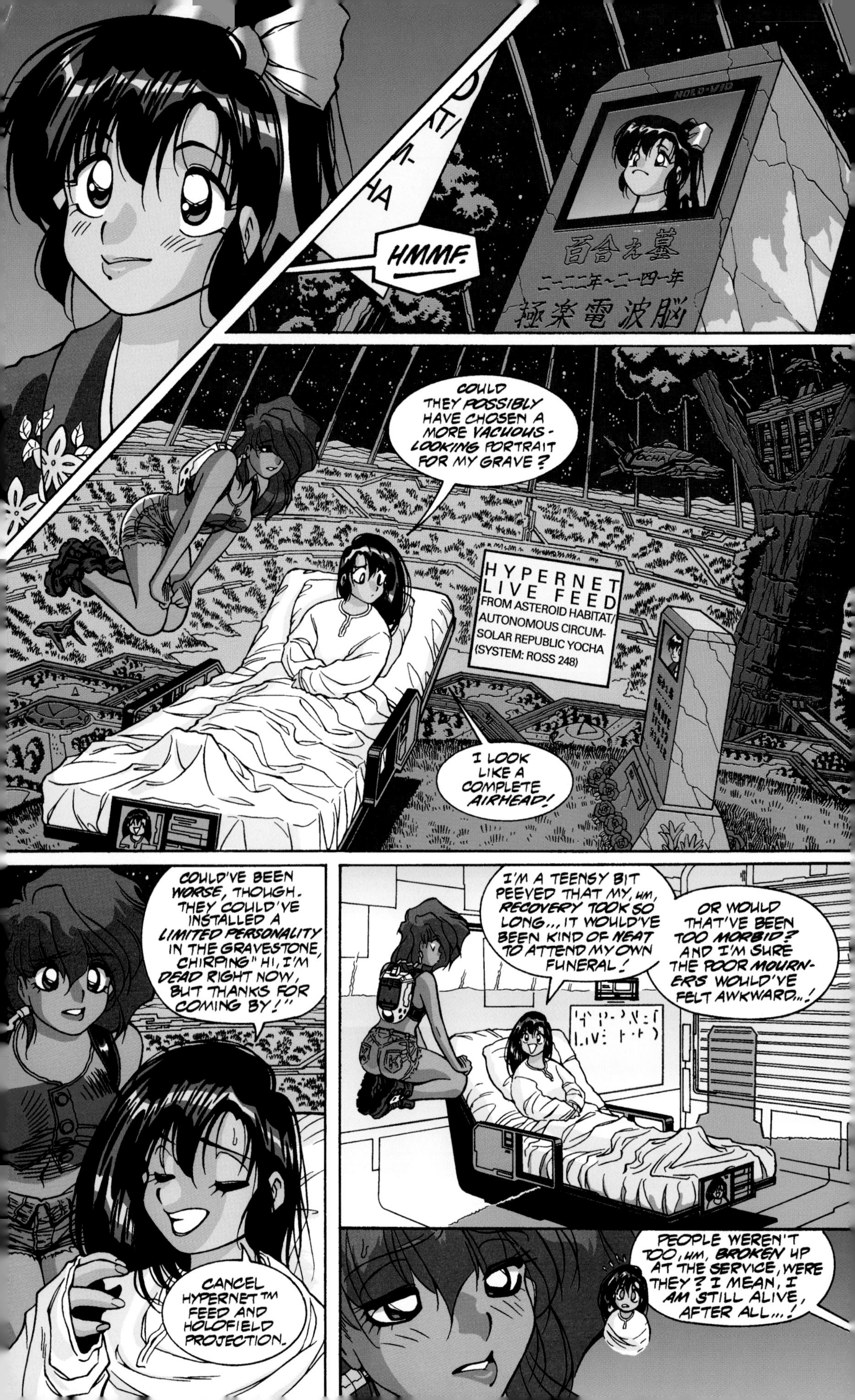
HMMF.
百合え墓
二一二二年～二一四一年
極楽電波脳
COULD THEY POSSIBLY HAVE CHOSEN A MORE VACUOUS-LOOKING PORTRAIT FOR MY GRAVE?
HYPERNET LIVE FEED FROM ASTEROID HABITAT/ AUTONOMOUS CIRCUM-SOLAR REPUBLIC YOCHA (SYSTEM: ROSS 248)
I LOOK LIKE A COMPLETE AIRHEAD!
COULD'VE BEEN WORSE, THOUGH. THEY COULD'VE INSTALLED A LIMITED PERSONALITY IN THE GRAVESTONE, CHIRPING "HI, I'M DEAD RIGHT NOW, BUT THANKS FOR COMING BY!"
CANCEL HYPERNET™ FEED AND HOLOFIELD PROJECTION.
I'M A TEENSY BIT PEEVED THAT MY, UM, RECOVERY TOOK SO LONG... IT WOULD'VE BEEN KIND OF NEAT TO ATTEND MY OWN FUNERAL!
OR WOULD THAT'VE BEEN TOO MORBID? AND I'M SURE THE POOR MOURNERS WOULD'VE FELT AWKWARD...!
PEOPLE WEREN'T TOO, UM, BROKEN UP AT THE SERVICE, WERE THEY? I MEAN, I AM STILL ALIVE, AFTER ALL...!

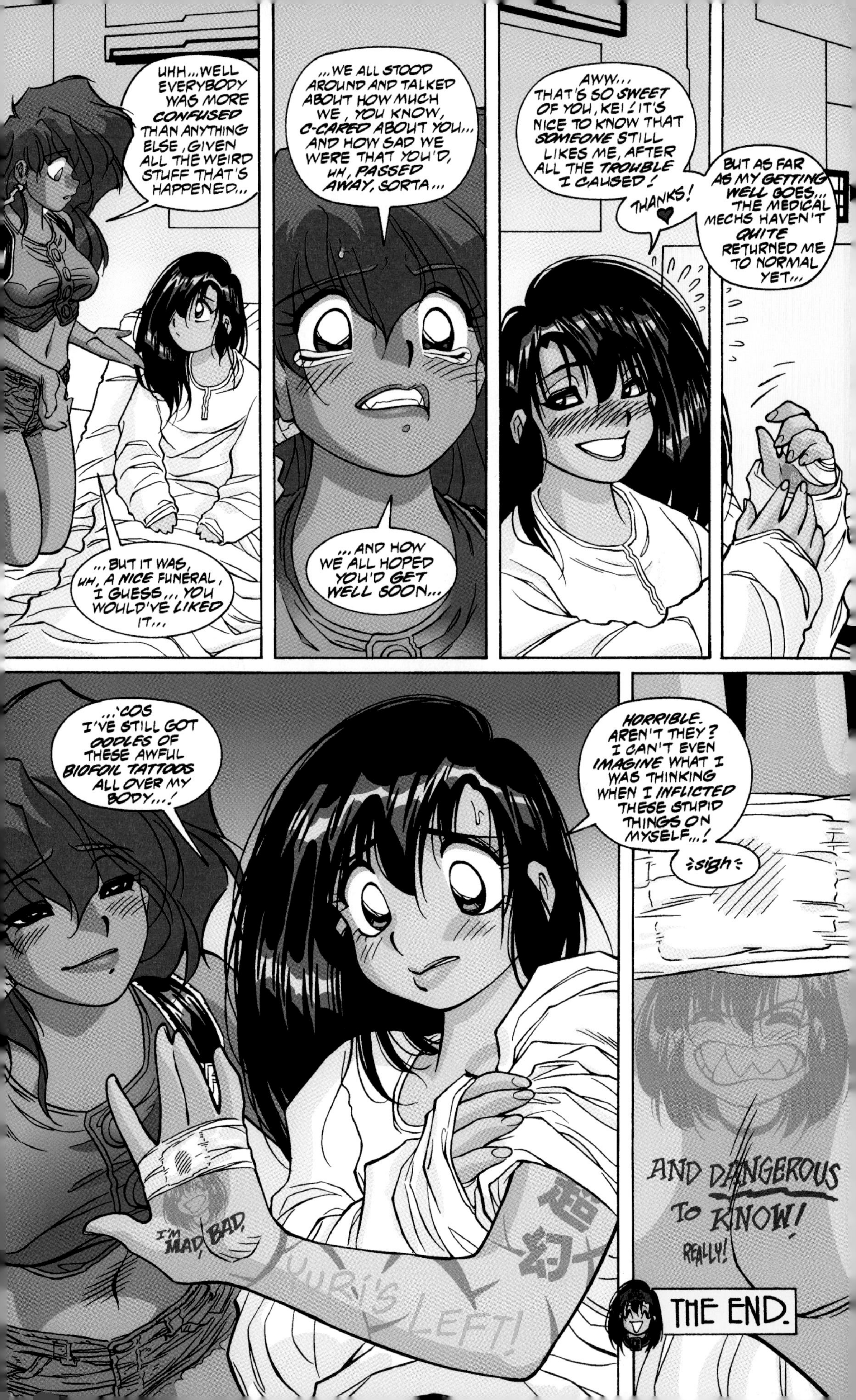
UHH...WELL EVERYBODY WAS MORE CONFUSED THAN ANYTHING ELSE, GIVEN ALL THE WEIRD STUFF THAT'S HAPPENED...
...BUT IT WAS, UH, A NICE FUNERAL, I GUESS... YOU WOULD'VE LIKED IT...
...WE ALL STOOD AROUND AND TALKED ABOUT HOW MUCH WE, YOU KNOW, C-CARED ABOUT YOU... AND HOW SAD WE WERE THAT YOU'D, UH, PASSED AWAY, SORTA...
...AND HOW WE ALL HOPED YOU'D GET WELL SOON...
AWW... THAT'S SO SWEET OF YOU, KEI! IT'S NICE TO KNOW THAT SOMEONE STILL LIKES ME, AFTER ALL THE TROUBLE I CAUSED!
THANKS!
BUT AS FAR AS MY GETTING WELL GOES... THE MEDICAL MECHS HAVEN'T QUITE RETURNED ME TO NORMAL YET...
...'COS I'VE STILL GOT OODLES OF THESE AWFUL BIOFOIL TATTOOS ALL OVER MY BODY...!
I'M MAD, BAD,
YUURI'S LEFT!
HORRIBLE. AREN'T THEY? I CAN'T EVEN IMAGINE WHAT I WAS THINKING WHEN I INFLICTED THESE STUPID THINGS ON MYSELF...!
sigh
AND DANGEROUS TO KNOW!
REALLY!
THE END.

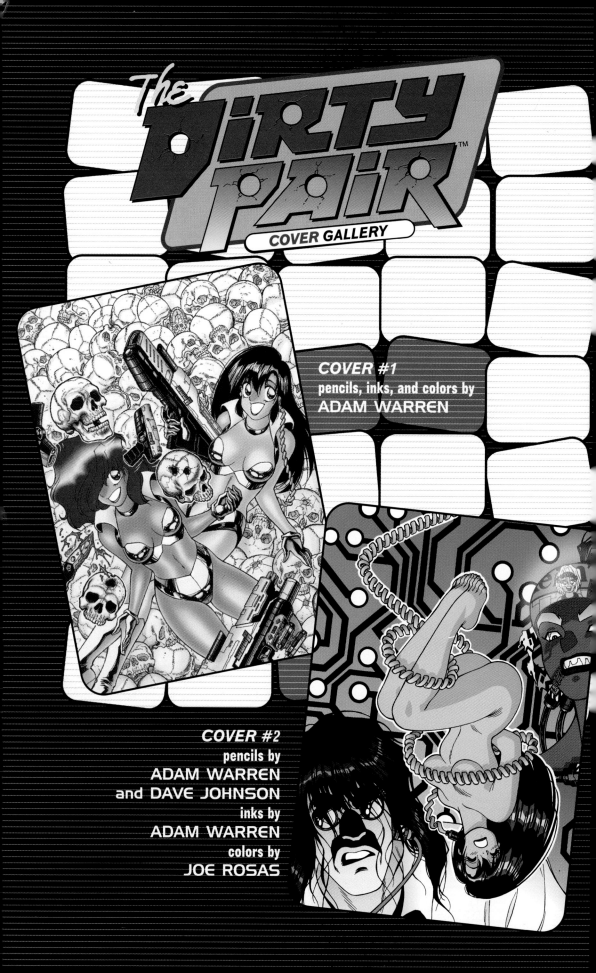

The Dirty Pair™
COVER GALLERY

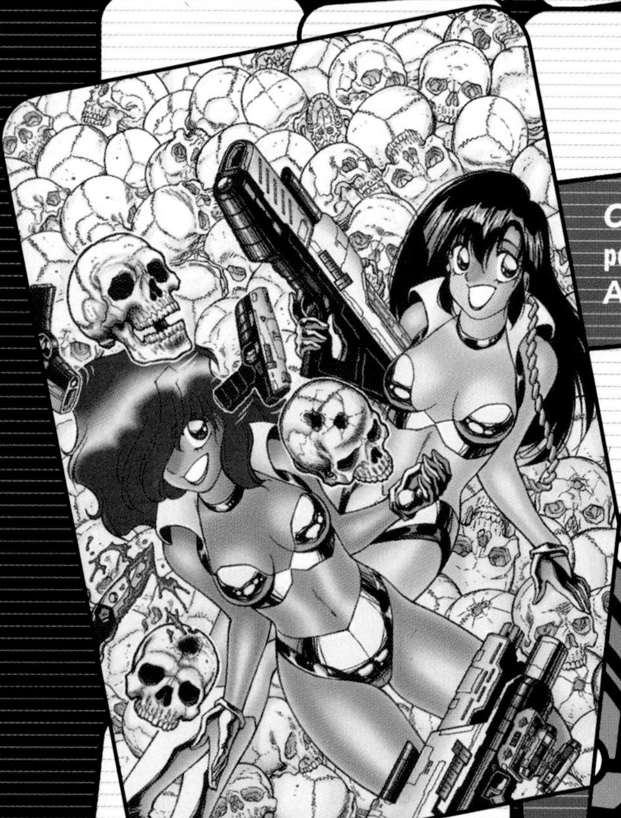

COVER #1
pencils, inks, and colors by
ADAM WARREN

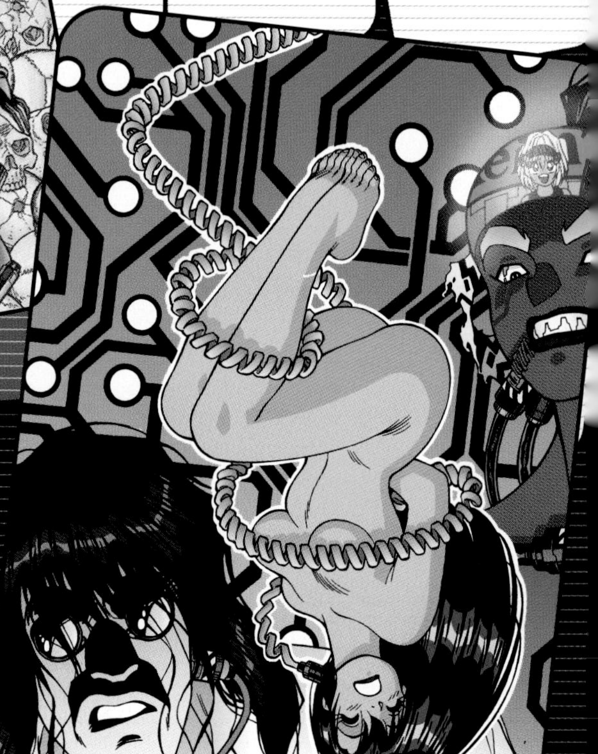

COVER #2
pencils by
ADAM WARREN
and DAVE JOHNSON
inks by
ADAM WARREN
colors by
JOE ROSAS

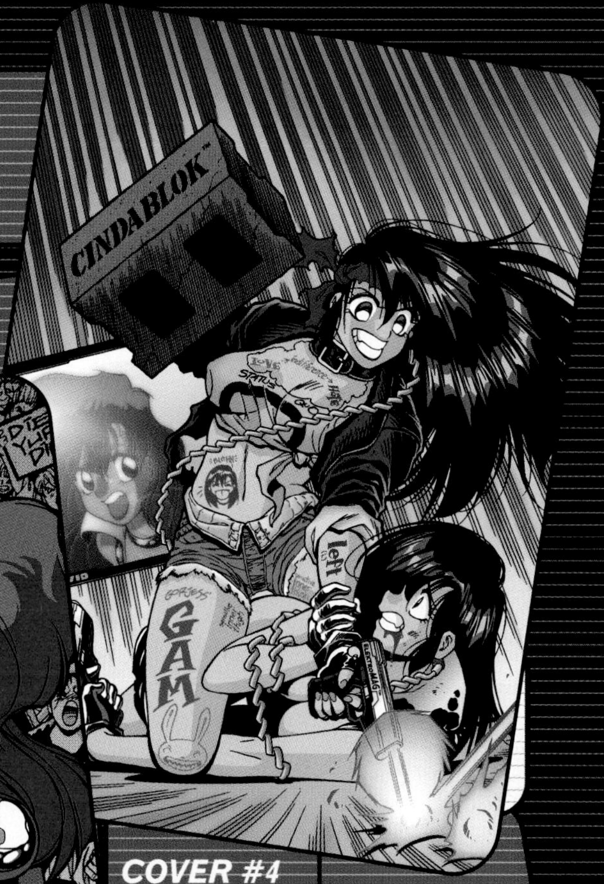
CINDABLOK
left
GAM

COVER #4
pencils, inks, and colors by
ADAM WARREN

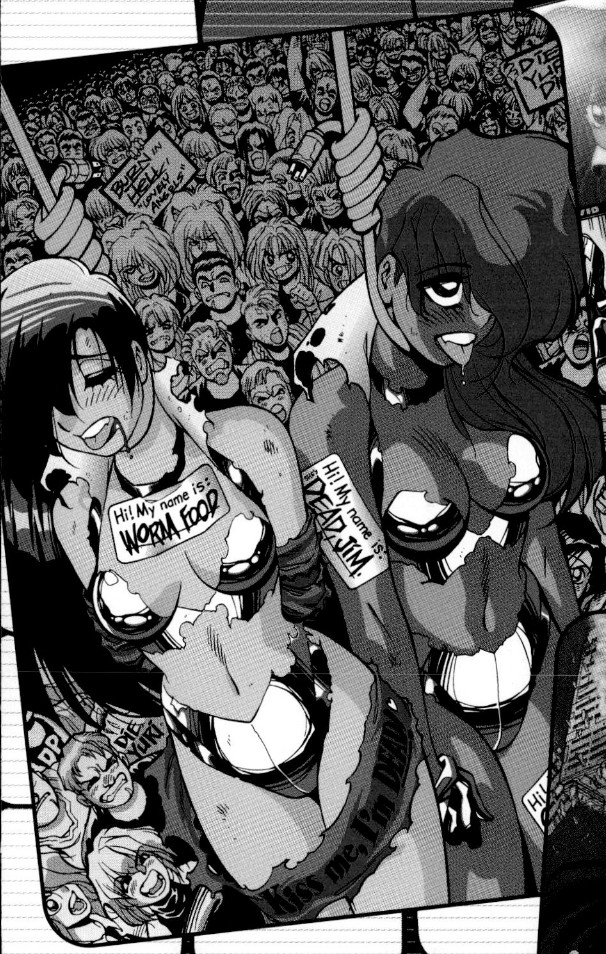
Hi! My name is: WORMA FOOD
Hi! My name is: DEAD JIM
Kiss me, I'm DEAD

COVER #3
pencils and inks by
ADAM WARREN
colors by
JOE ROSAS

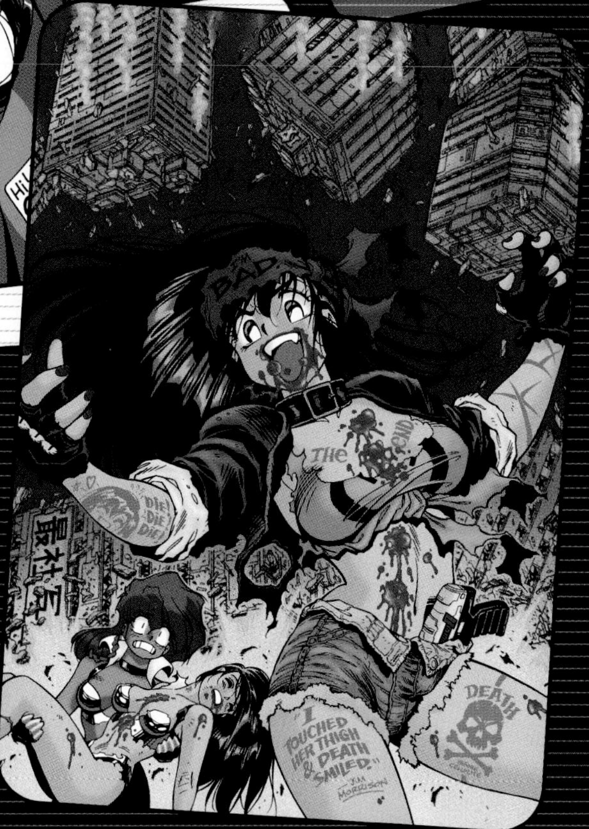
THE
DIE! DIE! DIE!
DEATH
"I TOUCHED HER THIGH & DEATH SMILED."
—JIM MORRISON

COVER #5
pencils and inks by
ADAM WARREN
colors by
JOE ROSAS

CALLING ALL KYOTAKU!*

A celebration of the 3WA's controversial "Lovely Angels" (a.k.a. "Dirty Pair")

KEI 'N' YURICON '41

is delighted to welcome this year's stunning, incredible,
you'll-think-you're-dreaming GUESTS OF SUPREME HONOR:

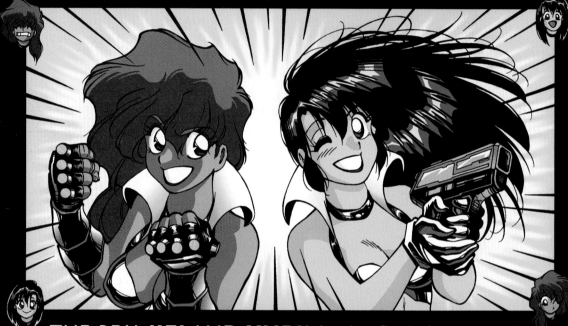

THE *REAL* **KEI** AND **YURI**! *In the flesh* (and how!)

SEPTEMBER 13-15, 2141

Krafft-Ebing Hotel and Convention Center
city Sparagmos, world New Eysenck, system Egawa
Hypernet™ node: Krafft-Ebing.Sparagmos@boring.corporate.zone.B82556

CONVENTION FEATURES

*KYConnect, our 24-hour official Hypernet™ node/omnimedia hub, allowing real-time on-line convention access and providing an informational overload of Kei 'n' Yuri-oriented media coverage, past and present!

*Fabulous live programming, featuring Kei 'n' Yuri (and other, lesser guests) in autograph sessions, lectures, panel discussions, media seminars, and other stunning displays of egotism!

*Poverty-inducing dealer's rooms, offering gray-market Kei 'n' Yuri paraphernalia from every corner of the United Galactica!

*Disturbing "Art" shows, displaying the best in Kei 'n' Yuri-inspired omnimedia "art" of all kinds . . . including a special showcase of unauthorized interactive simulations featuring the Lovely Angels (adults only)!

*And much, much, MUCH more!

For a free download of the official Kei 'n' YuriCon '41 Infopak™ (containing ALL relevant information, from registration to travel and hotel reservations to last will and testament filing**), contact Hypernet™ node: Kei 'n' YuriCon '41@goofball.convention.zone.A34563.

*__KYOTAKU__: A mildly demeaning term used to describe hard-core <u>devotees</u> of the "Lovely Angels" (or, if preferred, "Dirty Pair"). Derived by combining Kei and Yuri's initials (KY) with the Japanese term for a dangerously obsessed fan (otaku).

**Kei 'n' YuriCon '41 will not be held responsible for any injuries, deaths, or psychological trauma suffered by convention attendees. See Infopak™ for full details and mandatory legal waiver.